Melancholy and the Otherness of God

Melancholy and the Otherness of God

A Study of the Hermeneutics of Depression

Alina N. Feld

LEXINGTON BOOKS
Lanham • Boulder • New York • Toronto • Plymouth, UK

Published by Lexington Books
A wholly owned subsidiary of The Rowman & Littlefield Publishing Group, Inc.
4501 Forbes Boulevard, Suite 200, Lanham, Maryland 20706
www.rowman.com

10 Thornbury Road, Plymouth PL6 7PP, United Kingdom

British Library Cataloguing in Publication Information Available

Library of Congress Cataloging-in-Publication Data

The hardback edition was previously cataloged by the Library of Congress as follows:

Feld, Alina N., 1956–
  Melancholy and the otherness of God: a study of the hermeneutics of depression /
Alina N. Feld.
    p. cm.
  Includes bibliographic references and index.
  1. Melancholy. 2. Depression, Mental. I. Title
  BF575.M44F45 2011
  616.85'27—dc23   2011030980

ISBN 978-0-7391-6603-1 (cloth : alk. paper)
ISBN 978-0-7391-8207-9 (pbk. : alk. paper)
ISBN 978-0-7391-6605-5 (electronic)

Printed in the United States of America

Dedication

In memory of my mother, Hortensia, and my father, Ioan, whose loving sacrifice day after day constituted my first horizon and whose ideal of the intellectual heart has remained my primary inspiration.

Contents

Foreword

During the first decade of the twenty-first century, an enormous and continuously growing body of literature has been devoted to the topics of human happiness and depression. Whether produced by psychologists whose perspective has grown steadily more "positive" in recent years, or by contemporary Buddhists who seem to have concluded that the essence of life may be something other than *dukkha* (suffering), or by certain Christians who conceive of Christian "flourishing" in increasingly worldly terms—many of these works portray happiness as a fundamental desideratum (indeed, often as *the* desideratum in human life), and designate melancholy or depression as something to be eschewed. These moods or states of mind can now be pharmaceutically controlled to some extent, which adds an interesting twist to the discussion. Moreover, as a complement to or even apart from the use of medications, significant breakthroughs in cognitive behavioral therapy have yielded effective strategies for alleviating depression, at least in some of its manifestations.

Psychological and medical advances in the treatment of depression are most certainly to be celebrated. Moreover, the notion that happiness is the meaning and purpose of human life is not exactly a new idea, if not as old as Siddhartha Gautama, at least as old as Aristotle (with proper adjustment made, of course, for how differently Aristotle may have conceived of *eudaimonia* in contrast to modern views of what it means to be happy). Nevertheless, it is worth pausing to ask what insights might be obscured by the points of view presently dominating this discussion, what truths about the experience of melancholy may be elided. At the end of her remarkable study of *Melancholy and the Otherness of God,* Alina Feld affirms as true such claims as "the self knows its light only by knowing its darkness" and "a melancholy-less world is no longer a human world." Far from being a naively dangerous romanticizing of a debilitating form of mental illness, these claims represent the upshot of a lengthy, detailed and nuanced analysis of melancholy in all of its varieties. On Feld's account, deep sadness and boredom are not to be judged as positive or to be cultivated, but they are most certainly to be regarded as inevitable. Once experienced, one can divert attention away from them and also from the factors that precipitate them, with more or less success. Yet doing so can yield disastrous consequences in Feld's view, precluding the possibility of our learning whatever important lessons such troubling moods might teach us, not only about ourselves, but also (in a theological vein) about our relationship to the dark mystery of God.

William James certainly understood this to be the case when, more than a century ago in his lectures on the *Varieties of Religious Experience* (1902), he portrayed the "sick soul" as a necessary *yin* to the *yang* of the religiously optimistic "healthy minded" consciousness. While persons of the latter type may be more happy and often more productive, the former possesses a greater depth of religious insight. That insight (which he sometimes described as an awareness that there is a real "wrongness" in the world) was one that James regarded as being preserved rather than obliterated in experiences of religious conversion, that is, as surviving in the more complexly nuanced consciousness of the "twice-born." Yet the portrayal of the sick soul that James provided in his lectures, albeit brilliant and compelling, amounts to a crude sketch in comparison to the massively detailed mural that Feld's book supplies. This book traces historical treatments of the topic of melancholy that span several millennia, ranging from Plato and Aristotle to Michel Henry and Jean Baudrillard, from the ancient ascetical theology of Evagrius and Cassian through the medieval scholasticism of Aquinas to the modern death of God theology articulated by Thomas J. J. Altizer. No other work dealing with this topic (at least none with which I am familiar) displays a comparable range and erudition.

At the same time, this book is something more than simply a massive compilation of views about melancholy espoused by thinkers ancient, medieval and modern. Feld's representation of each one of these viewpoints is typically as probing and insightful as it is accurate. Even the juxtaposition of such a broadly disparate group of thinkers is a hermeneutical achievement of some significance. While the standard accounts of this topic would certainly embrace Cassian and Evagrius, Burton and Pascal, Kierkegaard and Heidegger, they might very well neglect Ficino, Hume, Kant, Hegel, Maine de Biran and others included here. I am especially appreciative of the way in which Feld is sensitive to the logic of vagueness that has governed historically much of the philosophical and theological discourse concerning the key terms that she is exploring. As the father of "fuzzy logic," Aristotle once warned that we should not strive to be more precise in our analyses than a given subject matter permits. Working with multiple languages and traditions, it is important not to focus attention too narrowly on any one term, but to be aware of each term's relationship to an entire "family" of cognates, near-synonyms and closely related concepts. Contemporary talk about depression and boredom must be examined against the backdrop created by premodern treatments of *melancholia, tristitia, ennui,* and *acedia.*

In my own considerably more limited study of the concept of boredom in particular, I chose to regard it primarily as a "semiotic" phenomenon. That is to say, boredom represents a failure to interpret certain signs as meaningful or to perceive them as signs at all; it signals a vacuum, the absence of meaning. So not only is boredom a semiotic response to something (or "no-thing"), it itself can be conceived as a sign inviting and open to subsequent interpretation. Feld takes a similar approach here but greatly expands the range of her interpretive activity. She is intrigued by depression, boredom and related moods as the *symptoms* of some basic human condition, pursuing the *readings* of such signs offered by numerous thinkers, here woven together in her own elaborate reading. But distinctive of her account is the profound insight that for all that our melancholy can tell us about what it means to be human, it is most eloquent when it exposes its own limits as a sign, resists reading and interpretation, and falls mute.

This feature of her account, underscored by the title of the book, is embodied in Feld's careful descriptions of the human encounter with "otherness," the confrontation with that which resists conceptualization, rationalization, interpretation. Of the many thinkers explored in the book, Schelling (as she indicates at one point) is most paradigmatic for her perspective, most crucial for the argument that Feld wants to develop. This is so, among other reasons, because what I have elsewhere called "semiotic breakdown"—the failure to find meaning that can precipitate these dark moods—is not simply an epistemological issue, but a deeply metaphysical one, for both Schelling and for Feld. The abject, the Other, is beyond semiosis. It limits, conditions, and challenges all interpretations, revealing itself in dark moods and as the dark mystery that forms the horizon of all human attempts to find and make meaning.

A book like this, because it introduces many more questions than it would ever pretend to try to answer, is a wonderful stimulus to further inquiry. Some of the key questions broached here encourage exploration of the relationship (1) between accounts of depression supplied by clinical psychologists/ psychiatrists and those embodied in philosophical and theological treatises;

(2) between depression and boredom, melancholia and acedia; (3) between the dark moods as existential signs and the impenetrable, mysterious limits of semioisis, the otherness that resists all signification; and finally (4), between melancholy/boredom as something that happens *to* us—also the relief from it as something experienced as gratuitous—and these same moods as fields of *agency*, something for which we are at least partially responsible, conditions that we can (sometimes) do something about. But this preview by no means exhausts the kind of questions raised in Feld's book, as she proves to be a reliable guide and engaging fellow traveler, a rare enough combination of qualities in any author.

Michael L. Raposa
Professor of Religion Studies and
E. W. Fairchild Professor of American Studies
Lehigh University

Acknowledgments

I wish to thank all those who directly contributed to bringing this book through the long process of conception, gestation, and execution to its present published state.

I owe a great debt of gratitude to my three mentors during my years of advanced study, who have deeply enriched my life: Thomas J. J. Altizer, whose passionate apocalyptic theology has been a ferment to my own thinking of melancholia; his confidence in my work, critical responsiveness, relentless support, and personal friendship have sustained and called me forth through the years. Ray L. Hart, for whom philosophy is a personal task of thinking and living with deliberation and art, whose subtly intricate vision sketched in *Unfinished Man and the Imagination*, progressively deepened in his more recent thinking on God and Nothing, opened up unsuspected horizons for understanding myself and the world. Alan M. Olson, who gave me sustained support and encouragement, generously sharing his intellectual and academic advice, encompassing conversation, and mindfulness of the other; his being among the few still tempted by transcendence in spite of all rumors of its demise has been a source of inspiration, especially for a writer on melancholy.

My profound gratitude goes to Lissa McCullough—a dear friend, scholarly advisor, and partner in existential conversation, whose thinking, writing, and life are marked by lucidity, probity, moral conscience, and compassion—for having taken upon herself the responsibility of copyediting this book. Turning editing into an art, she thoroughly and painstakingly brought this work into its present form and her enthusiasm for it helped to bring it to completion.

My deep thanks are due to Lexington Books, a wholly owned subsidiary of the Rowman & Littlefield publishing group: on the editorial side, to Jana

Hodges-Kluck, associate aquisition editor, and Eric Wrona, her editorial assistant, for their indispensable professional support, informed guidance, and abiding spirit of patience throughout the process of reviewing, editing, and publishing. I am also indebted to Della Vache, assistant managing editor, and Eric Hardy, from the production department, as well as to the design team and the typesetting team for their labor in bringing it forth. I owe particular thanks to Jonathan Sisk, senior executive editor at Rowman & Littlefield, for including this work in their list. In addition, a note of thanks to Sarah Stanton, acquisitions editor at Rowman & Littlefield, who referred me to Lexington Books. I would like to acknowledge, as well, the anonymous reviewer of my manuscript who supplied a most appreciated guidance.

I would like to express warm thanks to Michael L. Raposa, whose book *Boredom and the Religious Imagination* prompted me to think philosophically about boredom, for having honored my request to write the foreword. My gratitude is also due to Richard Kearney for sharing chapters of his manuscript *Strangers, Gods, and Monsters* and for the inspiration of his hermeneutics of the possible God, and Edward S. Casey and Tom Rockmore for their gracious willingness to help my project along. I acknowledge with gratitude William Desmond, always willing to discuss metaxic being, for encouraging thinking without intimidation, David G. Leahy, whose intellectual range and postapocalyptic vision have continued to call me forward beyond the death of God. Special gratitude is due to the Karl Jaspers Society of North America (KJSNA), in particular to Alan M. Olson and Helmut Wautischer, for help and guidance I received at conferences to which I delivered earlier versions of a couple chapters in this book. Thankful acknowledgments go to David M. Eckel, Peter S. Hawkins, Robert C. Neville, and the late Harold Oliver, for the intellectual stimulation their works has represented as well as for having manifested enthusiam for my work on melancholy and suggested publication.

I acknowledge my gratitude to Monique Pommier, whose depth of insight, grace of spirit, intellectual sophistication, and always unexpected vision have steadied my steps, straightened my path through uncertain terrain, and sustained my courage in the process; and Calin Vartosu, my fellow traveler in the quest for ultimate answers, whose ludic nature and mercurial spirit can instantly transform melancholy into pure joy.

Finally I owe thanks to my family for their inspiration and encouragement: to my brother Sorin-Alexander Bradford whose musical compositions and melancholic nature have presented me with a superior aesthetic ideal and a task of relentless self-questioning, as well as his wife Margot, an accomplished music producer and connoisseur, for their patient witnessing. Last but not least, Geza, my husband, a secret melancholic himself and poet at heart, engaged in a continual work of self-conquering, whose light-heartedness, perseverance, and faith have never failed to amaze and humble me. My deep gratitude goes to him for forbearance that seemed endless, unfailing assistance, and caring understanding throughout the period in which this work was completed.

PERMISSIONS

My thanks are due the following publishers for having granted permission to quote extensively from their texts: G. W. F. Hegel, *Philosophy of Mind*, translated by A. V. Miller (1970), by permission of Oxford University Press. Immanuel Kant, *Anthropology from a Pragmatic Point of View*, translated by Victor Lyle Dowdell, copyright © 1978 by the Board of Trustees, Southern Illinois University, by permission of Southern Illinois University Press. Karl Jaspers, *General Psychopathology*, vol. 2, translated by J. Hoenig and Marian W. Hamilton, with a new introduction by Paul R. McHugh, M.D. © 1997 The Johns Hopkins University Press, by permission of the publisher.

Oxford University Press kindly gave permission to republish two illustrations from *The Nature of Melancholy: From Aristotle to Kristeva*, edited by Jennifer Radden (2000): *Melancholy, An Allegory* (oil, 1532) by Lucas Cranach the Elder (fig. 3, p. 7), and *Melencholia I* (engraving, 1514) by Albrecht Dürer (fig. 6, p. 14).

A section of chapter 8 was published online in *Existenz: An International Journal in Philosophy, Religion, Politics, and the Arts* 3:2 (Fall 2008): 10–20, and is reprinted here in revised form with permission.

DISCLAIMER

This book does not intend to be a scientific investigation of a mental condition, but rather a selective study of hermeneutical hypotheses concerning melancholy from historical periods ranging from Greek antiquity until the present. The study refers to Western Judeo-Christian philosophical and theological theories only, and does not address the strictly medical aspects of the condition. Moreover, although the principle of selection is philosophical significance, a few major thinkers of melancholy are not comprehensively represented here. The most illustrious of these is certainly Søren Kierkegaard. The rationale for his absence is the monumental stature of the Danish philosopher as an exhaustive hermeneutician of melancholy whose work would demand an extensive study unto itself.

A.N.F.

Introduction

After the great syntheses of the Renaissance, up until the nineteenth century, mood did not figure overtly as a metaphysically or ontologically relevant philosophical theme but was relegated to theories of the passions, encyclopedias, and treatises of practical theology. Only with German idealism and philosophies of life (*Lebensphilosophie*), followed by twentieth-century existentialism, did dark and pathetic mood become increasingly significant philosophically. The condition commonly and medically known today as "depression" is arguably the ground for the mood ontologies present in contemporary continental philosophy, in such figures as Heidegger, Levinas, Michel Henry, and others.[1] This rather new philosophical interest, paralleled by similar developments in theology, psychology, psychiatry, neuroscience, sociology, cultural studies, women's studies, literary theory, and more recently economics, indicates a growing general concern with the disquieting epidemics in today's culture of depression, a state of mind that is often defined in terms that belong to the condition known in premodern periods as *acedia*[2] or melancholy.[3] Psychology and psychiatry are constantly solicited to respond therapeutically to the problematic of depression, the removal or alleviation of which challenges the inventiveness of research.

The principal intention of this investigation—which was initially prompted by my suspicion that depression may be a privileged locus of significant metaphysical, existential, and anthropological unveilings—is to discover how depression as we identify it today has been historically interpreted, and what role the dark mood has played in the development of consciousness. Indeed, understanding depression as a perduring condition of the human spirit rather than a contingent malady may contribute to a revision of modern anthropological conceptions such as those implied in the Cartesian axiomatic model of rationality as the human telos, a model later consecrated by Kant, and further qualified by British empiricism and analytical reduction.[4] By questioning the truth and value of modern models of rationality while reappropriating premodern models of sensibility and wisdom, the horizon of human self-understanding is open to being redefined and deepened. As part of this movement, an effort to retrieve depression's cultural past will lead to a deeper understanding of the profound meaning and complexity of being human.

TERMINOLOGICAL DECISIONS

Let us begin by analyzing the terminology of contemporary depression and its classical terminological incarnations: acedia and melancholy. The term *depression*, used in both medical and folk idioms to refer to a condition of psychic suffering, is a recent phenomenon. Prior to it, the condition had been known by a constellation of terms, among which acedia and melancholy had dominated thanks to a venerable tradition. In order to establish the economy of relations between contemporary depression and its classical incarnations, the latter two must be succinctly defined. Both as conditions and symbols, acedia and melancholia perplex the critical intellect by the excess of their connotations and metamorphoses. Siegfried Wenzel articulates the meaning of acedia thus:

> The name given to this special form of boredom was not invented by the monks. Αχηδεια or αχηδια, literally "lack of care, *incuria*," had a long history in Greek literature, from a work attributed to Hippocrates down to Hellenistic writers, although it apparently had never been in frequent use. . . ."Lack of care" can mean a negative as well as a positive state: carelessness or freedom from sorrow, and both uses are attested. A second meaning is "weariness, exhaustion, apathy," which in at least one passage is connected with the moral endeavors of Stoic philosophy.[5]

Whereas at the beginning of its history acedia would fare side by side with melancholy as the distinctive humors of phlegm and black bile, respectively, or as the mortal sins of acedia and tristitia, at a certain moment, perhaps due to their phenomenological concurrence and similarity, acedia and melancholy were fused. Subsequently the hybrid condition would be indiscriminately referred to as acedia or melancholy, and today as depression. Nevertheless, other terms would continue to be used, some corresponding to aspects more specific to acedia, such as sloth, hypochondria, or boredom; others to melancholy, such as sadness, tristitia, mourning, or despair; and yet others corresponding to both, such as apathy, fatigue, pusillanimity, *taedium vitae*, spleen, ennui, depression, even madness. Depression belongs to the third group, supplanting the two conditions taken in tandem.

Certainly, a decision on the terminology to be used throughout the present study is imperious. The term depression is the one used in today's culture, both medically and popularly. Compared to other candidates, it is superior in its suggestive quality since it symbolizes one pole of a relation, the low, the "valley," thus containing in itself the operation of comparison with its opposite, the elevated level, the "mountain"; thereby, it suggests a movement from high to low or vice versa: in other words, a deep fall below sea level, into the abyss, and perhaps, also, the beginning of an ascent. As a matter of fact, Schelling's interpretation of melancholy as a vestige of the abysmal groundlessness of God, which represents a momentous shift in the definition of the condition, is a definition that depression approximates more closely than does the term acedia, signifying a lack of care or self-forgetfulness, or even the term melancholy, named for the black humor (in Greek, *melanos*, black + *khole*, bile) considered the cause of the condition. Nevertheless, in order to preserve both the tradition of interpretation and the distinctive aspects of the complex condition of contemporary depression, I will use the classical terms melancholy and acedia, as adequately qualified.

Faced with this excess of determinations, the present study must identify a principle for organizing the profusion of constellations of acedic and melancholic hypostases of contemporary depression, which, under their different names and guises, compete for priority as the origin or centerpiece of this genealogy. In her anthology of texts dedicated to melancholy, Jennifer Radden emphasizes the categorization conundrum that baffles all attempts at interpretative coherence in the case of melancholy and acedia.[6] She notes that hermeneutic labor has been undertaken primarily toward detailed descriptions and intricate classification. Radden observes that the hermeneutics of melancholy has not notably advanced since the seventeenth century. With superb medical and philosophical expertise Radden has subsequently continued, deepened, and qualified her research into the intricacies of the condition. *Moody Minds Distempered* is a tour de force treatment of the intellectual and medical history of melancholy and depression, a thorough analysis of descriptivist and causal ontologies, as well as a comparative study of the two conditions.[7] In it Radden concludes that today's depression and past melancholia are erroneously and misleadingly equated (75–94).

Thus questions as to the intrinsic nature of the condition commonly known today as depression arise: is depression a psychological or existential constant across cultures? Is it an ontological or even a metaphysical condition? If the latter, is it grounded in Being or Nonbeing? In discovering the answers to these questions we could adjudicate between the different etiological accounts and remedies suggested by the range of diverse and potentially incompatible models jostling in the field of depression studies today.

THE THREEFOLD TASK OF THIS STUDY

The present investigation assumes three major intertwined tasks: genealogical, hermeneutical, and therapeutic. Since these three aspects of research can be separated only theoretically, observations pertinent to one will be immediately relevant to the others. The first task, the genealogical one, is fulfilled by considering melancholy's paradoxical ontology, exploring diverse historical hermeneutical insights into it and philosophical reflections on it. This re-collection undertakes to identify the principal hermeneutical paradigms of the condition, as well as to recover the symbol best suited to account for the depressive comportment, now viewed in the complexity of its paradoxical etiology and therapy. The original paradigmatic interpretations are identified as the medico-metaphysical, the theological, and the mythical. On this foundation, interpretations further proliferated and developed in multiple directions: alchemical, anthropological, ontological, metaphysical, phenomenological, existential, postmodern.

The second task is hermeneutical. As the life of melancholy gradually arises out of the symbolic roots of humor, sin, and Saturnine nature, two distinctive complexes emerge as its two principal destinies: the depressive (acedic) complex of sloth-boredom-emptiness, and the melancholic complex of sublime-tragic-nonbeing.[8] In order to illustrate these two complexes, I will consider Albrecht Dürer's and Lucas Cranach's allegories of melancholy (Fig. 1.1 and Fig. 1.2).

Figure 1.1

Figure 1.2

They illustrate the two distinctive symbolic identities, thus clarifying their respective compasses of meaning. Dürer's engraving *Melencolia I* (1514) presents Dame Melancholy as a massive, sculptural winged feminine figure of dark complexion, with a leafy crown, perhaps of laurel, on her head, compass negligently in right hand, resting her head on her left clenched fist, a bunch of keys loosely hanging at her waist. As if having been suddenly snatched away from her work in geometry, architecture, or construction by something ultimate, she is surrounded by objects, symbols of both her trade and of melancholy, in disarray: symbols of geometry and architecture—arts associated with melancholy—a brooding angel, an acedic dog, the corner of a building inscribed with a numerological square, probably Jupiter's to propitiate Saturn, the planet-god of melancholy, and a ladder leaning against the wall. In the distance there is arising a star that has been variously interpreted either as an ill-foreboding comet, Saturn, or the black Sun of melancholy (*sol niger*). Dame Melancholy's intensely frowning angered gaze is concentrated upward on an object that hovers above, invisible to the viewer. The nature and tension of the gaze suggest that the object may be invisible to her as well: her gaze is seemingly turned inwards. The winged figure is tensely sitting. Dürer's *Melancholy* may be cited as a suitable illustration of Burke's or Kant's melancholic sublime.

The other image, Lucas Cranach the Elder's painting entitled *Melancholy: An Allegory* (1531) signifies quite a different mood. She is also a winged and seated figure, surrounded by symbols of melancholy, but her face is expressionless and her gaze is downcast. She holds a broken cane in her hand; her whole postural attitude is one of weakness, fatigue, and despondency: the Dame is acedic or depressed. Although both works of art allegorize melancholy, Dürer illustrates the melancholic complex whereas Cranach presents the depressive (acedic) complex. Thus these two allegorical illustrations circumscribe the domain of melancholy with its distinct complexes: hypostases of bored apathy and sublime but tragic inspiration. These two complexes are fundamental configurations of hypostases of what we know now only as depression. The dialectical relation between them will be utilized as an organizing principle, for each complex helps to articulate the condition by absorbing similar hypostases and affirming or questioning the relevance of various theoretical attitudes. Different as they are, both complexes reveal *the nothing*; but their respective relations to the nothing are not identical since they represent two different modes of confronting it. As we shall see, the distinction is that between Schelling's concept of primordial "absolute indifference" on the one hand, and angry self-negation on the other. According to him, melancholy is a trace of God's otherness, of the abysmal nature of God; prompted by this interpretation, melancholy can be viewed as a trace of God's self-negation or death. Depression (acedia), by contrast, can be viewed in Schellingian terms as a vestige of the primordial groundless ground of absolute indifference.

This radical difference aside, both complexes affect time and the self. Martin Heidegger, Ludwig Binswanger, and Michel Henry contribute to a shift of interpretation toward temporality and subjectivity. If, as according to Schelling, melancholy is a reflection of otherness within God, or as according to Hegel, an inevitable negative stage in the dialectical evolution of the Idea—theologically expressed, the moment of the death of God in the history of God's revelation—then it could never be annulled, nor should it be. Schelling insists, as did Pseudo-Aristotle earlier, that the life of reason itself, its creativity, is a constant overcoming of melancholic madness; meanwhile, Hegel argues that the movement from nature and necessity toward freedom and creativity traverses all the forms of depression and melancholy. Later on Jung will discover the synthesis of Schellingian and Hegelian dialectic in the alchemical operation, during which the movement of consciousness toward healing as restoration of the self's totality always begins with the dark phase of melancholy. Thus Schelling and Hegel posit a correlation between the melancholy of human subjectivity and the suffering God: specifically, our melancholic suffering is a trace of a metaphysical principle of negation, of God's otherness as the ground of God's darkness and death.

Heidegger, Binswanger, and Henry contribute to a shift in interpretation toward temporality and subjectivity. Heidegger goes one step further. He considers anxiety and boredom as fundamental attunements of Dasein, respectively existential and ontological. As such, neither must be resisted or overcome, but rather consciously accepted, undergone, and deepened; anxiety lets Dasein appear as a being toward death, while profound boredom is the mood in which the nothing transpires as the ground of Dasein itself. Thus with Heidegger therapaeia has come full circle, reflecting an absolute reversal in the interpretation of the condition. Heidegger's ontology of the dark mood is endorsed by Jaspers's empirical-psychological research into pathological cases vis-à-vis intellectual-spiritual creativity: mental pathos is a condition for otherwise inaccessible insight, thus for deepening self-consciousness. The hermeneutics of melancholy as the stigmata in subjectivity of divine nonbeing and pathos irrupts in Thomas J. J. Altizer's death of God theology, first proclaimed in the 1960s. Since then, after a period of relative eclipse, the theme of God's otherness has resurfaced more recently in the thinking of Jean-Luc Marion, Gianni Vattimo, Slavoj Žižek, John Caputo, Richard Kearney, Ray L. Hart, and D. G. Leahy.

The third task is to decipher the range and significance of therapeutics and reflect on therapeutic recommendations traditionally associated with the condition. In opposition to classical remedies, a new mode of thinking about the negative moods emerged—corresponding to Schelling's metaphysical being of melancholy as well as to Hegelian dialectics of consciousness—effectuating a radical transformation in the understanding of melancholy and its therapeutics. In all the diverse hypostases of the condition, the therapeutic for depression entails forms of labor that ultimately partake of that labor which gives birth to the self, whose identity was decided by the system of meaning in which the remedy was inscribed. In all its forms, remedial labor was meant to reawaken and redress the slumbering, forgetful, and diseased melancholic. Accordingly, it ranged from manual work, to societal work, to working on the self through various activities: passionate engagement in life, self-remembering by reflection and understanding, or redirecting the will and imagination through cultivating Stoic *apatheia*, or the theological virtues of courage and hope, or the Jovial and Solar qualities. Work is also implied in the experience of the sublime; indeed, with the exception of grace, the traditional remedies pertaining to the strictly religious sphere—conversion and self-transcendence—are also forms of labor. Ultimately work is the process by which the self readies itself for God as the *tremendum et fascinans*.

As the present study does not venture into the territory of the medically pathological, the vast literature that has been generated on the basis of medical expertise will not be discussed, and competence in this area is disclaimed; this study nevertheless intends to sound a warning against all reductionist approaches, whether theoretical or clinical, as well as extend an invitation to question the philosophical and crypto-theological presuppositions of those approaches. Programs of exclusion of the dark mood in Western culture began with the banning of melancholy from Plato's ideal city, proceeded through the Renaissance quest to extract the stone of madness, and issued in modern utopias or dystopias that exile melancholy; these programs, which should not be taken too literally but viewed as ciphers in need of interpretation, will be treated in chapters 3, 5, and 9.

THE ORDER OF REMEMBERING

We will consult theological and philosophical texts that have presented paradigmatic definitions of the melancholic condition, have illustrated the two distinctive complexes, or can help indirectly with the hermeneutical task, according to the following outline.

Chapter 1, "Hippocratic Humors, Plato's *Chora*, and Pseudo-Aristotle's Question": In Hippocrates's theory of the humors we witness the genesis of acedia and melancholy out of the excess of phlegm and black choler. These humors, when excessive, unravel the harmony of the human cosmos. While Plato's *chora* is a double cipher of melancholy and the otherness of God, Pseudo-Aristotle's question, "Why are all remarkable men melancholic?" articulates the breaking up of cosmic harmony and initiates the long journey of individual consciousness toward maturity and integration. In this first irruption out of the harmony of the all, extra-ordinary individuality and excessive abnormal melancholy emerge as coeval: all subsequent developments in the life of the concept can be interpreted as hypothetical answers to Pseudo-Aristotle's question and reflections of Plato's *chora*.

Chapter 2, "The Mortal Sins of Acedia, Sadness, and Sloth": The first section reflects on the original genesis of the concept of acedia (boredom) and melancholy as sins with Evagrius Ponticus and John Cassian. Thomas Aquinas will later fuse these two sins into the single sin of spiritual apathy. The second section is devoted to Ricoeur's analysis of sin and its conditions of possibility inscribed in human fallibility. Melancholy emerges as the prevenient condition of sinfulness par excellence.

Chapter 3, "Children of Saturn": With Marsilio Ficino the phlegmatic (acedic or depressive) and melancholic hypostases are distinguished from each other and addressed. Ficino serves as an au courant guide through the labyrinth of melancholic dispositions because their genealogical origins are still uniquely visible in his *Three Books on Life*. The myth of Saturn, the planetary divinity and patron of melancholy, deepens the symbolic connection between melancholy and God's own otherness—as Saturn, the malign demiurge, becomes by homologation the devil himself.

Chapter 4, "Indolence and Ennui": Robert Burton's *Anatomy of Melancholy* is a pivotal reference in the career of the concept that offers a Rabelaisian vision of a cosmically projected melancholy. Burton elects as the most potent causes of this universal condition the dialectics of two hypostases of melancholy: idleness and boredom. His theory confirms the intuition of classical interpretations, according to which doing nothing literally reverses creation by generating the nothing. Blaise Pascal offers a theological counterpart to Burton's vision, in that the nothing defines the human condition without God. Thus the acedic complex of sloth, boredom, and the nothing emerges.

Chapter 5, "Infinite Will, Skepticism, and Sublime Terror": For Descartes, *tristesse* is the experience of evil that can be transcended only by detachment of soul from body or cultivation of infinite will; meanwhile, Hume's melancholic imagination leads to philosophical skepticism. The melancholic complex of the tragic sublime, or *melancholia gloriosa*, appears with Edmund Burke and Immanuel Kant. Kant's interpretation of melancholy as a temperamental attunement to the natural and moral sublime prompts him to conceive the Romantic theory of genius.

Chapter 6, "On God's Otherness": Hegel interprets melancholy as a sine qua non stage in the evolution of the Idea: the soul emerges out of the immediacy of nature into the realm of mind and freedom; the unhappy consciousness, infinite grief, and God's pathos are the principal moments of the negative to be overcome. With Schelling the metaphysical ground of melancholy becomes visible from a different perspective. Faithful to the Pseudo-Aristotelian theory, Schelling interprets melancholy as a trace of God's primordial dark nature of nonbeing. His theory of melancholy offers fundamental metaphysical insight into the life of this condition of the soul, paralleling and complementing Hegel's theory.

Chapter 7, "Boredom, Time, and the Self": Martin Heidegger's fundamental ontological attunement to boredom proposes a revelatory role for boredom and a new understanding of Being itself; care (*Sorge*) as the being of Dasein explains the significance of anxiety, temporalization, and the evil of forgetfulness. His notion of the "last god," meanwhile, inserts Schellingian metaphysics into Heideggerian discourse. Emmanuel Levinas's "horror of impersonal existence," which constituted an objection to Heidegger's anxiety toward death, is revealed in the experiences of fatigue and *paresse*. Michel Henry discovers that subjectivity itself is coeval with the melancholic pathos made evident in the exercise of Maine de Biran's "effort to be." With Heidegger, Levinas, and Henry, melancholy is accepted by the individual self as its own intrinsic condition: its incarnation in consciousness has been completed.

Chapter 8, "Psychic Pathos, Creativity, and Insight": Ludwig Binswanger bases his theory of melancholy as a sui generis creative self-therapeutic on Edmund Husserl's phenomenology of the triadic self. Karl Jaspers interprets the condition as a boundary situation that provides access into the abysmal territory of the psyche, thus explaining profound insight, both artistic and religious. Binswanger and Jaspers emphasize the creative dimension of the melancholic self.

Chapter 9, "Postmodern Depression and Apocalypse": This chapter introduces Thomas Altizer's recent theological reflections on the final act of the death of God and corresponding depression in late modernity. Jean

Baudrillard's melancholy of systems constitutes a cultural interpretative theory that, though divergent, witnesses to the same contemporary mood. The question of the destiny of theology after the death of God has received considerable attention in recent years in continental philosophy and has generated an intense debate and rethinking of God's nature and our theologically constructed identity. It is significant that this rethinking emphasizes God's otherness and humanity's fragility.

Chapter 10, "Therapeutics of Melancholy": Treated here are the therapeutic indications, distinguishing the constant essential features from the culturally and existentially contingent. Further discussion of Rene Le Senne's and Hubertus Tellenbach's studies testifies to the therapeutic value of labor in all its forms, as well as the value of a theology of atonement. Theories of melancholic therapeutics proposed by Renaissance thinkers Henry of Ghent and Cornelius Agrippa, and more recently Rudolf Otto, Karl Jaspers, and Paul Tillich, are adduced. Finally, the fundamental therapeutic throughout all these metamorphoses and interpretations may be discerned: that is, the labor of the self in confrontation with the other—with otherness itself—through self-transcendence, self-acceptance, and grace.

Conclusion, "Afterthoughts": The conclusion weighs the outcome of the foregoing investigation and evaluates the significance of the entire study for a more careful understanding of what it means to be a human being in a melancholizing postmodernity. What comes next?—this is the question still to be pondered.

NOTES

1. See in particular Martin Heidegger's analysis of boredom as a fundamental way of being for Dasein in *Fundamental Concepts of Metaphysics*, trans. William McNeil and Nicholas Walker (Bloomington: Indiana University Press, 1995); Emmanuel Levinas's analysis of fatigue, indolence, and weariness in *Existence and Existents*, trans. Alphonso Lingis (Pittsburgh: Duquesne University Press, 2001); Michel Henry's concept of the "pathetic subjective immanence" in *Philosophie et phénoménologie du corps* (Paris: Presses Universitaires de France, 1965), 254–307, and Jean Baudrillard's notion of "melancholy of systems" in *Simulacra and Simulation*, trans. Sheila Faria Glaser (Ann Arbor: University of Michigan Press, 1994), 162. Theologically I would note Thomas J. J. Altizer's recent reflections on contemporary depression and the nothing in "Postmodernity and Guilt," in *A Call to Radical Theology*, ed. Lissa McCullough (Albany: State University of New York Press, forthcoming), and "The Transfiguration of Nothingness" (unpublished manuscript written in August 2008, cited by permission of the author).

2. Among studies that address contemporary depression—traditionally known as *acedia* or melancholy—from its theological birth through its historical itinerary,

mainly through literary texts or works of art, two are to be mentioned as canons in the field due to their pertinence and comprehensiveness: Siegfried Wenzel, *The Sin of Sloth: Acedia in Medieval Thought and Literature* (Chapel Hill: University of North Carolina Press, 1967), and Raymond Klibansky, Edwin Panofsky, and Fritz Saxl, *Saturn and Melancholy* (London: Thomas Nelson & Sons, 1964). Following these two scholarly references there come, in chronological order, Reinhard Kuhn, *The Demon of Noontide: Ennui in Western Literature* (Princeton: Princeton University Press, 1976); Desmond Healy, *Boredom and Culture* (London: Associated University Presses, 1984); Patricia Meyer Spacks, *The Literary History of a State of Mind* (Chicago: Chicago University Press, 1995); Julia Kristeva, *Black Sun: Depression and Melancholia* (New York: Columbia University Press, 1989); Donald W. Livingston, *Philosophical Melancholy and Delirium: Hume's Pathology of Philosophy* (Chicago: University of Chicago Press, 1998); Michael L. Raposa, *Boredom and the Religious Imagination* (Charlottesville: University Press of Virginia, 1999); Wolf Lepenies, *Melancholy and Society*, trans. Jeremy Gaines and Doris Jones (Cambridge: Harvard University Press, 1992); Julius H. Rubin, *The Other Side of Joy: Religious Melancholy among the Bruderhof* (Oxford University Press, 2000); Jennifer Radden, *The Nature of Melancholy from Aristotle to Kristeva* (New York: Oxford University Press, 2000), and *Moody Minds Distempered: Essays on Melancholy and Depression* (New York: Oxford University Press, 2009); Andrew Solomon, *The Noonday Demon: An Atlas of Depression* (New York: Simon & Schuster, 2001); Max Pensky, *Melancholy Dialectics* (Boston: University of Massachusetts Press, 2001); Donald Capps, *The Depleted Self: Sin in a Narcissistic Age* (Minneapolis: Fortress, 1992), and *Men, Religion, and Melancholia: James, Otto, Jung, Erikson* (New Haven: Yale University, 1997); Peter Schwenger, *The Tears of Things: Melancholy and Physical Objects* (Minneapolis: University of Minnesota Press, 2006); and Kathleen Norris, *Acedia and Me* (New York: Penguin, 2008). In the French speaking world of philosophical and theological reflection, renewed scholarly interest in the history of depression has been recently occurring, a phenomenon explaining the sudden proliferation of studies on the subject such as Jean Libis, *Bachelard et la mélancolie: L'ombre de Schopenhauer dans la philosophie de Gaston Bachelard* (Paris: Presses Universitaires du Septentrion, 2000); Bernard Forthomme, *De l'acedie monastique à l'anxio-dépression: Histoire philosophique de la transformation d'un vice en pathologie* (Paris: Sanofi-Synthélabo, 2000); Claire Jequier, *La folie, un pêche médiéval: La tentation de la solitude* (Paris: L'Harmattan, 2001); Anne Larue, *L'autre mélancolie: Acedia ou les chambres de l'esprit* (Paris: Editeurs des sciences et des arts, 2001); Jean Clair, *Mélancolie: Génie et folie en Occident* (Paris: Gallimard, 2005); Hélène Prigent, *Mélancolie: Les métamorphoses de la dépression* (Paris: Gallimard, 2005); the latter two works are related to the exhibition *Mélancolie: Genie et folie en Occident*, organized by Jean Clair and Hélène Prigent (Grand Palais, Paris, October 2004–January 2005).

3. Note, for example, Paul Tillich's understanding of the end of the modern age as an age marked by "spiritual anxiety," which he further qualifies as "anxiety of meaninglessness and emptiness" (*The Courage to Be*, 2d ed. [New Haven: Yale

University Press, 1959], 46–51); and also Desmond Healy's view of the phenomenon of "hyper-boredom" as a symptom of the "collapse of meaning" consequent upon a "culture-wide breakdown" and a "metaphysical crisis," in *Boredom, Self and Culture* (London: Associated University Presses, 1984).

4. On the Cartesian model of rationality as the human telos see, for example, Husserl's phenomenological critique of the Galileo-Cartesian model in *The Crisis of European Sciences*, trans. David Carr (Evanston: Northwestern University Press, 1970).

5. Wenzel, *The Sin of Sloth*, 6–7. More important for the later history of the word was its appearance in the Septuagint. The term occurs nine times in the *Septuagint* and translates several different Hebrew roots. Its general meaning is faintness, weariness, anguish. One of these passages should be singled out because of its later importance as a bridge between the still very vague meaning of *acedia* in the Septuagint and its eventual application to a specific temptation: the passage is Psalms 119:28: "My soul has slumbered because of acedia." In *The New Jerusalem Bible* the translation is: "I am melting away for grief;/true to your word, raise me up." Reference to acedia as the "noonday demon" appears in Psalms 91:6: "You need not fear the terrors of night,/the arrow that flies in the daytime,/the plague that stalks in the darkness,/the scourge that wreaks havoc at high noon."

6. Jennifer Radden, "Introduction," in *The Nature of Melancholy from Aristotle to Kristeva* (see n. 2 above).

7. Radden, *Moody Minds Distempered: Essays on Melancholy and Depression* (Oxford: Oxford University Press, 2009).

8. *Complexe* is the term that Gaston Bachelard uses, following the psychoanalytic tradition, to capture the phenomenological emergence of the imaginal signature or stylistic structure of a specific mode of poetic imagination; it can be a recurring figure, image, *élan*, intuition that appears as a symbol or fragment of a myth. Northrop Frye attempts a definition: "What Bachelard calls a '*complexe*' might better be called something else, to avoid confusion with the purely psychological complexes of actual life. I should call it a *myth*, because to me a myth is a *structural principle* in literature. For example, there is, in Bachelard's sense, a literary Oedipus complex. . . . It is undoubtedly related to the Oedipus complex discussed by Freud, but can hardly be treated as identical with it. The "complexes" dealt with in this book are actually points at which literary myth becomes focused on its cardinal points of creation, redemption, and apocalypse" (Frye's introduction to Bachelard, *The Psychoanalysis of Fire*, trans. Alan C. M. Ross [London: Quarter, 1987], ix–x).

Chapter 1

Hippocratic Humors, Plato's *Chora*, and Pseudo-Aristotle's Question

The first most significant moments in the hermeneutics of melancholy are Plato's metaphysical notion of *chora*, introduced in his dialogue *Timaeus*, and Pseudo-Aristotle's question posed in *Problem 30.1*.[1] While Plato's *chora* interconnects melancholy, the absence of God, and time, Pseudo-Aristotle poses the question of the relation between melancholy and exceptional individuality that will reverberate throughout the entire hermeneutic tradition of the dark mood. Indeed, one could read subsequent interpretations of the condition as traces of Platonic chorology and responses to Pseudo-Aristotle's question.[2]

MELANCHOLIA AND *PHLEGMA* IN HIPPOCRATES'S THEORY OF THE HUMORS

In order to understand the background of both the Platonic and Aristotelian discourses, a brief incursion into the humoral theory of Hippocrates (460–370 B.C.E.) is appropriate. The medical treatises that form the Hippocratic corpus are rooted in the metaphysical assumption of the perfect harmony of the cosmos to which the human being naturally belongs. The complete correspondence between the macrocosm and human microcosm, which will resurface once more in the Renaissance, appears to be self-evident and available for experimental verification. The author (though it is likely there were several authors belonging to the Hippocratic school of thought) establishes invisible connections between the human dimensions of being—organs, humors, thoughts, emotions, dreams, sexuality, age, food, exercise, constitution, diseases—and the natural universe—the time of year or day,

1

geography, climate, the nature of the four elements, no less than the aspects of stars and planets.[3] *Regimen I* adopts the Heraclitean theory of ultimate reality as an everlasting becoming whose symbol is fire, and postulates two metaphysical principles, fire and water, in whose various forms and combinations everything in the universe, including the human body and soul, participate.[4] The constitutional or contingent differences in the quality, quantity, and combination of fire and water explain the infinite variety among individuals. The ideal condition is one of perfect complementariness between the constitutive elements, whose formula is one of musical harmony since the cosmic law is one of Pythagorean attunement. The perfect attunement is "the finest moisture" kept in movement by "the best fire."

According to this theory there are six basic conditions, of which two are the ones that require our attention, to wit, "the thickest water and finest fire [that] gives a cold and moist nature, unhealthy in winter, aging rapidly," and "the rarest fire and driest water [that] gives a dry and cold nature, unhealthy in autumn and when forty."[5] Childhood is moist and warm, youth is warm and dry, maturity is dry and cold, and old age cold and moist as a progressive cooling is taking place during one's lifetime. Melancholy (black choler, or bile) indicates the critical condition of maturity, is grounded in a cold and dry constitution, and corresponds to autumn; *acedia* is not termed a-cedia (carelessness) but *phlegma*, its physiological cause. The latter is the final attunement on the musical scale, the disharmony therefore of the last stage of life, human and seasonal, old age and winter; it is the final condition of the life spectrum. Within the Hippocratic worldview, sleep and inaction are indicated as the causes or aggravating agents of the phlegmatic condition, while thinking and labor are recommended as the cure; prolonged sleep "heats and melts the flesh, dissolves and enfeebles the body," while inaction "moistens and weakens the body"; by contrast, "thinking and labor dry and strengthen the body."[6] In the case of an excess of phlegm the indications concerning the compensatory preventive or therapeutic regimen are interesting in light of subsequent therapeutics.

According to Hippocrates, all senses, since warm and dry, must be exercised to compensate for the cooling effect of aging: in exercises for sight, hearing, and voice, the soul must be moved and warmed.[7] Beside the gymnastics of the senses, a sui generis gymnastics of the mind is also recommended for having the same warming and drying effect. Since exercise is a form of "work," the validity of later prescriptions against the sin of acedia or secular boredom, by Cassian, Burton, Burke, or Hegel, is confirmed centuries earlier in the Hippocratic corpus. The ideal in Hippocrates is one of harmonious attunement of the individual and the natural cosmic environment. Any excess causes disease and must be tamed and adjusted. Excessive melancholy and phlegm appear as pathological conditions, harbingers of death.

PLATO: THE ENIGMA OF *CHORA*

One of the most discussed, controversial, even contested of Plato's dialogues, *Timaeus* is a complex metaphysical, cosmological, and political treatise that also provides the philosophical-mythical foundation of the Hippocratic theory of the humors and is the first source of a hermeneutics that interrelates melancholy, primordial nature, the absence of God, and time before time.[8] Interestingly, like *Problem 30.1*, whose Aristotelian authenticity has been questioned, the *Timaeus* has been suspected of being a forgery.[9]

Introduced as an astrologer, Timaeus is principally a metaphysician interested in the primordial elements and principles operative in the universe beyond the visible manifestation. The metaphysical impulse drives him toward speculation on the beginning. He postulates before the creation of the heavens the existence of three primordial eternal kinds of being: being (the being of the Ideas), becoming (the being of generated copies), and *chora* whose common dictionary translation is space or place. As the theorists of *chora* have observed, the dialogue is a metaphysical and cosmological palimpsest of at least two beginnings. Timaeus refers to God's creation of the heavens as one beginning; then he regresses to another, more primordial beginning, prior to the creation of the heavens, one from which God is absent, when fire, water, air, and earth, "first principles and letters" of the whole, are generating themselves, appearing and disappearing endlessly in a circular movement within *chora*. The four natures are in a condition of chaos as one may expect whenever God is absent, in chaotic and painful contrariety (53b-c). God's creating act consists in bringing measure and order from primordial chaos. Timaeus advances the reasons, modes, and order of creation—or rather of the second beginning, chronologically. God creates the universe out of the four natures of fire, water, air, and earth by infusing measure and order into them; he gives the soul intelligence and seven distinctive qualities; out of these ingredients, he fashions the heavens: first the fixed stars, then the seven moving stars or planets (the Greek term *planetai* means "wanderers"). The whole universe emerges as a perfect living animal, one and solitary, spherical, moving perpetually with a circular motion. Planets and time are created simultaneously, the planets being instruments of time, their heavenly dances making up time. He begins the creation of man by planting in him the seed of divinity. Having this divine seed as foundation, man is created by the planets out of the four elements, an operation that places the immortal soul into a mortal body in perpetual influx and efflux, "a nature subject to irresistible and terrible affections," pleasure and pain, rashness and fear, anger and hope, all mingled with irrational sense and love (43ab).

In this divine and stellar economy, disease is a regress to a pre-creational stage, a regress into the disorder of the four primordial elements in the womb of *chora* when God was absent, before God's work of cosmicizing chaos.[10] Disease undoes the work of God, an undoing that is also a rejection of God, a mode of being without God, a return to chaos that also means a return to the primordial when time was not, but only *chora*, space. The interpretation of disease as a regression to a space before divine creation and time is pertinent especially in the case of melancholy, so much so that melancholy has been interpreted as primarily a disorder of the sense of time. Melancholic time suffers an intriguing metamorphosis, seems slow, stagnant, in other words, becomes spatialized: it regresses into precreational primordial *chora*, space and receptacle of all.

CHORA AND CONTEMPORARY CHOROLOGY

The discourse on *chora* is indirect, oblique, metaphorical, imaginal, since *chora* cannot be said or spoken of except in the medium of a "bastard discourse" that mixes together logos and mythos. Timaeus introduces the new kind of being that requires a regress to a more originary metaphysical beginning and a new discourse:

> This new beginning of our discussion of the universe requires a fuller division than the former, for then we made two classes; now a third must be revealed. The two sufficed for the former discussion. One which we assumed was a pattern intelligible and always the same, and the second was only the imitation of the pattern generated and visible. There is also a third kind which we did not distinguish at the time, conceiving that the two would be enough. But now the argument seems to require that we should set forth in words another kind which is difficult of explanation and dimly seen. What nature are we to attribute to this new kind of being? We reply that it is the receptacle, and in a manner, the nurse, of all generation. (49ab)

Besides the two ontological orders of being and becoming, of reality and appearance, there is a third kind of being, *chora*. *Chora* cannot be described either by logos or mythos, but rather by a third form of analogical and metaphorical discourse according to which she/it is likened to a receptacle, nurse, mother of all generation; she/it is like the gold out of which the moving figures of the elements are made, the "formless, invisible being," the "similar principle circulating through each and all" (49e-50b). Timaeus explains:

> For inasmuch as she always receives all things, she never departs at all from her own nature, and never, in any way or at any time, assumes a form like that of any of the things which enter into her; she is the natural recipient of all impressions, and is stirred and informed by them, and appears different from

time to time by reason of them. But the forms which enter into and go out of her are the likenesses of eternal realities modeled after their patterns in a wonderful and mysterious manner. . . . That which is to receive all forms should have no form" (50c-e).

Chora or space is introduced as the third nature, eternal and indestructible, providing a home for all created things and "apprehended, when all sense is absent, by a kind of spurious reason," and "hardly real"; it is seen as "in a dream," and since "neither in heaven nor in earth," has no existence" (52b). If the three kinds of being—being, *chora*, and generation—existed before God's act, *chora* is described in relation to the four elements as the "nurse of generation . . . moistened by water, inflamed by fire, receiving the forms of earth and air, experiencing all the affections corresponding to these" (52d). Now if *chora* appears as the cosmic womb, invisible being in-forming itself, the matrix of the world of becoming, she/it is not in equipoise, but is shaken by the perpetually moving forms and affections and shakes them in turn, "swaying unevenly hither and thither" like a "winnowing machine" (52e-53a), already acting as a selective principle of attraction of the similar and repulsion of the dissimilar, although without reason and measure, in a chaos on the verge of perishing and of aborning. This is an image of the primordial chaos one may expect to find "whenever God is absent." The state of disorder is interrupted only when God becomes present to it and fashions it "by form and number," thus making "the fairest and best out of things which were not fair and good" (53bc). Although Timaeus continues his speculations without further mention of *chora*, we have enough grounds to assume, John Sallis argues, that she/it is always there, "the irreducible remainder" in all melancholic conditions.

Thus according to Timaeus, *chora* is paradoxical and mysterious: she/it holds the all, pervades it, and cannot be separated from it; like a mother, she/it animates the four elements as well as the celestial bodies. She/it is invisible but becomes visible only in her/its forms. She/it continuously gives birth and shape to the things of the world by her/its invisible influence and visible rays. Her/its ontology is unclear, that of a dream, between being and nonbeing, informed by being, and giving rise to becoming. A spurious reason corresponds to this metaxic ontology. Quite significantly, reflecting on *chora* has been at the center of contemporary debate on God and God's otherness in theological thinking after the demise of ontotheology and the death of God theology of the 1960s. Julia Kristeva, Slavoj Žižek, Jacques Derrida, John Sallis, John Caputo, Richard Kearney have joined in the conversation.[11] In "God or Khora," Richard Kearney discusses the different competing interpretations of Plato's *chora* that are proposed by psychoanalysis and deconstruction; the former is represented by Kristeva and Žižek, the latter by

Caputo and Derrida.[12] According to Kearney, for Kristeva *chora* represents the "primordial matrix of the unconscious," the nonego, presymbolic and prelinguistic, the site of chaos and abjection, "when deity is absent," while Žižek homologizes *chora* to the pre-ontological and Schelling's primordial "that which in God himself is not yet God," of "monstrous drives" and the "spectral real." For both, while *chora* indicates the absence of God, it is a paradox of negation and a ground or precondition of self, speech, meaning, and—by allusion to Schelling—God.[13]

To clarify the nature of the relation between *chora* and God, Kearney attends to Derrida's and Caputo's deconstructive reading, engaging in a critical evaluation of their either/or separation and atheistic theological choice of *chora* over God. For both Caputo and Derrida, *chora* is a-theological and a-donational, a radical alterity, in spite of Plato's metaphors of mother and nurse; it seems that *chora* recalls Levinas's *il y a,* the impersonal, nocturnal existence, and absence of God and of any being.[14] Kearney admits the "khora-esque experiences" as the "most unspeakably traumatic limit experiences of things that exceed our understanding," the "most sublime of horrors," since *chora* is experienced as misery, terror, loss, and desolation, the "insomniac dark, blind Oedipus, Sisyphus in Hades, Prometheus in chains, Iphigenia in waiting; *tohu bohu* before creation, Job in the pit, Jonah in the whale, Joseph at the bottom of the well, Jesus abandoned on the cross, or descended into hell; Conrad's heart of darkness, Hamlet's stale worlds, Primo Levi's death camp"; Kearney then asks, "more basically still, is khora not that pre-original abyss each of us encounters in fear and trembling when faced with the bottomless void of our existence?"[15]

If the experience of the "bottomless void of our existence" indicates the archetypal presence of *chora*, then melancholy and *chora* are indelibly united: melancholy in all its different hypostases appears as the experience of god-less, abysmal *chora*. At the beginning of the history of the hermeneutics of melancholy, outside both logos and mythos, Plato's unspeakable and incomprehensible enigmatic *chora* already reveals while concealing the metaphysical arcanum of the melancholic hybrid of being and nothing, as well as of experience of the otherness of God.

CHORA AND ARISTOTLE: THE COMPORTMENT OF EARTH AS A METAPHYSICAL PRINCIPLE

Aristotle's cosmology essentially participates in Hippocratic metaphysics of the humors and provides, through further qualifications, a metaphysical ground for the hermeneutics of melancholy while also providing the blueprint of the heavens that will be adopted by Aquinas and Dante. According to Aristotle, the universe has an extremity and a center, an up and a down; the number of the elements is finite, and since their generation cannot come from something incorporeal, the elements are generated from one another.[16] The moving stars within the first heaven are ungenerated and indestructible; they move the simple bodies of the four elemental metaphysical principles and the bodies composed by them.[17] Although there are four elemental substances (air, fire, water, earth), the "extremes and purest" are fire and earth, while the other two are intermediaries.[18] The properties of these two extremes are particularly revealing. According to the Empedoclean law of universal correspondence "like to like," metaphysical earth and the bodies in which it predominates sink to the bottom of things and move toward the center, while metaphysical fire moves upward and to the outer limit.[19]

Aristotle goes further into deciphering the metaphysical constitution of the world and elaborates on the originative source of the all. He agrees with Plato's conception of *chora*, but reduces it to primary matter and substratum for the four elements, while establishing three originative sources: namely, the potential body, the contrarieties, and the four elements.[20] Aristotle's elevation of humoral qualities into metaphysical principles and his metaphysics of the earth will prove significant in the theory of melancholy. Metaphysical and physical earth effectuates a centripetal movement to the centre and into the depth; it is defined by heaviness and the effect of "dissociation" whose cause is "Strife rather than Love" (333b). The individuals in whom the principle of earth predominates will exhibit the telluric nature with a propensity for deep and profound matters and an insight into the center of being. Aristotle's metaphysics of the earth sanctions Hippocrates's theory of the humors of phlegm and melancholy and establishes the genesis of the symbol of melancholy in relation to the metaphysical telluric principle, a relation that explains, as chapter 3 will indicate, the symbolic connection of melancholy with the myth of Saturn prevalent in the medieval and Renaissance intellectual worldviews.

PSEUDO-ARISTOTLE'S QUESTION INITIATING THE HERMENEUTICS OF MELANCHOLY

The genesis of the ancient concept of melancholy comes forward with the question posed in *Problem 30.1*, a text in Aristotelian vein that became the first illustrious landmark in the interpretation of melancholy.[21] Beginning with the question of the relation between melancholy and exceptional destiny, the treatise proposed a hermeneutical alternative to the negative interpretations of the condition present both in previous medical theory of the humors and in the dark traces of *chora*.[22] More important though, this question initiates reflection on the nature of melancholy that will eventually reverberate through the entire hermeneutic tradition of the dark mood. Indeed, one could read subsequent interpretations of the condition as hypothetical responses to Pseudo-Aristotle's question.

Against the previous metaphysical background, *Problem 30.1* limits itself to questioning the connection between melancholy and the exceptional individual. As Raymond Klibansky, Erwin Panofsky, and Fritz Saxl, the authors of the erudite scholarly study *Saturn and Melancholy*, remark, the text of *Problem 30.1* is a fruit of the union of Platonic myth and Aristotelian natural science that gives birth to the notion of the melancholic genius as the abnormal—literally exceptional—individual, a notion that will be developed during the Renaissance with Marsilio Ficino, then later with Kant and the Romantics, and will also be considered by Karl Jaspers.

Problem 30.1 begins with the observation that all remarkable men are melancholic and undertakes the task to find the answer to the question: "Why is it that all those who have become outstanding in philosophy, statesmanship, poetry or the arts are melancholic, and some to such an extent that they are infected by the diseases arising from black bile, as the story of Heracles among the heroes tells?" (155). To support his claim, the author adduces examples of mythical heroes (Heracles, Ajax, Bellerophon), philosophers (Empedocles, Plato, Socrates), as well as political figures and poets. He discusses in particular Heracles and Bellerophon as melancholic figures par excellence, whose destinies will indelibly mark the meaning of melancholy.[23] Both Heracles's melancholic madness and Bellerophon's damnation indicate particular uncommon conditions. Heracles historicizes himself principally as a man of great labors to the glory of Zeus's wife Hera, of great suffering and apotheosis. A simple man unaware of his semidivine descent, he is submitted to extremely difficult and dangerous tasks meant to test his character and valiance and initiate him into the world of the gods. He assumes the tasks, each of which implies a confrontation with a deadly other, a confrontation that calls forth both physical exertion and moral strength: courage, endurance, and honesty. Although, Heracles is also known for having fallen into deep depression or madness, he remains the "idealized representative of combative strength; the symbol of the victory of the human soul—and of its high price—over its own weaknesses."[24] Bellerophon is a tragic hero, victim of divine punishment for the hubristic transgression of the limit imposed on mortals. Innocent, he is wrongfully and secretly accused, providing the reason for which his benefactor sets up forbidding tasks meant to kill him. Most challenging is his confrontation with and vanquishing of the Chimera. Because he succeeds in all his tasks, his innocence is revealed and rewarded. But what seems to be a happy ending is only a final test, one that, unaware, he fails. Although not immortal, he undertakes a forbidden flight on the winged horse Pegasus to Mount Olympus, thus incurring Zeus's wrath. Having been thrown back to earth, he "wandered about the earth, lame, blind, lonely, accursed, avoiding the paths of men until death overtook him," forsaken and betrayed by all.[25]

The mythic figures used by Pseudo-Aristotle to illustrate melancholic destiny share several features: enormous difficulty and effort both physical and moral; exceptional trajectory of supreme elevation followed by abysmal fall; divine wrath and forsakenness as punishment for hubris; artistic nature or simplicity and melancholic psychological symptoms: distress, despair, guilt, madness, anger. It appears that the melancholic destiny is a tragic destiny par excellence, as cathartic fear and pity arise at the spectacle of disproportionate or undeserved suffering. The role of tragedy and passion in the therapeutics of the soul represents a locus of contention between Platonism and Aristotelianism, between two opposed interpretations of melancholy. For Plato, since the world of Ideas can be reached only through the containment, control, and sublimation of the passionate nature by the higher intellect, tragedy, by its nature a provocation to passion, must be exiled from the ideal city since it is not conducive to the philosophical life. Pseudo-Aristotle proposes the opposite therapeutic for the soul: tragedy awakens and intensifies the fear-and-pity complex that circumscribes the entire spectrum of passion, then sublimates it into awe before the *mysterium tremendum et fascinans*: catharsis of the passions facilitates the experience of the sublime. Tragedy, melancholy, genius, and the sublime are introduced as interconnected categories—connections that will be further explored with Burke and Kant.

There is another aspect of Heracles's and Bellerophon's destinies that indirectly refers to melancholy: both heroes excel in confronting the monstrous other that mythically represents the dark side of the self, or melancholy. While Heracles excels in his twelve works, Bellerophon, with the help of the winged horse Pegasus, tramples over the Chimera, a hybrid monster with a lion head, goat body, and dragon tail, which like Medusa cannot be fought face to face, whose mother is sister of the Gorgons and a subterranean monster. The Chimera is a complex symbol of the nocturnal creations of the abysmal subconscious, according to Paul Diel, "a disease of the psyche, characterized by a fertile and unrestrained imagination," which expresses the "perils of exalting the imagination."[26] Bellerophon is unfortunately intoxicated with his victory over the Chimera, falls victim to enormous hubris, wishes to seize Zeus's throne, and suffers the consequences. Significantly, among the melancholic heroes Pseudo-Aristotle does not mention Perseus, the hero of a myth parallel to Bellerophon confronting the Chimera: the reason is that

Perseus is not presented as melancholic himself. Perseus's heroic deed does symbolize, however, by its moral and psychological translation, the successful conquering of deadly melancholy (see Dante's Medusa in chapter 3).

Problem 30.1 represents a crucial moment in the life of the concept of melancholy by inaugurating philosophical reflection on the nature and meaning of this condition. Besides the exemplary models illustrating melancholy, Pseudo-Aristotle also mentions its lesser instantiations caused by excess. While anybody may suffer temporarily from a melancholic disorder of excess or defect, or even a melancholic disease, it is only the individual of melancholic temperament who is the permanently abnormal, the exception. For the naturally melancholic temperament, according to the thermodynamics of black bile and its quantity, there are three principal possible types: if bile is considerable and cold, it produces sluggish and stupid characters; if excessive and hot, it gives rise to characters that are mad, clever, amorous, easily moved by passion and desire, and talkative; it is only black bile of moderate heat and quantity that gives birth to the ideal melancholic condition. In this latter case, characters are "more intelligent, less ex-centric, superior to the rest of the world in education, the arts, statesmanship" (163).[27] As Klibansky, Panofsky, and Saxl remark, the melancholic genius embodies the paradox of measure and control within excess:

> Only the Aristotelian conception of the "mean" made it possible to conceive an effective equilibrium between the poles of this antithesis, a "eucrasia within an anomaly" which justified the apparently paradoxical statement that only the abnormal was great. The miracle of the man of genius remained; but it was conceived no longer as an irruption of mythical forces into reality but as nature surpassing herself by following her own immanent laws, making man, though necessarily very seldom, a superman.[28]

By this gesture, melancholy becomes the condition for the possibility of exceptional destiny. The question of the nature and justification of such an elevated status is posed as a philosophical provocation or invitation to speculation. The author provides his own Hippocratic interpretation and the thinking experiment will be continued through other times and modes until the present.

Although there are several presuppositions that the *Problem* shares with the Hippocratic corpus, in the latter melancholy and phlegm were held to be two distinct humors and conditions, whereas the former refers only to melancholy and subsumes the etiology and problematic of phlegm under the extended category of black bile: phlegm becomes a colder hypostasis of black bile. Apparently, then, at the very beginning of their history, phlegm and melancholia were considered separately as distinct conditions. Yet already in the *Problem* they became fused together, making subsequent hermeneutic attempts at definition or therapy difficult. An admirable exception to this unfortunate state will be Marsilio Ficino's *De vita triplici* (*Three Books on Life*).

NOTES

1. This possibly spurious text is available in the Loeb Classical edition of Aristotle's works as question 1 of "Book 30: Problems Connected with Thought, Intelligence and Wisdom," in *Problems II, Books 22–38* and *Rhetorica ad Alexandrum*, trans. W. S. Hett; Loeb Classical Library, no. 317 (Cambridge: Harvard University Press, 1983), 155–69. Hereafter this portion of the text will be referred to as Pseudo-Aristotle, *Problem 30.1*. Nearly all the works of Aristotle intended for publication have been lost; the few extant ones are lecture materials, notes, and memoranda, some of which are spurious. Although *Problem 30.1* is today generally considered suspect or spurious, its authenticity was never doubted or questioned by the major figures in this study such as Ficino, Agrippa, Schelling, and Jaspers. In *Saturn and Melancholy*, the coauthors Klibansky, Panovsky, and Saxl construct a convincing argument in support of the high probability that *Problem 30* is genuinely Aristotelian (see Raymond Klibansky, Erwin Panofsky, and Fritz Saxl, *Saturn and Melancholy: Studies in the History of Natural Philosophy, Religion, and Art* [London: Thomas Nelson & Sons, 1964], 15–41).

2. I have adopted John Sallis's usage of the term "chorology" in relation to Plato's *chora*, which will be discussed in this chapter. See Sallis, *Chorology: On Beginning in Plato's "Timaeus"* (Bloomington: Indiana University Press, 1999).

3. Hippocrates, *Regimen 1*, in *Hippocrates*, vol. 4, trans. W. H. S. Jones; Loeb Classical Library, no. 150 (Cambridge: Harvard University Press, 1931): "If in dreams heavenly bodies appear disfigured or disappear, arrested in revolution, in mist cloud, rain, hail—all these are indicators of moist and phlegm like secretions arising in the body" (427). Also dreaming of heavenly bodies wandering about at random signifies "disturbance of the soul arising from anxiety" and the remedy is devised accordingly as "rest, and contemplation of cosmic things" (ibid.).

4. Hippocrates, *Regimen 1*: "But all things both human and divine are in a state of flux upwards and downwards by exchanges. All the same things and not the same things. Light for Zeus darkness for Hades, light for Hades, darkness for Zeus. The things of the other world come to this and those of this world go to that" (237).

5. According to Hippocrates in *Regimen 1*, finest water-rarest fire is the healthiest; strong fire-dense water is strong, robust but needs caution; thickest water-finest fire gives a cold and moist nature, unhealthy in winter, ages rapidly, least healthy in old age; moistest fire-densest water gives a moist and warm nature, sick in spring, unhealthy when young; strongest fire-finest water gives dry and warm nature, sick at the onset of fire, healthy in old age, long life; rarest fire-driest water gives a dry and cold nature, unhealthy in autumn, and when forty (xxxii–xxxiii, 273–79).

6. Hippocrates, *Regimen 2*, 347.

7. Hippocrates, *Regimen 2*, 349.

8. Plato, *Timaeus*, trans. Benjamin Jowett, in *The Collected Dialogues of Plato*, ed. Edith Hamilton and Huntington Cairns; Bollingen Series 71 (Princeton: Princeton University Press, 1961).

9. John Sallis, *Chorology*, 146–54. Sallis refers to the skepticism about Plato's authorship of the *Timaeus*, such as Diogenes Laertius's contention that Plato in fact reinscribed or even copied out a book composed by Pythagorean Philolaus; and also Proclus's theory that Plato copied *On the Nature of the Cosmos and the Soul*, a work of Middle Platonism allegedly composed by Timaeus of Locri, but in fact a forgery itself.

10. For Timaeus, the pain of the soul comes from an ill disposition of the body, evil government, evil discourse, bad education; while the evil of the body is caused by phlegm and bilious humors. "For where the acid and briny phlegm and other bitter and bilious humors wander about in the body and find no exit or escape, but are pent up within and mingle their own vapors with the motions of the soul, and are blended with them, they produce all sorts of diseases, more or fewer, and in every degree of intensity, and being carried to the three places of the soul, whichever they may severally assail, they create infinite varieties of ill temper and melancholy, of rashness and cowardice, and also of forgetfulness and stupidity" (87ab). The liver is the mirror of mental images, which it translates into emotions. According to the images reflected, pain or joy is produced, and correspondingly bitter bile or divination in sleep (71b-e). "There is also another cause of disease, i.e. the lack of proportion between soul and body: an excessive soul in a weak body causes madness while an excessive body and a small soul leads to ignorance—stupidity, dullness, forgetfulness—the greatest of diseases" (87d-88b). "The stars construct nature subject to irresistible and terrible affections (pleasure-pain, rashness-fear, anger-hope), mingled with irrational sense and love: man is the result" (69c-e).

11. Sallis, *Chorology* (n. 2 above); Jacques Derrida, *On the Name*, trans. David Wood, John Leavey, Jr., and Ian McLeod (Stanford: Stanford University Press, 1995).

12. Richard Kearney, "God or Khora?" in *Strangers, Gods, and Monsters* (London and New York: Routledge, 2003), 193–211.

13. Kristeva and Žižek are discussed in Kearney, *Strangers, Gods, and Monsters*, 194–97. Apropos at this point is John Sallis's discussion of the ambivalent destiny of *chora*, thus of dialectical thinking and ontotheology: Sallis notes Aristotle's and Plotinus's departure from Platonic *chora* and its reduction to matter, as well as its more faithful reappropriation by Schelling as the dark nature of God that becomes definitive in his *Treatise on Freedom*. Sallis's analysis in the final chapter of his *Chorology*, "Reinscriptions: Reduction and Appropriation," will be discussed in chapter 6.

14. Levinas's *il y a* will be discussed in chapter 7.

15. Kearney, *Strangers, Gods, and Monsters*, 204.

16. Aristotle, "On the Heavens," trans. J. L. Stocks, in *The Basic Works of Aristotle*, ed. Richard McKeon (New York: Random House, 1941), 308ab.

17. Aristotle, "On the Heavens," 293a–294a.

18. Aristotle, "On Generation and Corruption," trans. Harold H. Joachim, in *The Basic Works of Aristotle*, 330b-331a.

19. Aristotle, "On the Heavens": "There is an absolutely light, one which of its own nature always moves upward, and an absolutely heavy body, one which of its own nature moves downward" (311a-312a).

20. In "On Generation and Corruption," Aristotle writes: "What Plato has written in the *Timaeus* is not based on any precisely-articulated conception. For he has not stated clearly whether his 'Omnirecipient' exists in separation from the elements; nor does he make any use of it. He says indeed that it is a substratum prior to the so-called elements—underlying them, as gold underlies the things that are fashioned of gold. . . . Nevertheless he carries his analysis of the elements—solids as they are—back to planes and it is impossible for the '*Nurse*' (i.e., the primary matter) to be identical with the planes. Our own doctrine is that although there is a matter of the perceptible bodies (a matter out of which the so-called elements come-to-be), it has no separate existence, but is always bound up with a contrariety. . . . We must reckon as an originative source and as primary the matter which underlies, though it is inseparable from, the contrary qualities: for the hot is not matter for the cold, nor the cold for the hot, but the substratum is matter for them both. We therefore have to recognize three originative sources: firstly that which is potentially perceptible body, secondly the contrarieties (heat and cold), and thirdly Fire, Water and the like. Only thirdly however: for these bodies change into one another (they are not immutable as Empedocles and other thinkers assert since alteration would then have been impossible), whereas the contrarieties do not change" (329ab).

21. Details concerning this text are given in n. 1 above.

22. Sallis, "Traces of the Chora," in *Chorology*, 125–45.

23. Aristotle, *Problem 30.1*. In the case of Heracles: his epilepsy which was named after him the "sacred disease," his frenzy toward his children, eruption of sores, his disappearance on mount Oeta; Ajax went insane, and Bellerophon "craved for desert places, was hated by all gods, wandered alone, eating out his heart, avoiding the track of men" (156).

24. "Herakles," in Jean Chevalier and Alain Gheerbrant, *The Penguin Dictionary of Symbols*, trans. John Buchanan-Brown (Oxford and New York: Penguin, 1996), 496.

25. Robert Graves, "Bellerophon," in *The Greek Myths* (New York: Penguin, 1993), §75, 252–56.

26. "Chimera," Chevalier and Gheerbrant, *Penguin Dictionary of Symbols*, 191.

27. It is in this category that Pseudo-Aristotle includes the divinely inspired Platonic Sibyls, soothsayers, inspired persons. He explains that heat is near the seat of the mind and provokes madness and frenzy.

28. Klibansky, Panofsky, and Saxl, *Saturn and Melancholy*, 40–41.

Chapter 2

The Mortal Sins of Acedia, Sadness, and Sloth

There are three defining moments in the theology of acedia and melancholy. The first moment is the genesis of both conditions as the sins of acedia and sadness with Evagrius Ponticus in the late fourth century. The second moment is their translation into Western Christianity by John Cassian shortly thereafter, when acedia becomes hypostasized as sloth. The third moment occurs in the thirteenth century with Thomas Aquinas, who unifies acedia and sadness. Once acedia (manifested as boredom and sloth) and sadness (or melancholy) are identified as symptoms of the condition of modern depression or traditional melancholy, they will be followed in their distinct though intertwined destinies. It is important to emphasize from the beginning that these are different terms for aspects or hypostases of the condition that were constructed by the fusion of phlegm and melancholy, the two humors that with Evagrius and Cassian became acedia and sadness; therefore maintaining distinctions among them is necessary to understand them clearly, interpret them correctly, and make adequate therapeutic choices.

EVAGRIUS: THE DEMONS OF ACEDIA AND SADNESS

In the fourth century, the conditions known in antiquity as phlegm and melancholy were identified as *passionate thoughts* (*logismoi*) and named acedia and sadness, respectively, by the Greek intellectual and desert father Evagrius Ponticus (345–399 C.E.). Given the profound significance of this classification for the subsequent tradition of deadly sins, it is essential that we attend to Evagrius Ponticus as well as his theological system in which the two Hippocratic humors were conceived as sins. Their specific role and

15

significance will gradually emerge against the background of fourth century desert monasticism.

A sophisticated Greek intellectual who converted to Christianity, Evagrius lived in the second half of the fourth century in Constantinople, then Jerusalem, and finally later in his life in the Egyptian desert of Nitria, where he moved to become a monastic. His thought is a synthesis of the Greek philosophical tradition and of the orally transmitted tradition of desert monasticism. As a consequence of his condemnation by the Church for his Origenist and Gnostic leanings, his name entered a long period of eclipse. His theoretical thought nevertheless survived concealed in translations or under more orthodox names, while his practical teaching on asceticism lived on unhindered under two modalities. On the one hand, it continued to be followed and applied in monastic circles; on the other, through the writings of John Cassian, it laid the foundation of the Western ascetic-mystical tradition.[1]

Evagrius is a practical theologian with Gnostic inclinations and a mystic interested in attaining *theosis* through knowledge of secret metaphysics—that is, gnosis—and a well-structured program of spiritual exercises. While the Stoics considered *apatheia* the goal of their practice of detachment from passions, for Evagrius it is the first station on the path leading to divine knowledge and contemplation. The first step on this journey is the elimination of all obstructions that would interfere with the ultimate telos. In *The Praktikos*, he engages in a consideration of the passionate thoughts that constitute, according to him, the main hindrance in the progress of purification of the passionate and intellectual natures. Along with gluttony, impurity, avarice, anger, vainglory, and pride, acedia and sadness figured on his list of eight *logismoi* or thoughts with emotional content.[2] Evagrius thus generates the concept and list of the mortal sins, eight according to him, later reduced to seven by Pope Gregory I (known as Saint Gregory or Gregory the Great, 540–604 C.E.) by the union of acedia and sadness.

The etiology of all passionate thoughts is demonic; indeed, demonic agencies are the instigators of the thoughts with passionate content. In the case of acedia it is the noonday demon, the only one that has a name:

> The demon of acedia—also called the noonday demon—is the one that causes the most trouble of all. He presses his attack upon the monk about the fourth hour and besieges the soul until the eighth hour. First of all, he makes it seem that the sun barely moves, if at all, and that the day is fifty hours long. Then he constrains the monk to look constantly out of the windows, to walk outside the cell, to gaze carefully at the sun to determine how far it stands from the ninth hour, to look now this way and now that to see if perhaps one of the brethren appears from his cell. Then, too, he instills in the heart of the monk a hatred for the place, a hatred for his very life itself, a hatred for manual labor. He depicts

life stretching out for a long period of time and brings before the mind's eye the toil of the ascetic struggle and, as the saying has it, leaves no leaf unturned to induce the monk to forsake his cell and drop out of the fight. No other demon follows close upon the heels of this one (when he is defeated) but only a state of deep peace and inexpressible joy arise out of this struggle. (*Praktikos* 18–19)

This paragraph dedicated to acedia, or phenomenological boredom—which was subsequently discussed and qualified in modernity by Kierkegaard and Heidegger—illustrates the surprisingly modern character of Evagrius's psychological insight, offering a phenomenological description avant la lettre. As has been remarked, it is mainly by his art of phenomenological description that Evagrius exercised his influence on the monastic tradition.[3] Like the other sins, acedia is a bitter fruit of the desert, of the gaping void left in the soul by the absence of God as sole object of desire, or by God's shadow. At noon, the ascetics who were readying themselves through continual vigil and prayer for divine nuptials, feel forsaken by the Beloved. The soul, desirous of the infinite object of desire, experiences the latter's absence as infinite emptiness. The absence of God affects time, emptying it of meaningful content. To compensate for the infinite loss, the soul substitutes for the one object of absolute desire the worldly objects of relative desire, thus falling into idolatry, which according to Tillich involves precisely the replacement of the ultimate concern by relative concerns held as absolute.

EVAGRIUS'S DEMONIC ETIOLOGY OF THE PASSIONS

Evagrius exits the phenomenological suspension of the description and claims that acedia has a demonic causality, that all acedic moods and thoughts are demonic delusions and temptations to abandon monastic life and lose oneself in the world or in sleep: the noontime demon either drives the monastic away from himself and from his home or defeats him through slumber. In order to understand the nature of acedia's detrimental effect on the human self and the need for remedial spiritual exercises, we must first consider Evagrius's notions of the life of the intellect and its telos, demonic being, and the nature of spiritual exercises. According to Evagrius's anthropology there are two kinds of representations that influence the intellect, namely, figural and abstract. The former refer the intellect to objects of sense while the latter fill the intellect with spiritual realities. Not being an object of the world, God is the prototype of nonfigural representations. Filled with representations of sensible objects, the intellect becomes suffused with worldly matter and incapable of containing God. To remedy this opaqueness to God, spiritual exercises are intended to progressively remove all figural representations from the intellect, enabling it to receive the divine nonfigural representation. In order to create space for God, therefore, the intellect must undergo the purging of all images.[4]

Although in his metaphysics Evagrius develops a form of neo-Platonism mixed with Gnostic elements, the positive Christian view of Creation and Incarnation prevails. Neither matter nor human nature is evil. While the intellect is in its essence the locus of the divine, its auxiliaries the passions— *thumos* (spiritedness) and *epithumia* (passionate desire)—in their natural activity are its appointed helpers. Thus figural representations in themselves are not evil; God appointed man "shepherd of his figural representations," over which he must constantly watch and which he must guard against foreign predators.[5] Evagrius calls the novice to be a "good shepherd" of his thoughts through attention and uninterrupted self-observation. He describes the phenomena emerging in consciousness and applies a provisional *epokhē* as to their truth and reality; this is the first stage of a hermeneutics of suspicion in the art of the discernment of spirits. For Evagrius, self-observation is a specific form of thought-observation and analysis of one's own mental and affective activity. In observing himself, the individual must constantly identify and separate, add and eliminate, understand and interpret thoughts, emotions, perceptions, impulses. He devises a strategic program of thought-analysis and discernment. First comes attentive observation. Once the details are all present in memory, there comes the second moment of the strategic work: analysis of the thought. In this phase, thought is deconstructed and each of its elements questioned (*Pensées* 220–21). Only when the particular demon is identified and its activity known with clarity may the vigilant observer unmask the demon. The unmasking is the third moment of the strategy. Shamed and infuriated, the demon, a being of the dark, cannot bear lucidity and vanishes.[6]

Evagrius's demonic causality was not a novelty. By the time of his writing, demonic existence was assumed to be a reality. For Evagrius, demonic agency intends to take over the soul by gradually insinuating itself into the victim and metamorphosing into a semblance of the latter: thus it becomes indistinguishable from one's own body. Demonic thought, Evagrius explains, is actually an image of sensorial man constituted inwardly, an image that is unfinished, with which the intellect carried away by passion talks or acts in secret. Since Evagrius's demonically induced thought is "an unfinished [faceless] image of man, formed inwardly" (185), with which the passionate intellect speaks or acts in secret, it appears to be man's own shadow—one inhabiting rather than following him. As a faceless and unfinished man, Evagrius's demon anticipates Freud's unconscious, Jung's shadow, and Hegel-Lacan's natural soul prior to its mirror encounter with itself. Thus, according to Evagrius, our common sense of the self is merely a form of naïve consciousness. Self-perception is by nature neither stable nor reliable. That is why Evagrius calls forth a sui generis radical *epokhē* of the entire perceptual and imaginal representational world. The natural cogito itself may be delusional since illusion does not stop at the gates of the cogito but can slip inside. Coextensive with all the phases of the spirit-discerning art is metaphysical reflection. It takes the form of remembering the metaphysical disposition of the world and of man's constitution, place, and telos. In the absence of this metaphysical mapping, the work on the self would be impossible. Nevertheless, for Evagrius, gnosis is salvific on the condition it is applied, practiced. The actualization of metaphysical knowledge about the self is a second dimension of the work that the monastic undertakes.

In the context of Evagrian ontotheology, one in which "theology is prayer and prayer is contemplation," passionate thoughts that entrap, obscure, and lead the intellect astray are demonized.[7] Among these, acedic thought is in total opposition to the divine destiny of the intellect because it induces torpor and dreamless sleep, indifference, abysmal forgetfulness—all forms of interruption of self-awareness and intellectual activity.

ACEDIA AND SADNESS AS DEMONIC TEMPTATIONS TO EXTINCTION

In the treatise *On Thoughts* Evagrius's exposition of the conditions of acedia and sadness offers interesting clarifications and additions to the more defined but succinct presentation of sadness in the *Praktikos*. The demon of sadness is unique in two ways: it is the one that blurs the clarity of the mind more than any other and it is the only demon that paradoxically tempts not by pleasure but by pain:

> All the demons teach the soul to love pleasure; only the demon of sadness does not attempt to do this but rather destroys all other thoughts, withdrawing and drying out all pleasure of the soul through sadness if it is true that the bones of the sad man are dry. It engenders thoughts which advise the soul to escape or force her to flee. It is what saint Job once meditated on and suffered when he was tormented by this demon. (*Pensées* 193)

The demon of sadness destroys all other thoughts, removes and dries up pleasure of the soul, even the bones—as Hippocrates already warned. As in the case of acedia, it gives birth to thoughts that tempt the soul to escape and run away. But sadness is double-sided: although excessive sadness swallows up the soul completely, in a moderate form it can help one toward repentance.

Sadness may also give rise to a chain of thoughts that shipwreck the soul in an abyss of forgetfulness (*Pensées* 233–35). In dreams, inconsolable sadness brings up images of loved ones in great distress or future tragedies, such as falling from high ladders or being blind and not finding the way (*Pensées* 253). The references to acedia in this text, besides the already familiar mode of restlessness and impulse to leave home, introduce new elements: fatigue, a sensation of humidity and cold, and cataleptic sleep; here we recognize Hippocrates's phlegmatic condition, of which Evagrius himself was a victim.[8]

The seeds of a complex relation between sadness—which will be subsequently most commonly termed melancholy—and acedia—which will be commonly referred to as depression, boredom, or sloth—are already present in this first blueprint of the conception of mortal sins. Elements of acedia are contained in sadness, such as emptiness, discontent, and escapist promptings, and elements of sadness are contained in acedia.[9] Although for Evagrius sadness and acedia are separate experiences provoked by different demonic agencies, they are closer to each other than to any other passionate thoughts in their temptation to extinction, or, in Freudian terms, they represent the death drive. If all demonic temptations aim at the death of the soul, with the exception of sadness and acedia, they first convolute into an appearance of life; the latter two, by contrast, represent the paradoxical dispassionate passion, or simply passion in its original meaning, pathos rather than pleasure, forgetfulness and abandonment of the ground of being, sleep or death rather than life. Both sadness and acedia effect the absolute reversal of the early medieval destination of the human being toward restoration of the intellectual contemplative essence. That is why the entire Evagrian corpus is conceived as an initiation into the art of the care of the self: in Ricoeurian terms, Evagrius's spiritual exercises constitute an art meant to prevent the sliding of the soul from mere fallibility into the evil of fault, sin, and guilt.

HADOT: SPIRITUAL EXERCISES AND ACEDIA

Pierre Hadot (1922–2010), French philosopher and historian of philosophy specializing in ancient philosophy, particularly Neoplatonism, notes the importance of the spiritual exercises for both pagan and Christian thinkers.[10] For Hadot, the presence of spiritual exercises in ancient philosophical texts is one of the key indicators of the essential nature of ancient philosophy, namely, philosophy as a way of life that aimed to reform and transform the whole being of the philosopher. Hadot explains that with the advent of Christianity and its claim to be itself a philosophy, philosophy restricted itself to philosophical discourse, losing its practical and transformative-salvific concern and ambition to Christian monasticism. He points to the thinking patterns common to pagan, especially Stoic and Epicurean, thinkers on the one hand, and early Christian monastics on the other. The monastic communities of the Christian Middle Ages preserved to a considerable extent the existential conditions of the pre-Christian philosophical schools.

Let us follow Hadot in what he has to say about spiritual exercises and their content and role in pre-Christian and Christian contexts. Hadot writes: "[In antiquity] these exercises have as their goal the transformation of our vision of the world and the metamorphosis of our being. They therefore have not merely a moral but also an existential value. We are not just dealing with a code of good conduct but with a way of being." The Christian spiritual tradition adopted and preserved the ancient philosophy and practice. Thus "ancient spiritual exercises were preserved and transmitted by an entire current of ancient Christian thought: that current namely which defined Christianity itself as a philosophy" (127). Hadot remarks that the tendency to assimilate Christianity as a philosophy manifested itself with the Apologists of the second century, with Origen, Clement of Alexandria, and the Origenist tradition, especially the Cappadocians (Basil and the two Gregories), a tradition to which Evagrius Ponticus belongs as well. Fourth century monasticism was presented as a *philosophia* by the Church fathers, especially by Evagrius, and continued to be viewed as such throughout the Middle Ages. The result of this tendency was the "notorious Hellenization of Christianity," which involved among other aspects the "absorption of spiritual exercises" along with "a specific style of life, spiritual attitude, and tonality which had been absent from primitive Christianity" (129–30). Hadot quotes Jean Leclercq: "In the monastic Middle Ages just as much as in Antiquity *philosophia* did not designate a theory or a means of knowledge but a lived, experienced wisdom and a way of living according to reason" (130).

Most significant is Hadot's comparative inquiry into the objective of the spiritual exercises of Stoic, Epicurean, and Christian writings. He writes:

The fundamental attitude of the Stoic philosopher was *prosoche*: attention to oneself and vigilance at every instant. For the Stoics the person who is awake is always perfectly conscious not only of what he does but of what he is. In other words he is aware of his place in the universe and of his relationship to God. His self-consciousness is first and foremost a moral consciousness. A person endowed with such consciousness seeks to purify and rectify his intentions at every instant. . . . Such self-consciousness is not however merely a moral consciousness; it is also cosmic consciousness. The attentive person lives constantly in the presence of God and is constantly remembering God joyfully consenting to the will of universal reason and he sees all things with the eyes of God himself. Such is the philosophic attitude par excellence. It is also the attitude of the Christian philosopher. . . . Such attention to oneself brings about *amerimnia* or peace of mind, one of the most thought-after goals in monasticism. (130)

If "attention to oneself, the philosopher's fundamental attitude, became the fundamental attitude of the monk" (131), then acedia emerges as its negation par excellence, a condition for the possibility of all sins, faults, and falls. If mindful attention is already the mark of conversion, inattention or carelessness will be the sign of a relapse. This mastery over the movements and objects of one's own mind is meant to eliminate the distraction of the intellect while holding it in perpetual remembrance and contemplation of God. What agency can control the intellect? One traditional answer was the will. But the will is always informed by the intellect. In the neo-Platonic version the higher intellect informs the will, which disciplines the lower intellect. Hadot's thesis is that with the adoption of spiritual exercises—the main designer of which is Evagrius Ponticus—Egyptian and Syrian monasticism was penetrated by Greek philosophy of a neo-Platonic inspiration. Since neo-Platonism had already adopted Stoic concepts, both the metaphysical and the ethical-practical constructions of the monastic-theologians well-versed in Greek philosophical culture such as Origen, Evagrius, and Cassian are marked by a Stoic and neo-Platonic mixture that had been alien to less philosophical monks trained exclusively in the Scriptures. In the Stoic-neo-Platonic intellectual ambience in which Evagrius lived, as both its product and its creator, Christian perfection was equaled to *apatheia*, the complete tranquility of the passions, as the first stage of the soul's separation and flight from the body. Moral practice, physics, and theology remain the three main stages of knowledge and correspond to degrees of virtue.

It is in this Stoic-neo-Platonic context that the concept of acedia is born as a paradox and a question posed to the very tradition in which it becomes visible and which establishes it as sin. Acedia questions the fundamental presupposition and ideal of Stoicism and also of neo-Platonism: for what is the distinction between *apatheia* and acedia? Furthermore, what is the role of passion in the economy of perfection? What is the role of the body in the economy of spiritual striving? These are some of the questions that acedia, from its genesis onward, posed to the tradition. Hadot's investigation into the substance and trajectory of the spiritual exercises, indicates Evagrius as a nodal point of the encounter of several philosophical threads, officiating the resurrection of Greek philosophy in the new Christian body. Evagrius's corpus stands out amid both pagan and Christian texts thanks to the depth of psychological insight, detail of observation, and explicitness of method. Hadot observes that for the Christian monastics the remembrance involved in the spiritual exercises of self and God required a constant "examination of conscience" which was first mentioned by Origen as a series of self-addressed questions familiar throughout the tradition constituted by Pythagoreans, Epicureans, Stoics, a Plutarch, and a Galen (134). The methods of subjecting oneself to examination constituted an object of thorough study: the frequency (hourly, daily, seasonal), the medium (written or not), the state of consciousness (dreaming or awake) were aspects to be taken into account. Athanasius tells us that Anthony, the first monastic, much valued the written self-record for its therapeutic merits—which became the *journal intime* of later days. The quality of one's dreams indicated the spiritual state of the soul for Evagrius, as it did for Hippocrates, Plato, and Zeno. Attention to oneself was a sign of "self-mastery, the triumph of reason over passions," since passions caused distraction, dispersion, and dissipation of the soul. Hadot notes that these spiritual exercises, "repetitious actions, training to modify and transform ourselves," implied certain reflectivity different from evangelical spontaneity (135–36).

PROSOCHE: ATTENTION TO THE PRESENT MOMENT

What do attention to oneself and vigilance imply? They presuppose, Hadot writes, "a continuous concentration on the present moment which must be lived as if it were simultaneously the first and last moment of life" (131). There is an immediate relation between the degree of self-awareness and time, or rather the sense of time, according to Hadot. The call to total presence in the moment has an illustrious history. The condition for the possibility of such a total self-presence was thought to be an apocalyptic vision. The specter of one's own immediate annihilation effects an instant transfiguration of the self: it awakens the self from its slumbers. Death, attention to oneself, and time are tightly linked. For the Stoic and the monastic alike, mindfulness in the moment implies vigilance over thought and intentions, and is equivalent to "one of the fundamental themes of philosophical *prosoche*," that is, the spiritual exercise of the continuous presence both to God and to oneself (132). Hadot, like Nietzsche, considers the image of the Greeks that, according to Goethe, enjoyed the "healthiness of the moment" and had the gift of being able to live in the present a pure fiction (217–37). The Stoic and Epicurean philosophies in particular were meant precisely as therapies to remove the burden of the past, the uncertainty of the future, and the fear of death, in other words, the curse of existence. These philosophies were sui generis therapies intended to provide a cure for anguish, to bring freedom and self-mastery; their goal was to enable followers to free themselves from the past and the future so that they could live in the present. They imply a voluntary, radical transformation of one's way of living and looking at the world, and this philosophical *metanoia* is the true healthiness of the moment that leads to serenity (121–22).

Thus Hadot sees the common goal of Epicurean and Stoic therapeutics as the achievement of peace of mind by the self's integration into the cosmic order. This integration is made possible through the fullness and perfection of the moment, the *kairos*. The insertion in time requires a change in one's attitude toward time and oneself, bracketing past and future. For the Epicurean this is the condition for attaining wisdom since "the life of the foolish man is fearful and unpleasant, it is swept totally away into the future" (223). The passions steal our attention away from the present moment. The miracle of the present moment is lost through inattention and negligence caused by eccentric passions. It is only in the fullness of the lived present that eternity can be touched: the present is pregnant with eternity. What is the present? Hadot points to the Stoic double understanding of the present. First there is the "abstract, quasi-mathematical division, with the present being reduced to an infinitesimal instant"; it is "the limit between the past and the future." According to this definition "no present time ever actually exists since time is infinitely divisible" (227). Augustine had this elusive present in mind in his discourse on the impossibility of grasping the fugitive instant. It is Zeno's space in which the rabbit can never catch up with the tortoise. A second definition of the present is one in which time is defined in reference to consciousness. It is the present of lovers, human and divine, the all-encompassing fullness of time. On the one hand, the present is the only point of contact with reality, the only time under our control. On the other hand, a moment of happiness is equivalent to an eternity of happiness. That is the reason why one of the principal aims of both ancient and Christian spiritual exercises was a transformation in the perception of time.

FOUCAULT AND CARE OF THE SELF

In his study, Hadot also adduces Michel Foucault's reflections on the "care of the self" (206–13). Whereas both thinkers are interested in resuscitating the ancient understanding of philosophy as an "art, style, way of life," Hadot posits that their interpretation of this art differs somewhat (206). While both maintain that the cultivation of the self implied for Epicureans and Stoics an attunement of the self with the cosmos and with universal reason, respectively, which aimed at self-transcendence, Foucault overemphasizes—according to Hadot—the self and the principle of pleasure within the economy of the cultivation of the self. Foucault brings out aspects of the care of the self, however, that Hadot neglects. One such aspect is the relation between philosophy and medicine, which the art of caring for the self made visible. In keeping with a tradition that goes back a very long time in Greek culture, the care of the self is in close correlation with medical thought and practice. The rapprochement between the two fields is facilitated by their sharing one central element, namely, the concept of pathos which "applies to passion as well as to physical illness, to the distress of the body and to the involuntary movement of the soul; and in both cases alike, it refers to a state of passivity which for the body takes the form of a disorder that upsets the balance of its humors or its qualities and which for the soul takes the form of a movement capable of carrying it away in spite of itself."[11]

This acknowledgement of the correlation between the condition of the body and the state of the soul or mind initiates a series of correspondences between the two domains. Linguistically it is manifested in the use of medical metaphors for the description of therapeutics devised for the condition of the soul. Methodologically it expresses itself in the ethical ambitions and metaphysical presuppositions of a physician like Galen who, according to Foucault, believed it within his competence not only to "cure the great aberrations of the mind but to treat the passions and the errors of false opinion" (56). Foucault remarks that the attention given to the body in an ethos in which philosophy was seen as a preparation for death was somewhat paradoxical. Medically obvious, the correlation body-spirit imposes a relatively temperate attitude toward the body, neither discarding nor idolizing it. The object of attention, however, is not the body itself as the "crossover point" between body and soul, but rather the perception of oneself as diseased. This perception of oneself as weak, ill at ease, or dis-eased and in need of a cure emphasizes the idea of constant care of the soul. It also makes explicit the need for a hermeneutic skill of deciphering signs of disease in an otherwise unsuspecting, seemingly healthy organism. Foucault explains:

> And the establishing of the relation to oneself as a sick individual is all the more necessary because the diseases of the soul—unlike those of the body—do not announce themselves by the suffering that one perceives; not only can they go undetected for a long time, but they blind those whom they afflict. Plutarch remarks that the disorders of the body can generally be detected by the pulse, bile, temperature, and pains; and further, that the worst physical illnesses are those in which—as in lethargy, epilepsy, or apoplexy—the individual is not aware of his state. The insidious thing about the diseases of the soul is that they pass unnoticed, or even that one can mistake them for virtues. (58)

In the end all the exercises aim at knowledge of the self. They constitute the mental labor necessary for the acquisition of learning in the domain of the self. As in any other domain of knowledge, mastery over a particular subject or art offers the freedom to make wise and discriminate use of that subject or art. The most perilous condition is that of the organism diseased but unaware of it: delusion, unconsciousness, blindness—"the unreflective life is not worth living" (Plato)—from which only self-knowledge can liberate and save the soul.

CASSIAN AND THE SIN OF SLOTH

While Evagrius's spiritual exercises, intended as a self-applied exorcism, imply intellectual work, with John Cassian (ca. 360–433 C.E.) acedia emerges as the sin of sloth for which, correspondingly, manual work becomes the principal remedy. Cassian, Evagrius's closest follower, is the carrier of desert monasticism and the concept of mortal sin into Western Christianity. In the aftermath of the Church's persecution of the Origenist monastic society and Evagrius's death, Cassian left the Egyptian desert and founded the first monastic establishment in Paris. There he wrote two treatises of practical theology, *The Monastic Institutes* and *The Conferences*. While introducing the eight mortal sins into Latin theology, Cassian adopted the Evagrian phenomenology of acedia, as well as its specific distinction from, yet resemblance to, *tristitia*—two distinct terms rendered by the contemporary translator Jerome Bertram as "depression" and "melancholy" respectively.[12] The presentation of acedic deception is made in the mode *as if*: one feels *as if* heavy, exhausted, hungry, tied down, burdened, void of spiritual advance, empty, in mental turmoil, overwhelmed by gloomy darkness. These feelings are delusions provoked by demonic agency to trigger restlessness, a sense of futility, discontent with one's place, time, work, and a desire for other places, people, activities. The demon of acedia, a master of deception, begins its attack in the recesses of one's soul with hallucinatory perceptions of self and world. The attack occurs at noon. The phenomenological description of the noontide demon attack is patterned after the Evagrian model. The monk despairs of his salvation. He looks anxiously this way and that, goes in and out of his cell, looks at the sun, which seems to be slow in setting. He either consoles himself in sleep or leaves in pursuit of distraction. These two ad hoc remedies, sleep and distracting activity, are not simply false remedies but actually constitute the sin of acedia for which the true remedy is manual work. Cassian concludes that "the attacks of acedia should not be avoided by flight but resisted and overcome," and brings illustrative details into the portrait of acedia (161). He tells stories about idle monks, cites several references to sloth in Proverbs, and ends with examples of victory over the condition through ceaseless work, even work performed exclusively for its own sake as a therapeutic or preventive measure.[13]

Cassian's discourse on acedia comprises three progressively clarifying and reductive stages. Initially he covers the entire Evagrian territory; he perceives its paradoxical nature and reduces its effects to two opposing movements: idleness or sloth and restiveness. Since Cassian, like Robert Burton later, concentrates on idleness as the principal characteristic, he prescribes manual labor as the principal remedy. In the case of tristitia, or melancholy, Cassian, like Evagrius, distinguishes two forms: a beneficial one, a God-sent sadness that "comes to us through sorrow for our sins, the desire of perfection or the consideration of future bliss," and a demonic, deadly type that leads to despair and is "harsh, intolerant, cruel, full of rancor and futile gloom . . . breaks and drags [a man] away from any useful or salutary grief, being quite unreasonable."[14] The remedy for both types is filling the mind with divine things that would bring hope for the promised future bliss, joy, and equanimity.[15]

While apparently there is no disagreement between Evagrius and Cassian in their respective descriptions and valuations of acedia and tristitia, Cassian's treatment brings an emphasis that will subsequently establish a different identity, that of the sin of sloth, and will also help identify the specific nature of acedic boredom as distinct from melancholy. Whereas with both Evagrius and Cassian, acedic boredom appears as the *religiose Unlust* that provokes *horror loci* and *horror tempi* and whose ultimate effect is an encounter with nothingness on the threshold of total futility and despair, Cassian introduces a new accent in the interpretation of the sin.[16] Scholars have pointed out that the main transformation in the identity of acedic boredom from Evagrius to Cassian is its reduction to idleness-sloth-otium, which can be explained as a consequence of the change of habitat from desert to monastery.[17] Corresponding to this shift in the etiology of the condition, the remedy replaces intellectual work with manual work. The shift indicates an important modification of weltanschauung. In the translation from desert monasticism to Parisian coenobitism, the metaphysical presuppositions have undergone a fundamental transformation from the neo-Platonism of Evagrius to the Christian incarnationism of Cassian. While the symptoms remain the same, their interpretation evolves from a docetic to an incarnational approach.

When recommending the remedy of spiritual exercises, Evagrius intends the mind, while Cassian intends the entire being. Cassian does not reduce acedic boredom to sloth; rather he indicates a psychosomatic understanding of the role played by the body in the malady of the soul. Whereas for Evagrius, an intellectual well versed in Greek philosophy, the neo-Platonic tendency is undisguised and fashions both his theoretical work and his teaching of praxis, with Cassian, man appears as an integrated totality of body and spirit. Michel Henry will later refer to this as our "subjective pathetic body," while according to Ricoeur the acedic self, undergoing the experiences of heaviness, darkness, emptiness, appears as the *faille*, the locus where disproportion of the self is visible to itself as the revolt and revenge of the pole of finitude—matter and body—against that of the infinite—the spirit. Human nature resists the unnatural commandments of the spirit. As if angered by the prolonged *askesis*, the body rebels and emerges as a hostile resisting other, as the power of Saturn, the god of gravitation and petrification. It becomes the embodiment of unfreedom and inertia: slow, heavy, exhausted, depressed, burdened, falling into sleep as the death of the spirit; or it tries to escape the heaviness of the burden by flight into the world. It runs out of itself and its home. It becomes homeless, a wanderer, lost. Cassian warns: this fleeing oneself is not a cure but the perfection of the curse, an advanced stage of the disease. Since the disease causes solidification, a regression to a prehuman mineral state, manual work is therapeutic as a mode of attending to the materiality of the body, of enlivening it, thus appeasing its anger. Beyond differences and variants, the constant characteristic of acedia remains the peculiar nature of acedic time: the regularity of its attacks are indicative of its dependence on natural rhythms and, more importantly, its distorted perception of time.

THOMAS AQUINAS: SPIRITUAL APATHY

With Aquinas the union of acedia and tristitia is accomplished. Once these sins first leave the desert, then the courtyards of monastic enclosure, and enter the secular city, they are increasingly difficult to separate. With Gregory the Great's fusion of the two under the name of tristitia, the list of the eight mortal sins is reduced to seven. Aquinas will include tristitia under the category of acedia and create a division of gravity between acedia and despair. Aquinas's treatment of the sin of acedia occurs in *De Malo* and in the *Summa Theologiae*. In the format of scholastic debate, Aquinas marshals abundant evidence both for and against the consideration of acedia as a deadly sin. Aristotle, John of Damascus, Cassian, Peter Lombard, and Gregory the Great are the main authorities guiding his conclusions. Aquinas's acedia—translated by Thomas R. Heath as "spiritual apathy"—is an oppressive sadness about the divine good. It is a special sin in being opposed to spiritual joy; a mortal sin in being contrary to the command of keeping the sabbath holy, that is, keeping the repose of the mind in God; a capital sin in being the cause of other vices such as the wandering of the mind after illicit things, despair, sluggishness, faint-heartedness, pusillanimity, rancor, malice, anger, hatred, sadness, uneasiness of mind importunately rushing after this or that without rhyme or reason, idle curiosity, loquaciousness, bodily restlessness, instability, fluctuation of purpose. If it is an act of the sense appetite, a passion, acedia is only a venial sin and can affect even holy men. Aquinas writes: "A sense appetite has a bodily organ and corporeal changes make man more susceptible to certain sins. When a set of corporeal changes happens at set times, insistently, certain sins tempt us more. At about noon when people fasting really begin to feel the lack of food and the sun's heat, they are more bothered by acedia."[18]

For Aquinas acedia is a sin only if it involves the intellective appetite, the will, and if by indulging in acedic dialectics of mood "reason consents to the horror and loathing of the divine good and submits to the flesh's utter victory over spirit."[19] At this point becoming a mortal sin, acedia is the ground for despair, the sin opposed to the theological virtue of hope, the uniquely unpardonable sin against the Holy Spirit, and one of the three theological sins in addition to hatred of God and infidelity.[20] Certainly the sins against the three theological virtues—love of God, faith, and hope—are more serious than all other sins. Aquinas prescribes as remedy for acedia mental control over sorrow, resistance through steadying the mind, thinking about spiritual good, and cultivating joy in the divine good. According to him, acedia is particularly pernicious because, although it is both a capital sin by being the source of other sins and a mortal sin by killing the spiritual life, acedia appears as an unspecific spiritual apathy and tends to pass unnoticed. With Aquinas, acedia stands apart as the grey eminence among moral sins. Its ubiquitous presence is betrayed by the fact that, like a shadow, it follows or precedes all other sins, and occurs without apparent cause. Its deadliness consists precisely in a seemingly inconsequential manifestation—weariness, a passing loss of interest, a contextually justifiable boredom, and related restlessness—that is not a moral offense for oneself or the other, and thus does not call forth immediate intervention. If not attended to immediately, however, it continues unimpeded its invisible deadly work on the soul until it is too late for remedy: the falling away from the divine ground is accomplished.

Thus Aquinas's account makes several modifications to the original paradigm, modifications with seminal consequences for the interpretation of acedia. For Evagrius, acedia appears in the pure state of its Greek meaning of "carelessness." In following on the one hand the tradition of the Latin Vulgate, which translated grief by *accidie*, and on the other hand the authority of Gregory the Great, who merged the sins of sadness and of acedia into one, Aquinas fuses Greek acedia (carelessness) and Latin accidie (sadness or grief). To the semantic, resemblance was added a phonetic and terminological resemblance. As a consequence, the identity of the Evagrian acedia, as well as the distinction between it and tristitia, is obliterated. From now on carelessness, boredom, depression, sloth, anxiety, tristitia, and despair will fare together as a constellation of names and symptoms pertaining to the same condition of sin and differing only in emphasis and degree of intensity. Aquinas thus establishes the status of acedia, previously related exclusively to the monastic condition, as a mortal sin of the layman. His emphasis on the will in the task of resisting the temptation plays down demonic, bodily, and cosmic causation. With Aquinas, who is concerned with the movements of the will, acedia takes on a new identity and emerges as a mortal sin of the will for which the remedy is willful resistance and cultivation of joy.

The threefold therapeutics, ranging from the Evagrian work of the intellect and Cassian's work of the body to Aquinas's work of the will, indicate that acedia-melancholy, has been viewed as a complex condition that "infects" the whole being. The list of remedies is variegated: some address the body through purification (fasting, diet, hot baths, walking); others address the intellect, both inferior (reflection, readings from established authorities) and superior (mental concentration, prayer, contemplation); others engage the will (courage, fortitude), or the entire being (self-knowledge, the art of the discernment of spirits, music). What is common to all these spiritual exercises is the fact that they all imply exertion and effort, in other words, they are all forms of work.

According to a Ricoeurian reading, acedia-melancholy is not a sinful act, but rather a sinful condition, even the sinful condition par excellence. Indeed, the sinful temptation is the temptation to forget oneself in distraction or in sleep and return to a natural state, qua matter, become a stone, petrify; it is a negation of the spirit, an assault of the nothing and nonbeing. To resist this demonic temptation to nonbeing, a new creation is needed. Work with the hands puts the body in motion, brings it back to life from its slip of inattention into nonbeing. Movement is only a rudimentary first form of life. Becoming fully human requires an alchemical process; it involves a transfiguration of matter. To rise out of nonbeing presupposes a series of transmutations: from the inertia of the slothful body through manual work; from the inertia of the desireless heart through love; from the inertia of indifferent mind through reflection. The complexity and diversity of therapeutic suggestions is remarkable and constitutes an implicit commentary on the complex nature of melancholy.

RICOEUR: ACEDIA AS THE CONDITION OF SIN ITSELF

For contemporary consciousness, the idea that melancholy in any of its hypostases of acedia as *taedium vitae*, boredom, or depression, is a sin has neither credibility nor appeal.[21] In *The Depleted Self*, an insightful study of the problem of sin in our time, Donald Capps proposes the concept of shame as a more acceptable substitute for the concept of sin to explain the present condition of depletion experienced by the self.[22] Capps argues that the depleted self sees itself as a victim of shame rather than a perpetrator of sin. Arguably, it seems counterintuitive to consider depression as a mortal sin, even within a theological setting. The present chapter investigates the meaning and value for contemporary culture of the theology of sin in general and of depression in particular. In referring at this juncture to Ricoeur's reflection on fallibility and the symbolism of evil, I entertain several hopes: to understand the concept of sin with a view to clarifying what acedia may mean theologically in relation to fault, sin, and guilt; to recognize that acedia is more than one sin among others, but rather is the condition of sin; and to realize the complex nature of this condition by situating it within the four myths of the beginning, namely, the myth of creation, the myth of the fall, the myth of the tragic hero, the myth of the exiled soul.[23] Ultimately, we will seek to justify revisiting the concept of sin within the problematic of a secularized acedia.

Sin, according to the most general and theologically accepted definition, is the reversal or negation of the initiative of the love of God; it is essentially man's refusal to accept this relation to God, although it constitutes his being, and the history of salvation recorded in Scripture is the history of the tirelessly repeated attempt of God's love to restore it when man broke it.[24] Sin designates rupture from God, and is the original initiative that institutes and constitutes the human self. As a prototype of all subsequent sins, original sin reveals its intrinsic nature: conscious and voluntary violation of the divine commandment. The external act is the consequence of inner corruption, the radical perversion of the creature that refuses its dependence on its creator and becomes a rival instead. Nevertheless, while sin has commonly been understood as a voluntary act or attitude of refusal of divine law or love and has been identified mostly with arrogance, pride, or covetousness, already with John, but especially with Paul and Augustine, a different and even opposed interpretation emerges as well. According to it, evil appears as a mysterious reality in which the self always already finds itself. It is precisely the preindividuated presence of evil that is explained by the concept of original sin, an act that antedates individual agency. Indeed, the concept of original sin has two seminal implications: that the reality of evil and sin is embedded in the structure of the world and that the eclipse of consciousness inherent in sin is a mark of natural humanity, or, in mythical terms, a trace of the sin of the first human couple. Thus the paradigm of original sin presupposes both the enigmatic figure of the serpent and self-forgetting; it is on the ground of external temptation and interior dizziness that the will acts, therefore its decision is not fully free since original sin already clouds the mind and perverts the will. It is a condition in which the individual is born, the sinful condition par excellence, that inscribes itself in an individual history as the law of the "flesh" before and beyond any sinful act. This sinful condition in which humanity is captive and bound to a hostile other requires divine intervention, that is, grace. Outside of grace, the self remains unknown to itself, the enigma of a self in contradiction with itself.[25]

CONFESSION AS THE LOCUS WHERE EVIL BECOMES VISIBLE

Ricoeur argues the possibility and relevance of a philosophical study of the involuntary, pathos, and sin. Philosophy derives its existence, he thinks, from the substance of what has already been understood prior to reflection, therefore its task is a methodical elucidation of a nonphilosophical precomprehension.[26] This belief explains his recourse to symbol and myth. In answer to the question, "What is the point of insertion of evil in human reality?" he proposes a philosophical anthropology centered on the theme of fallibility. The concept of fallibility deepens the study of the voluntary and the involuntary into the more encompassing dialectic of human disproportion between the finite and the infinite (xliv).

Ricoeur maintains that although the origin of evil transcends the domain of the human, phenomenologically, evil becomes visible only in man because, irrespective of its origin, evil can appear and be recognized only by consciousness.[27] This state of affairs justifies the theological significance of confession. Confession of sins is the deliberate recognition and assumption of evil and, as such, the freedom of the will that takes evil upon itself.[28] What are the merits of assuming a foreign evil as one's own fault or sin? And more specifically, can modern consciousness still understand and accept melancholy in any of its hypostases—as depression, boredom, apathy—as sin? By assuming the agency of evil, Ricoeur proposes, confession is the locus where the interrogation of evil begins, an interrogation that in the end may dismantle the ethical vision itself. The ethical vision is a provocation to questioning, a hermeneutical tool for initiating an interrogation of freedom and evil in man. Thereby confession has been deemed an event of grace, a sacrament, as well as the beginning of a transition from self-ignorance to self-knowledge; it is the condition for the possibility of self-awakening, self-remembering, and self-understanding through the labor of self-reflection that assumes the past within an interpretation of the destiny of the self. Freedom can begin only with this assumption of responsibility for the evil either inflicted or suffered. The self-reflection induced by confession, Ricoeur argues, is constitutive of the self as undivided causality, as a primordial self beyond its acts:

> In joining together the temporal ecstasies of the past and the future in the core of freedom, the consciousness of fault also manifests the total and undivided causality of the self over and above individual acts. . . . Where it is a question of reflection attentive to projects alone, this causality divides itself in pieces and fritters itself away in a disjunctive inventing of myself; but in pertinent retrospection I root my acts in the undivided causality of the self. Certainly, we have no access to this self outside of its specific acts but the consciousness of fault makes manifest in them the demand for wholeness that constitutes us. This consciousness is a recourse to the primordial self beyond its acts. (xlviii)

The problematic of the self may be engaged from within an ethical self-interrogation. This self-interrogation begins with a confession of sins as the locus of reflection on both self and evil. The confession of sins provides the conditions for the possibility of forgiveness, the cleansing of consciousness from the stain that seems indelible, and creates the possibility of renewal of the self, its rebirth into the absolute novum. Grounded in these presuppositions, the act of confession itself also implies bringing into consciousness and language the shadowy crepuscular deed or the unfulfilled intention, thought, or mood. Confession liberates the victim-perpetrator by bringing the obscure mood into consciousness through its expression; the validation of the self through the other who hears the confession is also therapeutic. The psychoanalytic "talking cure" or today's various types of psychological counseling are its secularized variants. But religious confession goes deeper because, in the confession of sin, the depressed soul stands before God: infinite guilt or debt is forgiven, while the cleansed soul, unburdened and freed from the bondage to sin, is renewed by grace.

DISPROPORTION AS THE GROUND FOR FALLIBILITY

In thinking evil through the category of the ethical, the self is constituted as an enduring Kantian demand for totality, meaning, and ethical restoration. Consciousness of fault is certainly a paradox, the paradox of a servile will and a guilty victim. Since this paradox is an *aporia* of reflection, the symbolical-mythical domain must remain its natural residence, as only symbol and myth can allow for such resilient ambiguity. Ricoeur conceives the problematic of the symbolism of evil as a *pathétique* both of misery and of pure reflection, thus introducing fallibility as an experience accessible to pure reflection.

He considers and verifies two hypotheses: the rational approach is justified only if the idea that fragility and liability to erring designates an ontological characteristic of man's being. If this hypothesis is proven correct, the concept of fallibility will be made intelligible as a possibility intrinsic to man. The second hypothesis affirms the noncoincidence of man with himself, the disproportion of self to self. Faced with these two hypotheses, Ricoeur assumes the task of determining the point of departure for a philosophical anthropology placed under the idea of fallibility (1–4). He explains that a philosophical anthropology centered on fallibility needs two points of departure, prephilosophical and philosophical, or pathetic and transcendental: the pre-philosophical *pathétique* of misery given in myth and rhetoric is the substance that transcendental reflection takes up in thought. Certainly, the transformation of pure reflection into an equivalent of the *pathétique* of misery cannot but remain an ever retreating horizon to be approached via a hermeneutics of the fundamental symbols of fallibility (6); ultimately, the truth of human disproportion is confirmed by the impossibility of a perfect coincidence between pure reflection and pathetic precomprehension.

Once the two hypotheses have been proven correct, Ricoeur engages in the work of revising the history of thinking in light of this perspective. He identifies the preunderstanding of fallible man as a *pathétique* of misery in both Plato's myths and Pascal's rhetoric. Both instances evince the resistance to thought of prephilosophical narrative. The first case study is Plato. Plato's myth of Eros is a representation of the genesis and constitution of the soul. *Thumos*, the heart, is the locus of unstable and fragile function represented statically as the in-between, and dynamically as the mélange. Myth's resistance to thought resides in the aporetic nature of the mythicized condition: "Affliction is both primordial limitation and original evil . . . an undivided whole of limitation and moral evil" (9). A myth of fragility and a myth of downfall are fused into one; the trajectory slides from fragility to vertigo to fall, in the chiaroscuro of disgrace, forgetfulness, and perversion. He chooses Pascal as the second example. Pascal's spatial image of the two abysses as a figura of the human ontic identity is a representation of constitutive ontic fragility, whereas fault consists in distraction, diversion, and dissimulation. Fallibility appears as the fragility of an ontic condition of mélange that is the condition for the possibility of fault. Thus, fault is a hybrid of voluntary and involuntary movements of the soul. Plato's forgetfulness and Pascal's distraction are instances of this mixture of voluntary and involuntary that makes fault a hybrid of innocence and guilt.

The sin of depression inhabits this chiaroscuro. There is a distinction between depression as sinful condition and depression as sinful act that can be clearly seen in the distinction between fragility and fault: the former is a symptom of the fragility of metaxic being, the latter is the careless giving in to the compensatory impulse to distraction—which for Evagrius represented one form of the sin. Ricoeur's distinction between fallibility and fault helps clarify the depressive hypostases by discussing the anthropological implications of the old controversy between Pelagius and Augustine, the distinction between the theology of sin and the theology of grace. Pelagius's theology of sin insists in locating the sin in the will; its fundamental presupposition is the absolute supremacy of the voluntary over the involuntary. It implies confidence in the power of consciousness to detect the moment of insertion of evil and the subsequent ability of the moral will to intervene and prevent it. Conversely, the theology of grace has admitted, with Paul and Augustine, the impotence of the will to act according to the light of intellect, an impotence that makes the intervention of grace the salvific factor sine qua non. It posits an unruly resistance, an *otherness*—variously interpreted as matter, body, fallen nature, flesh, the will to evil, nonbeing, demons—that resides in the heart. It is interesting to note that acedia-melancholy has indeed been considered as a twofold weakness, to wit, of the human embodied condition generally and of the free will more specifically. In other words, it makes clearly visible the two moments of fallibility and fault, the sliding from the former into the latter.

The second origin of a philosophical anthropology of fallibility is located, according to Ricoeur, in transcendental reflection—in the Kantian sense of the term. By making the transition from mythos to logos, transcendental reflection is the condition for the transposition of the pathos of misery into a philosophy of fallibility. Within transcendental reflection, disproportion is located in the synthesis between understanding and sensibility effectuated by imagination. At this stage "the mélange of the pathos is called synthesis" (18). In order to understand the synthesis of the imagination as a fundamental disproportion—one conditioning the fallibility of man as consciousness—Ricoeur discusses the polarities of Cartesian infinite will and finite understanding, Hegel's certainty and truth, and Husserl's noesis and noema. The paradox embedded in the discovery of finitude is the fact that it is man himself who speaks of his own finitude (24). But finitude, knowing and expressing itself, has already transcended itself. This means that the discourse on finitude is a discourse on both the finitude and the infinitude of man (25). With respect to acedia, this self-transcendence through language is immediately visible since bringing pathos into language has been an important form of alleviation. Ricoeur explains, with Husserl, that we do not exhaust ourselves in the intentionality of fulfilled presence, but can speak of absence and signify emptily (28). The fact that we can say more than we see, that we can speak of the absent, that we are not exhausted in the intentionality of fulfilled presence points to our transcendence. As Ricoeur remarks, the synthesis of the imagination is only an intention, a presupposition. In itself it remains an enigma. Transcendental reflection on the power of knowing as the first stage of a philosophy of disproportion proves incapable of including pathetic understanding. Nevertheless, the importance of the attempt resides paradoxically in the reduction of the self to a thinking self. The reduced self is made problematic, thus visible.

Fallibility emerges as a constitutive ontological structure. It rends man's being across from the affective to the practical to the theoretical levels. It is the condition for the possibility of evil. It appears as the noncoincidence of self to itself, since disproportion is the specifically human form of disproportion between finitude and infinitude. Moreover, Ricoeur sees in this relation the ontological locus between being and nothingness (134). This limitation, specifically human, is synonymous with fallibility, the *faille*. But fallibility is merely the condition for the possibility of fault and not yet the reality of fault. Between the possibility and the reality of fault and evil there is a gap that is indicated by the difference between philosophical anthropology and ethics.

THE SYMBOLISM OF EVIL

Given that the enigmatic leap from fallibility into evil remains ever with us, Ricoeur proceeds from a phenomenology of fallibility to an exploration of the symbolism of evil. He maintains that primordial perfection is the original paradigm, and therefore fallenness can only be a pseudo-genesis (143). Nevertheless, according to Ricoeur, only the fallen is immediately visible, while primordial perfection remains inaccessible. In fact, the main presupposition of Ricoeur's entire enterprise is that access to the primordial is possible only through fallenness. The myth of the fall and the myth of creation presuppose each other. His recourse to a symbolism of evil is thus justified on three counts: first, it facilitates an encounter with originating affirmation; second, it makes visible the slide from fallibility into fault; third, it deepens the question of fallibility itself by showing the ambiguity of the transition from the mere possibility of evil to its reality. The latter transition is both a voluntary leap and an involuntary sliding; this ambiguity is represented by the paradoxical symbol of the servile and guilty will.

The symbolism of melancholy becomes visible in Ricoeur's work in the slide from fallibility into sin, and in the symbolism of defilement, sin, and guilt—of which melancholy is a mélange. The symbol of defilement is the most archaic of the symbols of evil and posits the evil of contagion and contamination, in other words, the evil of substance. It is the body that suffers evil by an infection coming from the outside. It is the most physical and objectified form of evil, one that is seen in its positivity and realism as an infectious power, literally a disease, and the external evil agency can extend to include a demonology. It is inscribed in the world of magic and possession, and the remedy is bodily purification. Interestingly, Ricoeur observes that the Greeks, who never arrived at the concept of sin, took over the symbol of purification in philosophical thought. The myths in which the symbol of defilement operates are the myths of primordial chaos and primordial dualism of good and evil. In modernity, it is German idealism that rethinks creation along the lines of the Babylonian mythical imagination by postulating the coeternal existence of the negative and the positive principles throughout divine life and creation. This paradigm of defilement is present in one aspect of the sin of acedia: the body is infected both by cosmic and demonic agency. The humor, the time of the day, the space of the desert, the heat of the sun, and bodily weakness, along with demonic intervention, constitute a complex external and physical causality. The medical terminology as well as the association with the noontide demon indicate acedia's original participation in the pre-Christian symbolism of defilement.

But this is only the most archaic meaning in interpreting melancholy; the symbol of sin is also present, and with sin we enter the universe of theology. Sin presupposes the existence of a dialogical relation with God, a relation that human agency interrupts precisely through willful desire. The sin of acedia preserves the involuntary dimension characteristic of defilement as well as the voluntary dimension characteristic of ethical sin. It is in weakness, carelessness, negligence, and passivity that the will inserts itself. The infection of defilement allows for the slide into sin; it is not a voluntary step but a slip of self-forgetfulness. The articulation of the infinite desire of God and transcendence and the finite desire of the world and its objects is, in the eclipse of self-consciousness, the condition for the possibility of sin. The mood in which the shift from infinite desire of God to finite desire occurs is the meontological feeling par excellence.

Guilt, the third symbol of evil, is also a principal component of acedia. As we will see further on, both acedia and melancholy are defined by what Hubertus Tellenbach and Ludwig Binswanger term the "delirium of guilt." With guilt replacing sin in response to the death of God, modernity emerges out of the theological dimension and the relationship with God toward a deepening refusal or denial of that relationship. The guilty consciousness has neither cause nor judging authority outside itself. Thus, acedia participates in all three symbols of evil as outlined by Ricoeur: defilement, sin, and guilt.

ACEDIA'S COMPLEX SYMBOLIC STRUCTURE

It has become visible that acedia as a condition and a sinful act of the will is a complex structure of meaning involving several dimensions of the human being. The demonic temptation to which the monastic may succumb, although present in Christian theology when the first list of sins appeared in written form, was a survival of the pre-Christian myth of primordial dualism. Demonic presence and activity are theologically presupposed by Evagrius, since by that time demonic temptation had been adopted by and adapted into a theology of the fall. The existence and activity of a nondivine and nonhuman element always carries with it the suspicion of a hidden extra- or intradivine dualism. A principle of negativity and nonbeing, an otherness exterior to divinity—or even more disquietingly, interior to it—overpowers both divine omnipotence and love. At the same time, Cassian and Aquinas refer to it, literally rather than metaphorically, as a disease that infects the will, the mind, and if not stopped, the soul itself. It thus appears that acedia preserves a trace of the fourth type of the myth of the beginning of evil as well: the exile of the soul into matter. The problematics of the myth of the tragic hero emerges as well, and with it the guilt and revolt about an evil committed unknowingly, and the specter of a God who permits and provokes evil, or of the absence of God.

A complex symbolic structure, the sin of acedia coalesces all the fundamental meanings of the symbols of evil and can be accommodated by all the four types of explanatory myths of creation. In light of Ricoeur's foregoing analysis it becomes possible to speculate that the noncoincidence of the self with itself creates the space where acedia becomes manifest: in the experience of the self in the desert, whether of medieval Egypt or late modernity, the horizon of infinitude sustained by transcendent words and the finite horizon of immediate perception clash. The individual intends to annul the pole of finitude by a total kenosis of the here-now-this. He intends to live in the transcendence made possible by the word. Certainly, this desire is understandable within a theology of the word. But the same theology pronounces grace as the only possibility of salvation. Acedia is the moment of human finitude experiencing the absence of grace, the crisis of relapse into the realm of dichotomy that calls forth a synthesis of the imagination. The impossibility of living exclusively in the category of transcendence and infinitude is the fallible self's cross to bear.

NOTES

1. John Eudes Bamberger refers to Bouyer's belief that there are reasons to believe that Pseudo-Dionysus, the father of Western mysticism, borrowed the basic elements of his theology from Evagrius; see "Introduction," *The Praktikos and Chapters on*

Prayer, trans. John Eudes Bamberger (Kalamazoo: Cistercian, 1981), lvii. Hereafter this work is cited in the text as *Praktikos*.

2. Evagrius, *The Praktikos*: "There are eight basic categories of thoughts in which are included every thought. First is that of gluttony, then impurity, avarice, sadness, anger, acedia, vainglory and last of all pride. It is not in our power to determine whether we are disturbed by these thoughts but it is up to us to decide if they are to linger within us or not and whether or not they are to stir up our passions" (16–17, §6).

3. John Eudes Bamberger, "Introduction" to *The Praktikos*: "One of the best instances of this more descriptive style is found in the chapter of the *Praktikos* dealing with the vice of acedia. In fact it was in the area of descriptive psychology that Evagrius exercised one of his chief influences on later monastic tradition" (lxvii–lxviii).

4. Evagrius, *Sur les pensées* (On thoughts), trans. Paul Gehin and Claire and Antoine Guillamont (Paris: Éditions du cerf, 1998), 293, 291. This Evagrian text is not available in English; all translations from the French are mine. Hereafter this work is cited in the text as *Pensées*.

5. Evagrius, *Sur les pensées*: "The Lord has given man the representations of this age like sheep to a good shepherd . . . night and day the recluse must guard this small flock for fear that one of these representations may become the victim of wild beasts" (211).

6. Evagrius, *Sur les pensées*: "Observe these details so that you can unmask him when he gets near: show him the place he keeps secret and also let him know that you will no longer follow him there. If you want to make him totally mad, unmask him as soon as he shows up and with one word tell him the first place he entered, then the second and the third; since he cannot stand shame, this is particularly painful for him and it is impossible for him to last once openly unmasked" (185).

7. *Chapters on Prayer* (n. 1 above): "If you are a theologian you truly pray. If you truly pray, you are a theologian" (65, §60).

8. Evagrius, *Sur les pensées*, 191, 213. "Demons touch the lids and the whole head making it cold by their bodies since the bodies of demons are very cold and like ice. Also we feel our heads as if it be sucked away with a gnashing sound. They act like this in order to attract to themselves the warmth of the cranium and then the lids loosened by the humidity and the cold slide over the pupils of the eyes. . . . Often when I touched myself I found my lids frozen/cold" (269).

9. Evagrius, *Sur les pensées*: Acedic effects are also provoked by the demon of the dawn. The latter makes the intellect roam from place to place, imagining chance encounters until the monastic insensibly moves away from virtue and the science of God and forgets his own profession. Acedia is also mentioned in the chapter on the demon of spiritual indifference as a possible offspring of the latter (189–91).

10. Pierre Hadot, *Philosophy as a Way of Life: Spiritual Exercises from Socrates to Foucault*, trans. Michael Chase (Malden, Mass.: Blackwell, 1995).

11. Michel Foucault, "The Cultivation of the Self," in *Care of the Self*, trans. Robert Hurley (New York: Vintage, 1986), 54.

12. John Cassian, *The Monastic Institutes*, trans. Jerome Bertram (London: St. Austin, 1999): "When depression attacks the wretched monk, it engenders a

loathing for his situation, dislike of his cell, and contemptuous disparagement of his brethren, whether they live with him or at a distance, as if they were lax and unspiritual. It makes him desultory and lazy at any task to be done within the walls of his cell. It does not let him sit in his cell and apply himself to his duty of reading; he grumbles that he has frequently spent such a long time at this exercise and profited nothing; he complains with sighs that he can gain no spiritual benefit as long as he is tied to such company; he laments that he is quite void of any spiritual advancement, and stagnates in this futile place; although he is capable of governing others to their great advantage, he has made no foundation and no one is profiting from his training and instruction. He makes much of monasteries situated far off, and talks about their more advantageous positions and healthier sites. He describes the community of brothers there, how friendly and how deeply spiritual they are; while in contrast everything to hand is disagreeable; not only are the brothers living in this place quite dis-edifying, but it is impossible to make a living here without enormous effort. In fine, he considers he cannot be saved if he stays where he is and he must leave this cell which would be the death of him if he stayed in it, and take himself off as soon as possible. And then the middle of the day brings such physical weariness and hunger that he looks exhausted as if by a long journey or heavy labor, or seems half starved as if deprived of food for two or three days. He looks anxiously this way and that unhappy because no brother is coming to see him; he goes in and out of his cell and continually looks at the sun as if it were slow in setting. Thus in an unreasonable mental turmoil, as if overwhelmed in gloomy darkness, he becomes idle and empty of any spiritual work until he thinks he can find no cure for this weariness except in visiting some brother or else in the easy consolation of sleep. The disease suggests that it would be permissible, nay, necessary, to exchange greetings with brethren, to visit the sick even far off at a distance. Thus the unhappy soul is vexed and assaulted by these wiles of the enemy as if it were battered by a weighty ram until it gives in to sloth or becomes used to leaving the enclosure of the cell and finding consolation from this burden in visiting other monks. What it uses as an immediate remedy soon becomes a dangerous complaint in itself. For the adversary will assault the victim more often and more severely once he knows that he will turn his back if engaged in close conflict and sees that he puts his hope in flight not in victory or resistance; thus little by little he draws him from his cell till he begins to forget that the obligation of his profession is no more than the rapt contemplation of that divine purity which exceeds all things and which cannot be found anywhere except in silence and in remaining constantly in the cell in meditation. Whenever *acedia* begins to overwhelm anyone in anyway, he either suffers languor and inertia and remains in his cell with no spiritual benefit or else he departs from his cell and becomes thereafter unstable, wandering about, useless for anything and constantly going around the cells and monasteries of other brethren, for no other purpose than to anticipate some further possibility of entertainment on whatever excuse" (145–47).

13. Cassian, *Monastic Institutes*: "A monk cannot remain happily in one place without manual labor, nor even rise to perfect virtue, so that even when the necessities of life do not demand it, he should perform it simply for the purification of his heart,

the control of his thoughts, perseverance in the cell and the defeat and overthrow of *acedia* itself" (160).

14. Cassian, *Monastic Institutes*, Book 9: "If morbid melancholy can gain mastery over our hearts through individual occurrences and unspecific chances, it will eventually cut us off from any insight of divine contemplation and cast the mind down from its general state of purity to weaken it and depress it. It does not suffer us to complete our prayer with the usual mental alertness, allows no healing to come through spiritual reading, prevents us from being peaceful or at ease with our brethren and makes us impatient and touchy in all our manual or divine work. When all sound discernment is lost and the heart is worried and perturbed, it makes us all but distracted and dazed and breaks us with overwhelming gloom. Melancholy often follows on the preceding vice, anger, and can also arise from failing to acquire what avarice yearns for when we find we have failed to attain what we have been hoping for. But sometimes it arises for no apparent cause which might provoke us to such depths but we are cast down by the enemy's insinuations and oppressed by such sudden sadness that we are unable to welcome even our nearest and best beloved with our usual cheerfulness and whatever conversation they make with us we find irrelevant and unwanted. We can give them no pleasant answer while our whole hearts are tainted with the bitterness of melancholy. . . . the soul eaten up with the attacks of devouring gloom . . . is useless like a garment attacked by moth or wood riddled by worm" (139–40).

15. Cassian, *Monastic Institutes*: "To build up the mind with meditation on divine things and fill it with the thought of hope for the future and the consideration of our promised bliss. In the prospect of eternity and our reward to come we shall always be joyous and remain steadfast neither cast down by present misfortune nor elated by good chance but considering both to be temporary and soon to pass" (143).

16. Reinhard Kuhn, *The Demon of Noontide: Ennui in Western Literature* (introduction, n. 2), 51.

17. Siegfried Wenzel, *The Sin of Acedia: Acedia in Medieval Thought and Literature*, 22; Michael Raposa, *Boredom and the Religious Imagination*, 23 (introduction, n. 2).

18. Thomas Aquinas, *Summa Theologiae*, trans. Thomas R. Heath (New York: Blackfriars in conjunction with McGraw-Hill, 1972), 25.

19. Aquinas, *De Malo*, 361–62; *Summa Theologiae*, 31.

20. Aquinas, *Summa:* "It is rather typical of despair to issue from acedia" (99).

21. Throughout this part of the chapter, I will use the term acedia to refer to the condition identified by Evagrius in separation from sadness to avoid confusing the two and for the sake of simplicity.

22. Donald Capps, *The Depleted Self* (introduction, n. 2).

23. Paul Ricoeur, "The Myths of the Beginning and of the End," in *The Symbolism of Evil*, trans. Emerson Buchanan (Boston: Beacon, 1967).

24. Stanislas Lyonnet, "Sin," in *Dictionnaire de spiritualité ascetique et mystique: Doctrine et histoire*; Volume Pays-Bas-Photius, nos. 78–79 (Paris: Beauchesne, 1984), 790–815.

25. This is the reason why the common Byzantine liturgical prayer prepares the faithful to receive communion by asking pardon for unknown sins and sins committed both voluntarily and involuntarily.

26. Paul Ricoeur, *Fallible Man*, trans. Charles A. Kelbley (New York: Fordham University Press, 1986), 4.

27. Ricoeur, *Fallible Man*: "It is by no means a decision concerning the root origin of evil but is merely the description of the place where evil appears and from where it can be seen. Indeed, it is quite possible that man is not the radical source of evil, that he is not the absolute evil-doer. But even if evil were coeval with the root origin of things, it would still be true that it is manifest only in the way it affects human existence. Thus the decision to enter into the problem of evil by the strait gate of human reality only expresses the choice of a center of perspective: even if evil came to man from another source which contaminates him, this other source would still be accessible to us only through its relation to us, only through the state of temptation, aberration or blindness whereby we would be affected. In all hypotheses, evil manifests itself in man's humanity" (xlvi).

28. Ricoeur, *Fallible Man*: "Evil's place of manifestation is apparent only if it is recognized and it is recognized only if it is taken up by deliberate choice. The decision to understand evil by freedom is itself an undertaking of freedom that takes evil upon itself . . . For if man were responsible for evil only through abandon, only through a kind of reverse participation in a more radical source of evil than his freedom, it would still be the avowal of his responsibility that would permit him to be in contact with that root origin" (xlvii).

Chapter 3

Children of Saturn

During the Middle Ages and the Renaissance, side by side with the theology of sin and the Hippocratic humoral theory, there emerged a mythological interpretation that subordinated the condition of melancholy-acedia to the planet and the god Saturn. Whereas in Dante Alighieri, the coming together of these different symbolic currents was implicit, Marsilio Ficino's *Libri de vita triplici* made visible the birth of a complex symbol out of the union of several traditions: the Greco-Roman myth of Cronos-Saturn, the astrological symbol of the planet-god Saturn, the metaphysical theory of the four elements, the medical theory of the four corresponding humors, as well as Plato's theory of divine madness, Pseudo-Aristotle's notion of the exceptional status of melancholy, and, last but not least, the theological concept of mortal sin. All these elements of symbol and myth were brought together within neo-Platonic ontology and cosmology to generate the richly textured Renaissance palimpsest of melancholy.

GENESIS OF THE RENAISSANCE CONCEPT OF MELANCHOLY: DANTE AND FICINO

Dante's portrait sketched by Boccaccio is that of the exemplary *typus melancholicus*, a medieval reactualization of Pseudo-Aristotle's tragic and sublime hero, one that will later be revisited by Kant. According to Boccaccio, from his dark complexion, to his thoughtful expression, to his manner, mood, and modes—silent, vigilant, withdrawn, solitary, superior, a metaphysician by inclination, wearied by vulgar crowds, attracted to the study of the occult, inconsolable for Beatrice's death—to his tragic fate,

Dante achieves fame but lives and dies in exile and refuses the long-desired crown of poet laureate Dante is a melanchilic, a man who goes down into hell and returns when he pleases."[1] Boccaccio's interpretation of the details of Dante's life as indicative of melancholy illustrates the powerful influence that the Aristotelian profile of melancholic genius played in late medieval intellectual imagination.[2] Boccaccio was keenly aware of this interpretation as he himself was a master of hermeneutics whose manual on the divinities of antiquity and their symbolic connotations had already been used by poets and artists.

Dante's melancholy aside, the *Divine Comedy* is an important document in the history of the symbol of melancholy, though it is often overlooked and overshadowed by the works of the Renaissance theoreticians of melancholy Marsilio Ficino and Robert Burton. Most significant in Dante's portrayal of melancholy is that it spreads over his entire three-tier universe, being present in its most characteristic hypostases from Limbo through Hell to Purgatory and Paradise. Thus a sui generis hermeneutics of melancholy and its dialectics is mapped in the *Divine Comedy*. On the one hand, the condition appears in its negative modes in the *Inferno* and the *Purgatorio*: the melancholic hypostases of sadness, anger, despair, and suicide reside in Hell, while the acedic hypostases of indolence and sloth, less severe, are assigned to Purgatory. On the other hand, melancholy emerges in its positive mode as Saturnine contemplation in the *Paradiso*. The way to Purgatory and Paradise passes through Hell; indeed, the climb to Purgatory starts at the bottom of Hell, via Satan's body used as a ladder (*Inferno* 34.1–139). Most insightful and disquieting is the revelation that ascending from Hell involves an intimate familiarity with Satanic anatomy. In other words, ascension presupposes the descent into abyss: the assumption and the transfiguration of ultimate otherness and negation.

The first hypostasis appears in Limbo. As a faithful follower of Pseudo-Aristotle's *Problem*, Dante assigns all significant figures of antiquity to Limbo, where they melancholize.[3] First come the poets: Homer, Horace, Ovid, Lucan. Virgil and Dante belong to the group (*Inferno* 4.84–96). Next come the Greek, Roman, and Arab philosophers, mathematicians, and physicians: Thales, Hippocrates, Socrates, Plato, Aristotle, as well as Cicero, Euclid, Ptolemy, Galen, Avicenna, among others (*Inferno* 4.132–44). The penitents of Limbo live in the in-between, between damnation and salvation, in eternal waiting for an impossible deliverance (*Inferno* 4.1–24). Sadness without torment, the feeling of being lost, longing without hope, living in a past without future all constitute the melancholic hypothesis of sadness. Here melancholy as a punishment for an ambiguous sinfulness revisits the Aristotelian interpretation from a Christian perspective. The great men of antiquity did not sin, Virgil comments, but having merit is not sufficient, for grace is needed. They are condemned for having been born untimely, before the Incarnation. Their condition is an illustration of Ricoeur's interpretation of sin as a hybrid of the voluntary and the involuntary, and as a condition rather than an act. It also indicates the disturbance in the relation to time which is characteristic of melancholy. The liminal melancholic punishment condemns the untimely birth as a paradoxical guilt for not having made haste to catch up with the fullness of time, for having lingered in the past.

The second hypostasis is encountered in Hell. The hellish punishment for the sad (sullen) and the angry is that of being submerged in a swamp.[4] As mentioned previously with Aquinas, being acedic (care-less) and *accidioso* (acrid, corrosive, sour, thus rancorous), due to their resemblance in form and content, were fused into a new hypostasis often characterized by sadness and anger. It is proof of Dante's familiarity with the by then established character of these conditions that he brought the sullen and the angry together under the same punishment. Anger, resentment, gloom, unsociability, and heaviness are all attributes of the dark mood. The sullen are immersed in the mud of their own mood, enveloped in a corrosive cloud of acrid fumes.[5] He makes visible the deserved punishment for the sin of melancholy, the hellish condition induced by a freely chosen or indulged-in dark mood.

The third hypostasis is introduced in the city of Dis, the depth of Hell, where melancholy takes the form of Medusa.[6] Aquinas discussed despair as the most aggravated mode of the condition. Medusa is a hellish creature and symbol of despair whose habitat is the city of Dis at the bottom of Hell. Despair takes over as Medusa changes the spectator into stone and irremediably compromises the possibility of salvation. As observed in chapter 1, vanquishing Medusa means escaping the Hell of despair and guilt and regaining the lucidity of a clear consciousness. Perseus represents the archetype of the individual who liberates himself from the atrocity of such Medusian hellish despair and delirium of guilt. In a parallel myth to Bellerophon's fighting the Chimera, Perseus, a demi-god, vanquishes Medusa by cutting off her head.

Originally a beautiful woman and a priestess of Athena, Medusa offended the goddess by her dalliances with Poseidon in the temple. Athena changed her into a monstrous Gorgon whose sight repels and kills all by turning them into stone. According to Jean Chevalier and Alain Gheerbrant, Medusa symbolizes the "spiritual drive perverted into self-satisfied sloth," whose guilt complex can be "overcome by recourse to harmony and the golden-mean" symbolized by Apollo. Medusa's effect is explained as the paralyzing effect of the delirium of guilt: "Whoever gazed on Medusa's face was turned to stone, perhaps because it reflected an image of personal guilt. However, acknowledgement of sin, in sound self-knowledge, may be perverted to an unhealthy degree, producing such scrupulousness of conscience as inhibits action."[7]

The delirium of guilt inhibits action and has a paralyzing effect. Let us remember that Dante places Medusa at the bottom of Hell as the archetype of despair. Medusa, the other of Athena, is the symbol of a melancholic self deformed by exacerbated guilt that kills by petrification. With the help of Athena, Perseus succeeds in his exploit and severs Medusa's head. His victory symbolizes the conquest through lucidity and courage of dark melancholic guilt resulting in a transfiguration of the self. It is also interesting to note that the dying Medusa gives birth to Pegasus, the winged horse, symbol of high inspiration and creativity: a latent creativity imprisoned in the vortex of melancholic despair, which the myth of Saturn illustrates as well. Ultimately, therefore, the confrontation of Perseus and Medusa is that between a divine being and divine Otherness, the image of absolute negation whose gaze kills (see cover image of Benvenuto Cellini's *Perseus Holding the Head of the Medusa*, 1545–1554, a bronze sculpture suggested by Cosimo I de Medici, now in the Loggia dei Lanzi Gallery on the edge of the Piazza della Signoria, Florence).

The fourth hypostasis of melancholy in the *Divine Comedy* is suicide, the effect of despair (*Inferno* 13.1–151). Suicides, having used violence against themselves, suffer the fate of Pier delle Vigne, perhaps the closest to Bellerophon's intense suffering that continues eternally without hope of deliverance. Pier is a melancholic: a poet, scholar, and courtier who is a faithful counselor to his king. Like Bellerophon or Boethius, he is a victim of calumny and shamefully punished. Imprisoned and in despair, he kills himself, thus becoming simultaneously victim and perpetrator. The souls of suicides, thrown away, fall on hellish ground, sprout like a grain of wheat and grow into contorted trees in whose veins run dark blood (the dark humor of melancholy). This eternal torment that only intensifies on Judgment Day is the revenge for the life they rejected.

Being less grievous, indolence, the fifth hypostasis, is encountered in *Purgatory* (*Purgatory* 4.1–139). Here Belacque is the image of inaction, immobility, indolence; his fetal position suggests regression: an unbecoming and a return to intra-womb existence. He will not move, casting glances without raising his head from between his bent knees. He thinks and articulates his words "slothfully." Accustomed to being attended to, he has forgotten the meaning of activity: he waits to be "served," taken care of, and even prayed for.

The sixth hypostasis is sloth (*Purgatory* 18.1–144). Images of delay, somnolence, and inattention due to insufficient love make up the landscape against which the frenetic activity of the formerly slothful takes place. They are running in circles while spurring themselves on by reciting stories evocative of the urgency of quick action. They accept their new condition with a fervor that makes up for the former negligence and delay.

The seventh hypostasis is profound contemplation (*Paradiso* 21.1–142). The sphere ruled by Saturn is the seventh, the highest and last before the sphere of the fixed stars. This is the crystalline sphere of contemplation and bears the name of Saturn, the ruler of the Golden Age, and Jacob's ladder is rising within the Saturnine sphere toward yet inaccessible heights. Dante remarks a number of surprising peculiarities: there is no music of the spheres; Beatrice has no smile. Peter Damian, the intercessor, explains the total reversal occurring in the seventh heaven of Saturn: it is the antithesis of earthly existence and values. Here there is a different mind shining, which on earth appears "dull," and spiritual senses are at work. Peter Damian is qualified to be an interpreter thanks to his mode of life on earth having been a negation of earthly life in agreement with the nature of the Saturnine world.

Thus, in the *Divine Comedy*, melancholy appears in seven hypostases ranging from longing, sadness and anger, Medusian despair, suicide, indolence, sloth, to sublime contemplation. With every sphere, its meanings are organized in new configurations, branching out into a vast efflorescence. Melancholy appears as a hybrid condition, ambiguously pernicious and sublime, while the new addition to the Pseudo-Aristotelian foundation is the Saturnine sphere of contemplation, which from here on establishes a connection between melancholy and Saturn. In order to investigate the symbolism of correlation between the medieval Dame Melancholy and the old god Saturn, we will adduce the illustrious Renaissance text devoted to this matter by Marsilio Ficino (1433–1499).

Marsilio Ficino's *Libri de vita triplici* (*Three Books on Life*, 1489) is a Renaissance work par excellence: a philosophical, scientific, medical, astrological, and poetic treatise in three parts for the consolation of melancholics, in particular for scholars and those experiencing aging of all times. An embodiment of the ideal of Renaissance humanism, Ficino is one of the most accomplished personalities of the Quattrocento: public figure, teacher, philosopher, theologian, translator, astrologer, medicus, Christian priest, and magus.[8] Like Bacchus he boasts of two progenitors: his natural father, a medicus and follower of Galen and Plato, and his father in spirit, Cosimo de' Medici, a medicus of the spirit. Ficino is also a "child of Saturn," however, and as a consequence of this mythical filiation, a melancholic. He laments his Saturnine nature and melancholy. He complains to his friends, the Italian humanists Guido Cavalcanti and Pico della Mirandola. Exasperated, Cavalcanti reprimanded, consoled, and advised him to write a recantation.

Taking his friend's injunction to heart, Ficino wrote *Three Books on Life* in the guise of a recantation. Here he aligns himself with the pseudo-Aristotelian interpretation of melancholy, adopts Hippocrates's theory of the humors, while his metaphysics is neo-Platonic: the Plotinian oneness of the world and theory of emanations is the metaphysical foundation for a *magia universalis* that justifies a complex system of correspondences. In fact, his entire treatise can be viewed as an extended neo-Platonic answer to the Aristotelian question.[9]

From the beginning of the treatise, Ficino identifies melancholy as the condition made up of the Hippocratic phlegm and black bile (in Latin *pituita* and *atra bilis,* in Greek *phlegma* and *melancholia*, respectively). He explains why scholars, and philosophers in particular, are victims of the professional hazard of being crushed between the Scylla and Charybdis of phlegm and black bile. By profession, the *litterati studiosi* have active minds and inactive bodies; as we remember from Hippocrates, the former leads to an excess of black bile, the latter to an excess of phlegm. He writes:

> For just as they are inactive in the rest of the body, so they are busy in the brain and the mind. From the former circumstance they are compelled to secrete *pituita* which the Greeks call phlegm, and from the latter, black bile which they call melancholy. Phlegm dulls and suffocates the intelligence, while melancholy, if it is too abundant or vehement, vexes the mind with continual care and frequent absurdities and unsettles the judgment. (1.3.1–10)

Phlegmatic-melancholy is a mélange of bodily torpor and intense mental concern. Torpor becomes manifest mostly as dullness and forgetfulness while excessive intellectual concern oppresses the mind with anxiety and even madness. Although Ficino makes the double peril clear, he will not consistently refer to the two separately (except when in the capacity of physician he must diagnose the specific condition and adduce the corresponding treatment) but, following Pseudo-Aristotle's lead, he will subsume phlegm under melancholia as one of the latter's complications. The original distinction is nevertheless paramount to the work of clarification in a domain that has seemingly been condemned to confusion and paradox.

The first stage of Ficino's recantation is to detect the place of melancholy within the infinite number of series of correspondences linking the stars to the center of the earth; finding its place in this series also means finding its reflections, echoes, causes, signifiers, effects, and ultimately its remedies. The correlations he makes between cosmic and human events, events of nature and the psyche, form the ground for both medical and philosophical insight, thus laying the foundations for a hermeneutic of symbolic signification as well as a sui generis alchemy of the psyche. Ficino thus developed an original metaphysics, incarnational and magical, that was to resurface in qualified form in the mystical theosophies of Jakob Böhme and Schelling. The method that Ficino used in binding the universe together is a hermeneutics based on series of correspondences among all the ontological categories and domains of the world, human anatomy, senses, affection, and intellect, meteorological phenomena, and cosmic bodies. The outcome is an all-encompassing symbolization of the world in which the causes of the condition operate at all ontological levels: they are celestial, natural, and human since, according to Ficinian Renaissance metaphysics, man is a microcosm, a quintessence of the all. The natural cause has to do with the soul and its activities, which by analogy call forth properties of the earth or celestial bodies.[10] The celestial cause of melancholy, which is cold and dry according to physicians, is the patronage of those planets that are cold and dry according to astrologers, that is, Mercury and Saturn. By connecting the darkest matter with the highest level of contemplation, melancholy functions as a symbolic *axis mundi* and a figura of *coincidentia oppositorum*. In Ficino's classification of the causes of melancholy, a unique hermeneutical event takes place: the genesis of the symbol of melancholy (phlegm included) out of the union of two symbolic traditions: the medico-philosophical and the mythological-astrological.

Ficino engages in the construction and elucidation of the symbol of melancholy, generating an anatomy of melancholy that is a precursor to Burton's. He explains that melancholy is congruent with both the center of the cosmos, according to Aristotelian metaphysics, and with Saturn, the highest planet, according to the medieval mythological synthesis. A melancholic mind is therefore prone to be drawn to high and hidden subjects, to explore eagerly, persevere in the investigation longer, find its answer easily, perceive it clearly, judge it soundly, retain the judgment longer. Access to divine influences and oracles, invention of new unaccustomed things, and original philosophy are the sweet fruits thereof, Ficino tells us in agreement with Democritus, Plato, and Pseudo-Aristotle. He qualifies this image as that of the good—the "white," as he calls it—face of melancholy, to be cultivated. The other face, though, is that of a bad daemon (1.6.25–35, 1.7.5–15). To avoid the latter, Ficino initiates melancholics into the art of exorcising demonic melancholy. Initiation involves the labor of purging and illuminating, a process that implies a radical transformation of the Saturnine-melancholic-phlegmatic nature, its alchemical transmutation.

The presupposition grounding this possibility of becoming celestial is the doctrine found in Timaeus's myth, according to which, since God appointed the planetary gods as co-creators of man, there exists an essential relation of mutual interdependence between the two.[11] Thus by modifying the quality of affective, mental, and spiritual attunement one can replace the connection to malign Saturn with one to more propitious planetary divinities (3.2.60–70).

MELANCHOLY AND SATURN

Throughout the Middle Ages and the Renaissance, Saturn was considered the patron-god of acedia and melancholy. With Ficino, the doctrine correlating melancholy and Saturn achieves its classic formulation. Melancholy belongs to a more originary creation remembered as the Golden Age presided over by Saturn. According to Klibansky, Panofsky, and Saxl, Ficino's treatise combines Dante's conception of Saturn as the star of sublime contemplation with the Pseudo-Aristotelian notion of the melancholic as exceptional individual, a synthesis emerging as *melancholia gloriosa.*[12]

Jean Seznec's study of the survival of the gods of antiquity into the medieval and Renaissance eras follows the metamorphoses of the ancient divinities after the advent of Christianity.[13] The identification of Greek and Roman gods with the planets, a fait accompli by the end of the pagan era, was the result of a long and complex process. While mythologization of constellations was already in place in Homer, the fusion of gods and planets was a later development and involved heteroclitic influences. Seznec opines that the correlation of the five errant stars with the Greek gods occurred during the fifth century before our era under Babylonian influence and was probably the achievement of Pythagoreans. By the time of Plato the planets were subordinated to the gods; but only gradually and by linguistic economy was the fusion between planets and gods perfected, such that the planets became gods. Seznec explains: "The absorption by the planets of the gods of mythology assures the latter's survival as a providential shelter: the great gods find in the planets an honorable refuge. Dethroned on earth . . . they become rulers of celestial spheres and men continue invoking and fearing them."[14]

The principle of causality in this cosmology is astrological and operates through a system of correspondences in which the planets and signs of the zodiac form the basis for the classification of elements, seasons, humors, temperaments, and corresponding arts and sciences. The moral tradition interprets stellar divinities as moral and psychological allegories. According to this system of interpretation, Saturn signifies Prudence as a relation to Time past, present and future: that is, in the form of Memory, Intelligence, and Anticipation. Seznec mentions a document of the fourteenth century, the work of a clerk at the court of Avignon, which, in the form of a map, unites the zodiac signs, planets, months of the year, minerals, bodily parts, ages of life, gifts of the Holy Spirit, and sins all around the Holy Virgin: an image that subsumes ancient gods and knowledge under Christian auspices. Although he maintained a tense relation with the new cosmology, Saturn is one of the seven planet-gods who, once translated into the heavens, continued to influence the sublunary worlds unhindered.

Saturn's place among the other planetary gods is ambiguous and belongs to two different traditions. On the one hand, in the tradition represented by Dante, Saturn is the god of sublime contemplation; on the other, he is the symbol of malignity; together they coalesce in shaping an ambivalent and contradictory symbol, whose uncanny meaning, due to the association of Saturn and melancholy, will be inherited by the latter. As an illustration of this double Saturnine nature, Seznec adduces the *Prayer to Saturn*, a medieval-Renaissance text dedicated to the god of melancholy:

Oh lord whose name is sublime and whose power is great,
Supreme Lord, Lord Saturn,
You the frigid, the sterile, the mournful, the pernicious,
You whose life is honest and whose word is true,
You the wise and the solitaire, the impenetrable,
You who keep your promises,
You who are weak and weary,
You who have more worries than all,
You who do not know either pleasure or joy,
Cunning old man who knows all the tricks,
You deceiver, wise and sensible,
Bringing prosperity and devastation,
Fortune and misfortune!
I conjure you, oh, supreme father, in your great benevolence and generous kindness,
Grant for me . . . [15]

The invocation addresses a disturbing divinity, a *coincidentia oppositorum* of God and God's alterity. The identity of Saturn and the nature of his gifts emerge as enigmatically disquieting. One wonders what kind of gifts this pernicious and weak God would grant his devotee.

According to Claude Mettra, when the humanism emerging at the end of the Middle Ages increasingly privileged man as the bearer of a culture that deepened his separation from nature, Saturn came to be interpreted as a symbol of Adamic nature itself, and by extension of the devil.[16] Mettra argues that the anti-*natura* tendency present in Judeo-Christian anthropomorphism became increasingly apprehensive about the secret powers of nature. The Church was relentless in punishing knowledge of herbs as witch gnosis. The time of Zeus is a "time of irremediable separation," whereas the "time of Saturn, the Golden Age, is a time of intimate fusion of all that aspire to being." Saturn came to signify the promise of "the impossible reconciliation between the life of nature and the human heart," the link tragically broken between the universe and ourselves. Mettra writes of Saturn: "Messenger of the absolute solitude, he also announces the end of our solitude. Messenger of death, he also affirms our possible victory over death since creation is this incessant generation through which we go on from kingdom to kingdom to our greatest enchantment" (196–98).

Mettra recalls Plato's Saturnine Golden Age: at that time men were born old and grew younger and younger by learning the lightness of being, until they would return infant-like into the womb of earth, thus merging with the principle of life. He echoes Nietzsche's idea of reconciliation through Dionysian harmonies beyond the Apollonian *principium individuoruum*. In this perspective Saturn, ruler of the Golden Age, would be another name for Dionysus. Saturn came to be homologized to Satan, to *deus otiosus* and *absconditus*, as well as to the crucified. He appears as a *coincidentia oppositorum*, a dialectical and tragic symbol, or according to Walter Benjamin's theory of melancholy, a rather baroque allegory.[17] Indeed, Benjamin adduces Pascal's figure of the melancholic king and Shakespeare's Hamlet as the principal prototypes of the melancholic nature and destiny. During the Renaissance, Saturnine melancholy emerged in its full dialectical complexity, when a revival of Pseudo-Aristotelian theories of humors and temperaments became endorsed by hermetic astrological tradition. Benjamin explains the Renaissance revival of the ancient valorization of melancholy vis-à-vis the Christian Middle Ages:

> The history of the problem of melancholy unfolds within the perimeter of this dialectic. Its climax is reached with the magic of the Renaissance. Whereas the Aristotelian insights into the psychical duality of the melancholy disposition and the antithetical nature of the influence of Saturn had given way in the Middle Ages to a purely demonic representation of both, such as conformed with Christian speculation; with the Renaissance the whole wealth of ancient meditations re-emerged from the sources. (138–58)

Benjamin maintains that both Ficino and Albrecht Dürer endeavored to separate the sublime melancholy, *melencolia illa heroica*, from the pernicious kind by a precise regimen of body and soul combined with astrological magic (150–51).

Evidently, the symbol of Saturn is fraught with contradictions as a product of several adventures in symbolic interpretation. Let us summarize the main events that compose the myth of Saturn. Before Saturn became the Roman equivalent of the Greek Cronos, he was a hero of cultivation and civilization, initiator in the art of agriculture.[18] Once fused with the Greek god Cronos, son of Uranus and Gaia, Saturn became the ruler of the Golden Age, the age before our time or beyond time altogether. The myth of progressive generations of Uranus-Saturn-Jupiter is the cosmogonic myth par excellence. Saturn and Rhea form the second divine couple after Ouranos and Gaia but the outcome of their marriage will lead to a new creation only via a melancholic detour: Saturn swallows his offspring to prevent being overpowered by them. Jupiter escapes thanks to Rhea's strategy: when she presents Saturn with a stone instead of Jupiter, Saturn bites into the stone and vomits his previously swallowed offspring, after which all the young brothers together war against their father; Saturn is emasculated and defeated. From his wounded genitalia Venus is born. Defeated, dethroned, dispossessed, he withdraws and lives alone in eternal exile from the time and space of the new creation. Jupiter is the victor over the old and the auspicious ruler of historical time. If the time of Jupiter is historical time, then some of the symbolic postures and episodes in which we find Saturn must indicate a precreational past existence. These symbolic moments defining Saturn may be helpful in unlocking interpretative knots in the theory of melancholy.

The first such moment is the myth of Saturn swallowing his own offspring. Saturn creates and then reabsorbs his creation in an unbroken circular motion. There is no issuing forth and no movement forward: only an unceasing rotation driven by Saturn's anger and sadness, his melancholy. In this self-devouring vortex, he imprisons divine creativity in himself instead of allowing its free manifestation. To the extent to which Saturn has been identified with time by the overlapping of Cronos with Chronos, the god of time, his self-devouring was interpreted as the action of time itself, creating and annihilating its creations.[19] There is, however, another possible interpretation. There is no time and no love in the Saturnine age, as Saturn does not allow either creation or time to begin. He hesitates and delays indefinitely his self-revelation. Thus the Saturnine age resembles the age of Plato's *chora*. Schelling will later give this Saturnine symbolism a metaphysical grounding, as we shall see, in the angry rotary motion prior to the beginning.

Another symbolic moment is Saturn's sacrifice. Saturn is vanquished and maimed, creation is liberated, time begins, love is born from his wound. Exiled away from the new creation, Saturn is forever wandering, sad and angry, jealous of Jupiter's kingdom, a forsaken king and god. He is old, weak, fatigued, beggarly, forlorn, desolate. He lives in the past to which he belongs, a lord of the past and nonbeing. The present and future belong to Jovial creation. Saturn is solitary, he does not belong to the community of history or of the living. He cannot live properly speaking, nor can he die: he is a medieval figure of death-in-life or life-in-death, a being-nonbeing. His spurious existence is boring: he has nothing to do, he is living in pure emptiness, in the desert, at the outskirts of being and history. His image par excellence is that of the melancholic exile, yes, but an exiled king and servant god: the myth of Saturn stretches comprehensively from the lowest to the highest; a reversal is always occurring, thus destabilizing the previous definition and scene. The dual image of the destitute exile and malign divinity is reversed by the scene of the Saturnine Golden Age. Saturn's kingdom of the Golden Age can never be taken away from him. There he is still a king and a god. To reactualize it, he must turn his back on Jovial time and creation and withdraw into precreational age; a beggar and exile in time, a king and god, outside time, in silent contemplation. As Ficino observes, we come under the influence of Saturn "by withdrawal from human affairs, by leisure, solitude, constancy, by theology, the more esoteric philosophy, superstition, magic, agriculture and by sorrow" (3.2.70–75). As an illustration of the Saturnine ambivalence, Ficino's portrait of Saturn, one familiar during the Middle Ages and the Renaissance, is pertinent: "An old man sitting on a rather high throne or on a dragon, his head covered with a dark linen cloth, raising his hands above his head, holding in his hand a sickle or some fish, and clothed in a dusky robe" (3.18.45–50).

In the *Divine Comedy*, Saturn appears as the most powerful of planets, the highest, thus the closest to the Primum Mobile.[20] Ficino, though faithful to this Ptolemaic tradition, acknowledges in addition the malignity of Saturn and therefore must account for the contradictory attributes belonging to the two identities: his depiction refers to Saturn as a king in distress, a servant-king. An arguably negative emblematic figure is evoked, that of a veiled and mysterious, erring, dethroned or exiled king; the head covered by a dark cloth, the attribute of the sickle symbolizing death and time—both distinguishing marks of the figure of Saturn at the time—together with the dusky robe and gesture of raised hands have the disturbing connotations of an obscure, hostile, and deadly power. Saturn evokes Dame Death, herself, a most familiar medieval allegorical presence; more significantly, as both Mettra and Benjamin emphasize, within an increasingly overpowering Christian world Saturn loses his dialectical nature and becomes reduced to the devil.

The observations on Saturnine nature allow for highly complex and contradictory hermeneutical possibilities. According to Ficino, Saturn wounds both "those whom he elevates to the heights above their physical strength and the customs of mortals" and "those he pushes down with world weariness, torpor, sadness, cares, superstitions" (2.15.80–83). The gifts of Saturn are ambivalent gifts of "care and contemplation," "duty of contemplation," and "labor of responsibility" (2.16.30–33). Care and contemplation, heavy responsibility, excess of mundane cogitations, and religious or scientific reflection—all belong to the category of the difficult. Essentially the Saturnine mode is not exuberant and light, but rather remains under the sign of the serious, the tedious, the sad, the old, the ponderous, the boring. Saturn does not sing like the other planets, he only speaks in a "slow, deep, harsh, plaintive" voice (3.21.120–22). He is propitious for the virtuosi, however, the initiates into the great mysteries, the great contemplators who have removed themselves from creation and the creaturely. Thus Ficino writes: "Lastly the contemplating intellect—insofar as it separates itself not only from things we perceive but even from those things which we commonly imagine . . . and insofar as it recollects itself in emotion, in intention and in life to supra-physical things—exposes itself somewhat to Saturn. To this faculty alone is Saturn propitious" (3.22.25–32).

Like him, melancholic individuals are kings in exile, turned away from the future and always lured into the past, toward the Golden Age. They are dead to the world and, if philosophy means practicing dying, they are the true philosophers. But they are also the immortals since Saturn kills in order to offer celestial and everlasting life. Thus Ficino uses two alternate perspectives, sublunary and celestial. From the latter perspective, ordinary life is already forsaken, Saturn and his melancholic children are the superior contemplators; from the former perspective, Saturn, faithful to the myth, is deadly especially to his children, whose destiny is tragic. Ficino notes that the domain signified by Saturn is that of the exceptional individual: Saturn cannot signify the common quality and lot of the human race, but only that of an individual set apart from others, divine or brutish, blessed or bowed down with extreme misery. Ficino's extension of the Pseudo-Aristotelian theory of the exceptional melancholic tragic individual constitutes an important hermeneutic node for a theory of melancholy that will later be adopted by Kant and the Romantics. Since Saturn signifies the individual, and also melancholy, individuality and melancholy become codependent. Indeed, Le Senne will later explain that subjectivity and self-consciousness are born with the melancholic individual, while for Michel Henry immanent subjectivity is inherently pathetic.

IMAGINAL TRANSMUTATION AS THERAPEUTIC

This complex symbolization of the exceptional and tragic Saturnine individual expands the horizon of meaning to the limits of space—the highest planet— and the limits of time—via the primeval god of the golden age—connecting meaningfully all the elements of manifestation. In this all-encompassing network of symbols, Ficino's compensatory therapeutic becomes a poetics of imagination. Imagination must be set free from the shackles of the dark mood and "redressed" towards a new imaginal universe. The mind, oppressed with cares and depression, is urged to shake off its load of darkness as the melancholic receives fresh food, white clothes, bathes in the air and sun of richly green pastures, delights in Apollonian melodies, cherishes fragrances of frankincense, rose, and violet, tastes pomegranates and ginger, drinks rose water from gilded silver vessels, wears sapphire and gold encrusted with Jovial and Solar emblems, gazes at a figure of a moving universe and begins to make gentle gyrations in imitation of the moving stars, while beholding and thinking about Light (3.11.1–20).

Ficino's therapaeia is an exercise in imagination, an abandonment of Saturnine habitudes, and cultivation of salvific Jovial and Solar ones. The outcome is an aesthetic art of being in which the body becomes a symbolic and magical corpus. As Seznec explains, such an art uses the Greek principle of *melothesia*, that is, the principle of correlation of planetary constellations and astrological signs to the geography of the body.[21] In Ficino's universe, everything in the inner and outer world is a symbol suffused with meaning; meaningfulness is excessive and overdetermining. The neo-Platonic metaphysics of light is salvific in the dark room of melancholy. According to this metaphysics, Ficino's remedial regimen covers a wide spectrum of advice ranging from down-to-earth to fantastic. Dullness and forgetfulness, a phlegmatic-melancholic condition, is treated with ginger seasoned with sugar, mixed with frankincense, adding honey of cashews, galingales, amber and musk, smell of incense, marjoram, fennel, nutmeg, rue, and clove, anointing of the head with specific oils, rubbing, arms, legs, neck, fomenting the top of the head with marjoram, frankincense, and nutmeg (1.25.5–25). He designs electuaries in which gold, silver, brightest pearls, sapphire, amber musk, emerald, hyacinth, and coral figure prominently along with rose and lemon water. The simple enumeration of the ingredients is mesmerizing; the melancholic is slowly lured into a magical world. It seems that the healing power of the prescriptions consists in their intrinsically poetic qualities, in the *magia* of words and images, a *magia* provoking a sui generis reconfiguration of imagination. Ficino would not disagree: after all he introduces himself— though apologetically—as a poet.[22]

In order to partake of the poetics of *magia universalis*, his hermeneutics prescribes the internalization of alchemical transmutation as indicated by an experiment in imagination. He elaborates the design and construction of the figure of the universe according to the astrologers' art. Once the figure is complete, the melancholic is asked to gaze at it, reflect upon it, live day and night in a chamber of this design, and, when away from it, to remember this figure rather than attend to the spectacle around him. In the end, he adds: "You, however, will fashion a better image within yourself when you know that nothing is more orderly than the heavens and that nothing can be thought of that is more temperate than Jupiter; you should hope at last to attain benefits from the heavens and from Jupiter if you have rendered yourself very orderly and temperate in your thoughts, emotions and mode of life" (3.19.54–58). This qualification makes clear that all the Ficinian paraphernalia proposes tools and props supporting an inner transfiguration, props that may be discarded once the latter has occurred. As a genuine alchemist, he uses the world of the senses only as a symbol for inner labor. The intuition of the secret correspondence between outer and inner nature, based on their participation in the same spirit of life, constitutes after all the ground for all alchemical endeavors.

At the time of Ficino's *De vita* the symbols of alchemy were not yet fixed, they had not become enigmatic ciphers whose original meaning is concealed by layers of superposed signification. They were still in formation, on their way to being congealed into cryptic signs. The genesis of new symbols and myths is here still visible—myths and symbol that, when mature, will lack the life and poetic profusion that exists only in the beginning.[23] It is no accident that Ficino intends to find a cure for melancholic philosophers: this endeavor is the aim of the *opus alchymicum* whose Magnum Arcanum, gold, the *lapis philosophiae*, is the symbol of the panacea and elixir of life. As Jung remarks: "The physical goal of alchemy was gold, the panacea, the elixir of life; the spiritual one was the rebirth of the (spiritual) light from the darkness of Physis: healing self-knowledge and the deliverance of the pneumatic body from the corruption of the flesh."[24] Beginning the work of inner transformation with melancholy is alchemically appropriate, Jung indicates, as *nigredo* is the first phase of the alchemical work:

> Confrontation with the shadow produces at first a dead balance, a standstill that hampers moral decisions and makes convictions ineffective or even impossible. Everything becomes doubtful, which is why the alchemists called this stage *nigredo, tenebrositas*, chaos, melancholia. It is right that the magnum opus should begin at this point, for it is indeed a well-nigh unanswerable question how one is to confront reality in this torn and divided state. . . . The *nigredo* signifies the *mortificatio, putrefactio, solutio, separatio, divisio*, etc., a state of dissolution and decomposition that precedes the synthesis. (497, 507)

But as Jung further explains, the medieval masters identified "*nigredo* with melancholia and extolled the opus as the sovereign remedy for all afflictions of the soul" (320). Moreover, *nigredo* is also a symbol of guilt and ultimately of the devil (420). He repeatedly emphasizes:

> Self-knowledge is an adventure that carries us unexpectedly far and deep. Even a moderately comprehensive knowledge of the shadow can cause a great deal of confusion and mental darkness, since it gives rise to personality problems which one had never remotely imagined before. For this reason alone we can

understand why the alchemists called their *nigredo* melancholia, a black blacker than black, night, an affliction of the soul, confusion, etc., or, more pointedly, the black raven . . . a well-known allegory of the devil. (520–21)

Thus for the medieval alchemists, melancholy, *nigredo*, guilt, confusion, affliction of the soul were symbolized by putrefaction, mortification, separation, dissolution, decomposition, chaos, the devil, Saturn, the raven, and *sol niger*. They were all interchangeable symbols belonging to the same family of meaning; they all signify the Other, choratic chaos, and the beginning of the great alchemical opus.

In Jungian terms, at the level of consciousness, the beginning of the movement necessary for self-knowledge and for the unification of consciousness is the most critical moment of the process of individuation. The work of gradual transmutation can only begin with *nigredo* or melancholy. That is why, according to alchemical tradition and Jungian psychoanalytic theory, melancholy is the sine qua non ground of any great work and why it must be carefully "attended to" and not be overlooked or dispensed with. It is only here in the dark night of the soul that the alchemical oeuvre can begin by which melancholy is transformed with the help of techniques of transmutation and sublimation, without which the perils of being engulfed by darkness are only too real. This also explains why at the first signs of melancholy the adept rejoices: melancholy is the *materia prima* in whose absence the alchemical process cannot be initiated. Jung could argue that both the alchemical and the theological traditions are profound therapeutic programs not to be discarded before substituting them with a system of symbols having equivalent meaningfulness and power. According to Jung, Christ's passion and Job's suffering are archetypal prefigurations representing the journey of transformation of the human soul undergoing the destiny to which it is called:

> In the furnace of the cross and in the fire, says the *Aquarium sapientum*, man like the earthly gold, attains to the true black Raven's head; that is, he is utterly disfigured and is held in derision by the world, and this not only for forty days and nights, or years, but often for the whole duration of his life. . . . Through this spiritual death his soul is entirely freed. Evidently the *nigredo* brought about a deformation and a psychic suffering which the author compared to the plight of the unfortunate Job's unmerited misfortune, visited on him by God, is the suffering of God's servant and a prefiguration of Christ's Passion. One can see from this how the figure of the Son of Man gradually lodged itself in the ordinary man who had taken the work upon his own shoulders. (353–54)

He explains that a valid therapeutic must necessarily include the following stages, of which the initial stage recalls Evagrius's method: first, recognition of the condition, naming it, attending to it, probing its depths, its source, its meaning, questioning it and listening to it; second, working one's way through it and out of it; and third, integrating it within a wider horizon.

Naming and thinking melancholy is already a stage of *therapeia*. To eliminate melancholic madness would mean to destroy the potential for healing and self-actualization that is the human task par excellence. This tragic hermeneutical error finds its illustration in a fifteenth-century hypothetical procedure involving trepanation and extraction of a stone thought to be the cause of madness, as depicted in Hieronymus Bosch's painting *The Extraction of the Stone of Madness*.[25] Bosch's painting depicts a charade in which two levels of meaning compete for attention: on the one hand, the presumed trepanation performed by a man with a funnel hat; on the other, the real meaning of the "stone," which appears not as a stone but a flower. The latter implies an interpretation that the stone of madness has the eudaimonic potential of a full actualization, a flowering of consciousness, thus effecting the culmination of the alchemical oeuvre precisely by means of the *other* of the philosopher's stone.

In light of this alchemical interpretation, Ficino's remedial program constitutes the alchemical work par excellence. His art involves the transmutation of *nigredo* (melancholy, chaos, and putrefaction) or the stone of madness into *albedo* (light, celestial purification), the flower and stone of philosophy. This transmutation is equivalent to a new cosmicization of primordial choratic chaos: another formulation of the alchemical work. Ficino's art is a sui generis imaginal therapeutics that has been recommended in more recent times, as we shall see, poetically by Bachelard and psychoanalytically by Desoille.

NOTES

1. Giovanni Boccaccio, "The Life of Dante," in *The Earliest Lives of Dante* (New York: Haskell House, 1974), 20–23, 42–43.

2. Boccaccio, "Life of Dante," 72–78. Boccaccio chose to interpret Dante's dream of his mother as well as all details in Dante's life as premonitions of the poet's genius and of a brilliant and unfulfilled melancholic course through life.

3. Dante Alighieri, *The Divine Comedy*, trans. H. R. Huse (Chicago: Holt, Rinehart, and Winston, 1954): "Thus he moved on and made me enter/the first circle which girds the abyss.//Here, so far as one could tell by listening,/there was no lament but only sighs/which made the eternal air tremble.//They came from the sadness without torment/felt by the great crowd/of children and of women and of men.//My good master said to me, "You do not ask//what spirits these are. Now,//I want you to know before we go farther//that they did not sin, but having merit/was not enough, for they lacked baptism,/which is a portal of the faith you hold;//and if they lived before

Christianity/they did not worship God rightly;/among such as these am I myself.// For such defects, not for other faults,/are we lost, and afflicted only/in that we live in longing without hope" (*Inferno* 4.23–42).

4. Dante, *Inferno*: "Fixed in the slime they say: 'Sullen were we/in the sweet air gladdened by the sun/keeping within the fumes of spite [*accidioso fummo*]/now we are sullen in the *black mire*'" (*Inferno* 7.97–130).

5. Anne Larue, *L'autre melancolie: Acedia ou les chambers de l'esprit* (Paris: Hermann, 2001), 108. Larue remarks that a smoky vapor characterizes the acedics: it is the screen that hid the sun from them, the screen of impossibility for them to live in the world, to love, and express their passions. Dante's acedic individual carries within the smoke of acedia (*accidioso fummo*) and is turned away from God.

6. Dante, *Inferno*: "Turn back and keep your eyes closed/for if the Gorgon Medusa shows herself and you see her there will be no returning" (*Inferno* 9.55–57).

7. "Gorgons" in Jean Chevalier and Alain Gheerbrant, *The Penguin Dictionary of Symbols* (see chapter 1, n. 24), 446–47.

8. A favorite of the Medici family and a prominent neo-Platonist, Ficino translated Plato and Plotinus into Latin for the first time, providing his own commentary, and also translated texts attributed at the time to Hermes Trismegistos. He founded a sui generis *republique des lettres*, the Academy of Florence, on the model of his masters, which functioned as a forum of spirited dialogue and intense personal encounter for the brilliant minds and complicated hearts of the Italian humanists. It is here in the Academy created around the charismatic personality of its founder that the quintessence of European Renaissance is distilled from the rich mélange of texts collected from remote times and places.

9. Marsilio Ficino, *Three Books on Life*, trans. Carol V. Kaske and John R. Clark (New York: Medieval and Renaissance Texts and Studies, 1989), book 1, chapter 5, lines 1–75. Hereafter references to Ficino's work will indicate book, chapter, and line numbers.

10. Ficino, *Three Books*: "Now to collect oneself from the circumference to the center, and to be fixed in the center, is above all the property of the earth itself, to which black bile is analogous. And being analogous to the world's center, it forces the investigation to the center of individual subjects, and it carries one to the contemplation of whatever is highest, since, indeed, it is most congruent with Saturn, the highest of planets" (1.4.15–20).

11. Ficino, *Three Books*: "We ourselves and all things which are around us can, by way of certain preparations, lay claim to celestial things. For these lower things were made by the heavens, are ruled continually by them, and were prepared from up there for celestial things in the first place" (3.2.1–5).

12. Klibansky, Panovsky, and Saxl, *Saturn and Melancholy*, 254–74.

13. Jean Seznec, *La survivance des dieux antiques* (London: Warburg Institute, 1940). Seznec (1905–1983) is known for his valuable studies as a French historian and mythographer.

14. Seznec, *La survivance des dieux*, 40; my translation.

15. *Prayer to Saturn*, quoted in Seznec, *La survivance des dieux*, 53; my translation.

16. Claude Mettra, *Saturne ou l'herbe des âmes* (Paris: Éditions Seghers, 1981), 195; the translations below are mine. Mettra (1922–2005) is author of valuable works in the domain of art history and philosophy.

17. Walter Benjamin, *The Origin of German Tragic Drama*, trans. John Osborne (London, New York: Verso, 1998; reprint, 2003). Benjamin (1892–1940), a German-Jewish intellectual active as a literary critic, philosopher, sociologist, translator, and essayist, was most appreciated for his work in aesthetic theory and Western Marxism.

18. "Saturn," in Chevalier and Gheerbrant, *The Penguin Dictionary of Symbols* (see chapter 1, n. 24), 828–29.

19. "Cronos," in Chevalier and Gheerbrant, *The Penguin Dictionary of Symbols*, 246–48.

20. Ficino, *Three Books*:s "You should certainly not neglect the power of Saturn. . . . For he is of all planets the head of the widest sphere. Saturn is also neighbor to the innumerable fixed stars; and indeed he is very similar to the Primum Mobile because he travels a lengthy circuit. He is the highest of planets; hence they call that man fortunate whom Saturn fortunately favors" (3.22.60–65).

21. Seznec, *La survivance des dieux*, 50. Ficino, *Three Books:* "Accordingly you must remember that Aries has power over the head and face; Taurus over the neck; Gemini, the forearms and shoulders" (3.10.43–46).

22. Ficino, *Three Books*: "But I beg you, good-natured Lorenzo to pardon these books of medicine if while trying to be a doctor, I am, somehow or other, willy-nilly a poet and often not a good one. For one and the same Phoebus is the discoverer of medicine and the master of poesy and he gives us of his life not only by herbs but through the lute and music" (Proem 33–37).

23. On the cooling of meaning see Ray L. Hart, "Afterthinking Meister Eckhart," in *The Otherness of God*, ed. Orrin F. Summerell (Charlottesville: University Press of Virginia, 1999).

24. C. G. Jung, *Mysterium Coniunctionis: An Inquiry into the Separation and Synthesis of Psychic Opposites in Alchemy*, trans. R. F. C. Hull; Bollingen Series 20 (Princeton: Princeton University Press, 1989), 90. All further quotations of Jung in this chapter are taken from this text.

25. Hieronymus Bosch (1450–1516), *The Extraction of the Stone of Madness* (oil on wood, 1475–1480), Museo del Prado, Madrid.

Chapter 4

Indolence and Ennui

With Robert Burton (1577–1640) and Blaise Pascal (1623–1662) the dialectics of idleness, boredom, and the nothing, the full complex of acedic or depressive hypostases emerges. Pascal's discourse on ennui and diversion is an echo of Evagrius's theology of the sin of acedia. Both Pascal and Evagrius intend to prevent the Ricoeurian slide from fallibility to sin, from the acedic condition to the sin of acedia. Nevertheless, Pascal's discourse belongs to a different time—the time of the transition from the Renaissance to modernity—and is addressed to a different audience. The audience is the layman caught in the infinities of unknown worlds without the support of faith, modern man in the absence of God. Phenomenologically though, the principal moments of the condition are similar: in the absence of God, the individual, whether in the desert of Egypt at noon or alone in his own chamber, faces his ontological nothingness or meontological ground and is prompted to flee it in diversion. For Pascal, being active in the world serves as an escape from facing oneself. He, too, calls the seers of nothing to refrain from taking refuge in the world but, swerving from Evagrius, he calls them to contemplate the nothing before beginning the search for the true remedy. This "tarrying in the nothing" is a new moment, unnecessary for Evagrius's monastic, who has already found the truth. In this tarrying, Pascal realizes— well before the German idealists, Schopenhauer, Kierkegaard, or Poe—the repelling creativity of the nothing. It is with Pascal that the repelling mood becomes evident as *ennui*: it is a form of what Heidegger would call "profound boredom" (*tiefe Langeweile*), the experience of a growing nothing as void or emptiness that is the principal acedic (depressive) hypostasis.

Pascal's dialectics of the sin of acedia and Robert Burton's discourse on the evil of idleness seem to refer to the same condition. But while Pascal inhabits

63

the Evagrian tradition, Burton is a continuator of Cassian. He contemplates the nothing made visible in idleness and, like Cassian, emphasizes work as a remedy—though unlike Cassian, and with a modern secular social awareness, Burton considers only socially purposeful engagement as work. In this distinction between Pascal's remedy and Burton's—that is, between the call to contemplation of the metaphysical ground, or rather groundlessness, and the call to work as salvific avoidance of such—appears in contrasting existential vocations. Work, which is advocated as therapeutic by both Cassian and Burton, constitutes the sin itself for Evagrius and Pascal. This difference aside, the discourses of these four figures establish the hypostases of idleness and boredom as forming the acedic complex par excellence and make visible the metaphysical ground, or groundlessness, of acedic boredom and depression: the nothing at the center of one's being.

BURTON: THE ENTIRE WORLD MELANCHOLIZES

Robert Burton's *Anatomy of Melancholy* (c. 1621) is a vast discourse on melancholy of encyclopedic and Rabelaisian proportions, as well as a political satire of the English society of the time.[1] The domain circumscribed by Burton's melancholy is excessive, ranging from melancholy and acedia properly so-called, to socio-political contradictions to the folly of the human condition, to universal madness: for Burton, the entire world melancholizes. Burton begins with the acedic-melancholic humor and studies its numerous hypostases, its causes, symptoms, and effects according to the stages of life and life involvements. Burton brings two distinctive novel features to the discourse on melancholy, namely, melancholy in secular society and melancholy as a cosmic principle of malignity. Against this horizon, melancholy is viewed as a contagious disease spreading over all social strata and professions, but principally as a socio-political disease emanating from the forces representing the past and the old regime. Characteristic of the old aristocracy and the Catholic Church, the virus threatens to infest the entire world unless society is sanitized by bourgeois spirit and work.

It is within this frame of reference that Burton comes to prioritize the hypostasis of acedic idleness as cause of melancholy. At the same time, Burton expands the boundaries of interpretation of melancholy, projecting it onto a cosmic scale. No longer merely a human disease, it is an active metaphysical *otherness*, a hellish and perverse agency that does not simply kill but torments. Thus Burton considers melancholy both in its widest definition as malign cosmic power, and in its narrower one as a splenetic disposition of the mind that, although present in all human beings and affecting them all to a certain degree, is constitutive only of the melancholic temperaments. The causes and symptoms of melancholy coincide for the most part, pointing to melancholy's constitutive circularity, the self-imprisoning character of the condition. In its double hypostasis of sadness and fear, the two cause-symptoms established by the Hippocratic tradition, enriched and transmitted by Galen, it figures prominently as melancholy. Burton especially emphasizes the hypostasis of boredom, and the new complex of idleness-boredom is thereby articulated: "Opposite to exercise is idleness (the badge of gentry) or want of exercise, the bane of body and mind, the nurse of naughtiness, stepmother of discipline, the chief author of all mischief, one of the seven deadly sins, and a sole cause of this and many other maladies, the devil's cushion, as Gualter calls it, his pillow and chief reposal" (242).

Burton refers to idleness as the deadly sin of sloth, and explains that it can affect both mind and body. Following Ficino and Hippocrates, he notes the effects of physical idleness, such as the accumulation of phlegm and "gross humors" that grow "as fern . . . in untilled grounds and all manner of weeds" (243). Idleness of mind, moreover, the condition of a mind unoccupied with "some honest business," is an even more serious condition, for ultimately it is the idle mind that is the productive cause of the condition. He enumerates the effects of "wit without employment":

> Idleness of the mind is much worse than this of the body; wit without employment is a disease, *aerugo animi, rubigo ingenii*: the rust of the soul, a plague, hell itself, *maximum animi nocumentum*, Galen calls it. "As in a standing pool worms and filthy creepers increase" (*et vitium capiunt ni moveantur aquae*, the water itself putrefies, and air likewise, if it be not continually stirred by the wind) "so do evil and corrupt thoughts in an idle person," the soul is contaminated. (243)

While the symptoms and causes of its perniciousness will later be discussed extensively by Edmund Burke and René Le Senne, Burton provides a naïvely empirical but insightful dialectical explanation of the degradation and decomposition caused by phlegmatic idleness:

> In a commonwealth, where is no public enemy, there is, likely, civil wars, and they rage upon themselves; this body of ours, when it is idle and knows not how to bestow itself, macerates and vexeth itself with cares, griefs, false fears, discontents, and suspicions; it tortures and preys upon its own bowels, and is never at rest. . . . When we are left to ourselves, idleness as a tempest drives all virtuous motions out of our minds, and *nihili sumus*; on a sudden, by sloth and such bad ways, we come to naught. . . . These men are devils alone, as the saying is, *Home solus aut deus, aut daemon*: a man alone is either a saint or a devil. (243–248)

For Burton, a social thinker with liberal-bourgeois views—representing the progressive force at the time—idleness is the prerogative of aristocracy and melancholy emerges as a political sin or disease of the old regime. Accordingly, the treatment he recommends for idling aristocracy is socially purposeful work. Even if physically and intellectually active, the nobility are not engaged in purposeful social work. For Burton it is evident that what is lacking is not activity per se but progressive social purpose and a corresponding passionate engagement. Nobility becomes for him a symbol of the past, of disengagement from any socially relevant cause, and thus of passivity or absence of passion.

In comparing Burton's explanation of the evil of idleness with Pascal's, there emerge common phenomenological elements as well as significant interpretative differences. Although each sees the nothing in the depths of being in accordance with his respective weltanschauung, they differ in their interpretations and the corresponding remedial strategies. For Pascal the nothing is the ultimate ground of one's being, a ground that is ordinarily hidden from view by "diversion" or "distraction" (*divertissement*) and contemplation of it terrifies the self, throwing it into despair. Burton has an interpretation of worldliness similar to Pascal's distraction: he calls it madness or melancholy. In his attempt to explain it, Burton anticipates Hume's observation concerning the incessant activity of the mind, only Burton goes further: unless properly trained and usefully employed, the mind turns against itself to consume itself. Burton cannot explain this turning against oneself; he can only illustrate it by analogy to the fate of a commonwealth that, when no outside enemy threatens, turns against itself in civil war. Without an external or internal other, the self splits itself in two and creates inside itself an other for itself. Burton has therein the metaphysical intuition of the dialectical necessity of otherness and negation that is later fundamental to the theosophical thinking of Böhme, Hegel, and Schelling.

PASCAL: THE REPELLENT CREATIVE POWER OF ENNUI

Pascal also sees the nothing in the recesses of being that idleness makes visible. Idleness clears away all objects of desire, such as distracting thoughts, passions, and activities. In the clearing thus created, one faces the abyss of one's being. The contemplation of the nothing of oneself suspended between the spatial and temporal infinities provokes an immense ennui and anguish—Heidegger's boredom and anxiety. Certainly, diversion only masks the abyss, it does not fill it: without God, the nothing always remains in the depth of one's being. What Pascal recommends is to arrest the impulse toward diversion, and, alone with oneself, contemplate the void. It is only then, face to face with this absolute emptiness that, he believes, the contemplator will realize that the nothing is tragically one's own groundless ground of being and will begin the search for authentic remedy. For Pascal, the only authentic remedy for the dread and despair of the nothing is *metanoia* as a way to faith and God's grace. Indeed, it is only God as Being-itself that can fill out the nothing of our fallen condition. There is a note in Pascal's contemplation that is Heideggerian avant la lettre. Like Heidegger later, Pascal lets ennui appear since it is in the inner space opened by it that one can see the truth. Contrary to Burton, Pascal encourages boredom and idleness as the conditions for the possibility of seeing the nothing, because the metaphysical nothing must be acknowledged and confronted, not avoided in distractions.

There is a radical distinction between Pascal's and Burton's remedies, a distinction grounded in their different interpretations of both the meaning of the metaphysical nothing hidden in the human heart and the ultimate telos of human life. When Burton exhaustively reviews the different theories of melancholy from antiquity to his own time, as well as the innumerable etiological hypotheses, he ultimately designates idleness as its fundamental existential cause. For Pascal, that idleness creates the perfect conditions for the possibility of contemplating the unredeemed human condition. His conviction that the tragedy of man comes from not knowing how to stay unoccupied in his room is a reformulation of Evagrius's theology of the sin of acedia, where the sin is indulgence in the desire to flee the boredom and anxiety of the nothing discovered in oneself in the absence of the absolute object of desire. If the failure to stay unoccupied in his room is the effect of the demon of acedia, then what Pascal really affirms is that the tragic condition of man is the acedic condition of ennui, or rather, the disquieting reality that becomes visible only in the acedic condition. His reflections on the cause of man's restlessness are reflections on the cause of the sin of acedia: boredom. Indeed, Pascal believes that man is like a bored king, or a king constantly under the threat of boredom, whose entourage employ themselves with entertaining and distracting him from the vision of the abyss of being, thus making impossible the search for an authentic solution. He writes: "There is nothing so insufferable to man as to be completely at rest, without passions, without business, without diversion, without study. He then feels his nothingness, his forlornness, his insufficiency, his dependence, his weakness, his emptiness. There will immediately arise from the depth of his heart weariness, gloom, sadness, fretfulness, vexation, despair."[2] Pascal deplores the negative creativity of boredom: he interprets all human work and play simply as distraction from being at home with oneself. He explains the impossibility of the self to be with itself by the disproportion of the human condition (§72,

127, 126, 139, 109), an interpretation that Ricoeur will subsequently adopt and develop. The human being, defined by the misery and glory of a thinking reed that dies—and knows that it is dying—is metaxic, caught at the crossing of the infinitudes of time and space, between the nothing from which it comes and the nothing toward which it goes (§347, 72). In one utterance he relates boredom, blackness, darkness, emptiness, sadness, grief, sorrow, resentment, forlornness, desperation; they are all forms of the nothing that reside naturally in the human heart (§139). In order to avoid the encounter with the nothing of his own being, man becomes ex-centric to himself and works at building the "tower of the world" meant to give him the stability and security he longs for. Pascal classifies all achievements and failures, significant or trite, in the category of diversion whose aim is to cover up the nothing. The human self temporarily hides from himself the ontological nothing by killing the time of his already short life (§183). He thus succeeds in avoiding knowing himself and searching for a more solid means to escape the nothing of his being (§139, 164, 171). As with Heidegger later, this is the rationale behind the consideration of diversion as the great evil: it is unmistakably the mortal sin of acedia itself. Diversion distracts one from proper thinking and knowledge of oneself; knowledge of oneself means knowledge of the human ontological lack or meontological ground. It is metaphysical knowledge and proper thinking that are the specifically human attributes, the greatness and dignity of man (§146). Pascal affirms that "proper thinking" implies thinking of three principal objects of thought, oneself, one's creator, and one's end. A life of diversion is a life of Kierkegaardian despair, in which one does not even know that one is in despair, an existence in which the spiritual has been repressed. Pascal laments the consoling power of diversion since it prevents man from confronting his condition seriously. He calls man back from the consolation of diversion to boredom in tones echoed by Kierkegaard's praise of acknowledged despair and Heidegger's invitation to an attunement to profound boredom.

RAPOSA: BOREDOM AS A SIGNIFICANT SIGN

As contemporary scholar Michael Raposa observes, Pascal's conception of the nature of boredom, "a feeling of nullity without realizing it," explains the interminable list of hypothetical or experimental interpretations as well as the temptation to avoid it in distractions.[3] As a matter of fact, Raposa's entire project in *Boredom and the Religious Imagination*, a Peircean semiotic analysis of boredom, centers on the ambivalence and metamorphoses of boredom understood as a sign that requires discernment and adequate hermeneutic labor. His pertinent observations on Pascal, Kierkegaard, and Heidegger address precisely this absolute task of reading and listening to boredom, a condition whose true signification is revelatory for the human condition. Such a task is a "spiritually edifying exercise." At the end of his study Raposa concludes:

> I have tried . . . to portray boredom as a sign. It is a sign that can be interpreted in various ways, sometimes as a sign of sin, a sign of failure. It can be a sign of fatigue, a healthy sign marking as trivial those objects on which we ought not wastefully to spend our attention. Boredom can also be interpreted as a trial, in its deepest and darkest manifestations, as a terrible trial of our love, so that it too, becomes like a balance on which our hearts are weighed. (166)

If boredom is this multivalent sign or cipher revealing while concealing a most significant truth or reality, Raposa identifies Pascal, Kierkegaard, and Heidegger as its lucid and skilled semioticians who have relentlessly applied a hermeneutics of suspicion to all its conventional and theological readings and diagnoses. Thus for Pascal, recognizing its true essence, a "feeling of nullity" requires the patience of waiting, Raposa notes, resisting the impulse to act as a form of self-deception and dangerous forgetfulness, and enduring the pathos of the infinite abyss of one's own being that only God as infinite object can fill (46–47).

SCHOPENHAUER: DIALECTICS OF PAINFUL STRIVING AND BORING RELIEF

The leitmotif of Schopenhauer's lamentation was already present in Pascal. Indeed, Pascal and Schopenhauer seem to be tormented by the same mood, by deadening mortal boredom, and inspired by it, their reflections strike surprisingly similar notes. With Schopenhauer boredom is postulated as a metaphysical principle. The Will to life objectified in the phenomenon of man manifests itself in the dialectics of pain and boredom. Boredom is the joyless relief from painful striving after the object of desire; it is satiety in the aftermath of the paradoxical and tragic loss of the object precisely through the fulfillment of desire. For Schopenhauer, the phenomenal world is an illusion: it is the veil used by the Will to life to hide its nakedness from itself. For the mind clouded by this frenzy of manifestation, life is the ever renewed chasing after elusive objects of desire whose possession promises the peace of fulfillment. But possession of the object means the loss of the object and of its promise. The ensuing relief from the pain of striving proves to be a curse rather than a blessing. The anticipated joy of fulfilled desire is only a mirage, as the Will to life can never be still. In the absence of objects of desire, the Will turns against itself in a Böhmian-Schellingian gesture, one that Burton intuited as the essential moment of melancholy provoked by idle imagination. As Schopenhauer describes it, "the will's passion itself remains, even without any conscious motive and makes itself known to [the individual] with desperate pain as a feeling of terrible desolation and emptiness."[4]

There is no natural exit from the Will's domain, not even in death. The battle of the two metaphysical powers of pure knowledge and Will ravages man's consciousness. The world sighs and moans in the grip of the Will and only esthetic or ethical contemplation and pure knowledge—because they are not bound to the Will—can penetrate the veil of illusion. This true gnosis, the Vedantist-Buddhist detached contemplation that Schopenhauer had recovered by way of Indian thought, is in accord with Stoic *apatheia* and Christian neo-Platonism in its condemnation of Will's madness.

Loss of hope is intrinsic to *tedium vitae* and can lead to suicide. The desperate suicide, trapped in illusion, is unaware that death kills only the phenomenon but not the Will itself. Boredom, the abandonment of hope, means entering hell, since, according to Schopenhauer's interpretation, Dante's Hell is the world as Will.[5] Hellish time is time that cannot be either filled or killed. Schopenhauer's theory of time is adapted to fit his Gnostic acosmism. Time is a constant dying, a present always disappearing into the past, a tangential point on the life-sphere, the sun at noon. A nondimensional blink of the eye, it comes from nothing and goes toward nothing. Under the whip of the Will to life, man forever strives to stretch out time. The irony of malicious Will is that, when in boredom time finally becomes long, it turns into an unbearable burden. The time of boredom is no longer a nondimensional point, a blink of the eye: it will not die into the past, but lingers precisely at noon. While the time of boredom is in excess, the time of eternity as the lightness of the present is inaccessible. The nature of boredom as absence of love or desire, reminiscent of Dante's hypostases of indolence, sadness, and anger, becomes visible. Deadening tedium is a Janus with two faces, apathy and acedia, just as Purgatory is coupled with Hell, making the walls between damnation and salvation porous, the first swallowed up in world-illusion, the second moving toward the only salvation, the only possible cure of the disease in Schopenhauer's philosophy of life: for only a complete denial of the Will produces the contentment that can never be disturbed and redeems the world (224). Boredom's ambiguity—which was implied in all Stoic humoral pathologies—comes forth again. Only gnosis distinguishes the good from the bad loss of desire.

LE SENNE: IDLENESS AS THE GROUND OF
MELANCHOLIC EVIL

With René Le Senne's theory developed in *Traité de Caractérologie* (1946), we reach a different perspective on the deeper layers of meaning of the dialectics of melancholy.[6] The treatise accounts for Democritus's principle that "character is destiny," and places itself in the humoral tradition. It constructs a metaphysics of the psyche, opening up a new stage in the understanding of the human self's complexity, its concrete hypostasis defined by the configuration of genetic tendencies which Le Senne terms *caractère*, traditionally known as temperament.[7] Within the limits of its temperament, the self evolves as a Hegelian actualization of the Idea, or a Ricoeurian hermeneutic project, from nature to freedom. Temperament is a form of embodiment, and one of the forms of predestination or necessity that the self confronts. The differences among temperaments are accounted for by the different degrees of actualization of the psyche's fundamental constitutive properties, namely, *emotivité, activité*, and *retentissement*.[8] This metaphysical triad, which forms the armature of the psyche, differs in its economy according to the individual temperament. One can detect in Le Senne a crypto-Trinitarianism applied to the psyche, especially inasmuch as the three properties are three and one at the same time while proceeding from the first, sensibility (*emotivité*). In establishing sensibility as the primordial ontological source of the self, Le Senne initiates an epistemological reform.[9] He also explains that in the theory of psychic hypostases, sensibility as affective responsiveness is actually the "essence of psychic life," "the capacity to be moved by outer and inner events" (63–64). Sensibility as affective responsiveness designates the psyche, as subject, as primordially receptive toward the object (75). The intensity of sentiment, excitability, impulsivity, the degree of attachment to the affecting object, the inner mobility, and readiness—these are the general modes of its manifestation; they are instances of the life of the self, its levels of life force. This source of life for the self modulates into the second mode of manifestation, which is readiness for action in the world as its object. These two, sensibility as affective responsiveness and activity as readiness for action, are the sine qua non constituent properties of the psyche. Metaphysically they represent the termini of the original subject-object relation (86).

The third constitutive property, one of Le Senne's original conceptual discoveries, is capacity for retrospection. The capacity for retrospection indicates the relation of self to time. We commonly refer to the self's living either in the present and future, or in the past. The former condition is termed by Le Senne's *primarité* (now-consciousness) and the latter *secondarité* (past-consciousness).

> In each person every representation possesses its double, resounding or repercussion, immediate and posthumous. When the effects of a mental given present to consciousness in the moment reject the effects of past givens, the now-consciousness (*primarité*) prevails over the past-consciousness (*secondarité*). If, on the contrary, the persisting influence of past experiences prevails over that of the present, masking it, repressing it, subordinating it to itself, then the person is characterized by past-consciousness. . . . The individual lives in the present, renews himself through it: the now-consciousness is a fountain of rejuvenation. By contrast, the past-conscious individual slows down the present as if by a steering wheel, by a structure that oppresses him and opposes the present event with the repercussion of a multitude of past impressions unevenly operative. (89)

In Le Senne's theory, the basis of temperamental constitution is defined by the particular combination of the three fundamental constitutive properties (*emotivité, activité, retentissement*), conceived as modes active in different degrees. Although he adopts Hippocrates's taxonomy of temperament, according to Le Senne's classification there are eight, instead of four, significant variations of the three modes. The eight variations are (1) choleric (sensibility-activity-now-consciousness), (2) nervous (sensibility-inactivity-now-consciousness), (3) sentimental (sensibility-inactivity-past-consciousness), (4) passionate (sensibility-activity-past-consciousness), (5) sanguine (insensibility-activity-now-consciousness), (6) phlegmatic (insensibility-activity-past-consciousness), (7) amorphous (insensibility-inactivity-now-consciousness), and (8) apathetic (insensibility-inactivity-past-consciousness). Besides the traditional three humors—choleric, sanguine, and phlegmatic—the remaining five are constellations of melancholy and inactivity. Inactivity is the predominant constitutive feature of the sentimental, the nervous, the apathetic, and the amorphous that correspond to the melancholic and acedic in the traditional humoral classification; the constant of all these variations is inactivity, while sensibility and retrospection are present in different degrees.[10] It becomes obvious that for Le Senne as well as for Burton and Pascal there is an intrinsic and direct relation between melancholy and inactivity. Le Senne explains the active mode and its negation:

> The term activity refers only to an individual who acts through an innate disposition toward activity that comes spontaneously from himself. The inactive one acts too, but against himself, his body opposing, with pain, often grumbling and lamenting; he acts because he is afraid or hungry. The naturally active one is on the contrary the one to whom the words of Ribot, taken over

by Malapert, apply: "he has to act, he needs to act." External events are for him only occasions, opportunities, pretexts; if they did not exist, he would look for them, would provoke them, since he lives to act. (77)

The psychic property of "activity" implies activity for its own sake, in spontaneity, with the joy and inalienable inner necessity to act. Le Senne illustrates spontaneous activity by the child's natural impulse to play. Nietzsche had intuited the value of spontaneous activity that is its own causality; in his *On the Uses and Disadvantages of History for Life,* both the child and the cow live in the moment, forgetting all past and future, being absorbed in the activity of the present.[11] Activity combined with now-consciousness is the makeup of Nietzsche's master race. It bears the marks of the innocence of the present, with its clarity, freshness, and hope. The spontaneous act is young and optimistic since it never broods over the past. The old man dreams of being a child, the slave of being a master, the Dionysian of Apollonian beauty and serenity. Nietzsche figures in Le Senne's speculative typology as a tormented passionate soul. What Nietzsche abhors is resentment, a complex of inactivity and past-consciousness, creating infinite "rumination" that suggests the impossibility of forgetting and, thereby, the impossibility of self-renewal by living innocently in the present. The Eternal Recurrence or the joyous acceptance of each moment is a psychological possibility only for the one who is not fatigued by recurrence through rumination, since there is no real recurrence for the one living in the present, the one not burdened by the weight of time and the inactive self, the one who is light, and can "play" like the child always in the present.

INNER OTHERNESS AND THE GREAT MELANCHOLICS

Thus, activity and inactivity circumscribe the range of possible attitudes toward the other qua obstacle. Le Senne explains that the inactive self is the one discouraged by obstacle while the active one is titillated by it. He defines the obstacle as the primordial other, that is, the self itself in the mode of inactivity.[12] There is an essential relation between inactivity and melancholy. As Le Senne notes, it is the melancholic that was the first, best known, and well defined of all the temperaments. Melancholics problematize their condition: it is they who tend to confess, complain, discourse about themselves and their unhappy state. The literary form of the *journal intime,* which Le Senne believes is the mode of expression par excellence of the melancholic, as a subjective record of the life of the self, is a valuable document of identity in this case. Le Senne illustrates specific features of the melancholic by adducing philosophical tendencies and attitudes of the great melancholics—such as Maine de Biran, Kierkegaard, and Heidegger—as the most prominent philosophical actualizations of melancholy. Their inactivity is the active negation of activity, the inner obstacle, the permanently resistant inner other that operates as a "brake, a coefficient of friction and inertia imposing a quantum of impotence and ineffectiveness" (79). The obstacle qua hostile other nested inside oneself develops its perverse schemes of resisting all movement. It is a deadly sickness of the soul: it kills all desire, religious fervor, enthusiasm, hope for the future, optimism, and joy. Inactivity deflates, discourages, paints the vision in dark and gloomy colors, leads to impotence of the will, incapacity to make an effort or reject a temptation. It converts all positive determination into its negative; it is the power of negation, of opposition, Schelling's power of the negative, the power of the devil.

What Le Senne calls *dyscolism*, namely, "sad and morose humor, pessimism, disposition to melancholy," is the "affective expression of inactivity" (188). Statistics have shown the presence or absence of the activity trait to make the difference between the active fashioners of historical destiny and the "dreamers": artists, poets, contemplatives. The latter mostly participate in the melancholic typologies. Inactivity is responsible, moreover, for the great boundary between objective and subjective philosophical attitudes, the turn toward the object or the subject respectively. Inactivity arrests or delays the manifestation of emotion in the world of objects; detoured from its natural outlet, emotion folds back on the self, becoming self-consciousness. In this tarrying, as Nietzsche has already observed, there emerges self-consciousness but also the possibility of degradation, of soul sickness, and fall. Le Senne remarks that it is precisely in the case of the melancholic that the hiatus between the self's essence and existence is experienced as painful and unbridgeable. In other words, the pathetic consciousness, whether religious or not, is the melancholic consciousness par excellence, where melancholy is the effect of inactivity.

Le Senne is aware of the scandal of such psychologism raised to the level of a metaphysical principle. Unlike Burton though, he is not a pragmatic ideologist calling humanity to work. He emphatically notes that the psychic propensity for activity is not identical with the proliferation of acts. On the contrary, such a proliferation may be precisely a symptom of a feverish inactivity. Or, it may as well be an exogenous or false activity, an activity provoked by external contingencies. Contrary to false activity, the meaning, motivation, and telos of natural activity actualize themselves in the act itself whose agent has no concern for the outcome—a fact that precludes all sense of fear of failure. Nor are there present the conditions for the possibility of self-condemnation. The act is forgotten once it disappears from the immediate horizon of the future, being pushed back into the past by subsequent acts rushing into being, thus making history. The naturally active individual lives in the present and toward the future, while the inactive one has his face turned toward the past. Inactivity resists present manifestation and lingers inside, outside the actual and the immediate. Precisely therein, however, lies the magia of sublimation, transmutation, and transfiguration. Inactivity sublimates raw emotion, polishes events of their roughness, absorbs the otherness of the obstacle into the subject. This total reversal of manifestation has theological and religious implications. Inactivity as inner obstacle discontinues the instinctive, natural movement from the self to the world. By reabsorbing the impulse to manifestation, the centrifugal drive of the self returns to itself and intensifies consciousness, complexifying it as Hegel, Nietzsche, or Pierre Teilhard de Chardin knew. Le Senne confirms the significance of Hegel's dialectical necessity of confronting the other as the radical modality of self-becoming and self-knowing.

As Le Senne notes, melancholy is present in the active character in a latent form. It can be aroused and awakened by a dramatic change of life situation. Such an exogenous circumstantial melancholy will remain a "borrowed" condition, lacking the purity of the natural propensity. Le Senne illustrates this with the case of Napoleon in exile, who took up writing his memoires— memoires that were not a *journal intime* à la Maine de Biran, Rousseau, Thoreau, or Kierkegaard however—a difference that is accounted for by the original difference in temperament and destiny.

In Le Senne's reflections on the great melancholics, Maine de Biran is analytical and an introvert, situated in a central position within the family of melancholics (287). Biran is moderate in his sensibility, inactivity, and past-consciousness. He is not rendered impotent by his inactivity, although his relation to it is one of constant painful struggle. The aspects that make Biran a perfect representative of the melancholic temperament are his resort to the *journal intime*, his emphasis on coaenesthesia (a general feeling of wellbeing or malaise arising from the totality of organic sensations), the role of the body in his theories of mood, his preoccupation with subjectivity, and his religious fervor. Kierkegaard and Heidegger, by contrast, are the tragic melancholics (288). Le Senne briefly notes that past-consciousness and the capacity for abstract and systematic thought lean toward philosophy, while sensibility gives this philosophy the substance and allure of a meditation on existence. It is again inactivity that tips this existential meditation over toward the category of the tragic.

THE INNER VOID OF BOREDOM

Le Senne looks for an even deeper understanding of inactivity. When inactivity or blocked activity weighs heavily on sensibility, the subject is prone to anxiety and depression, both hypostases of melancholy (679). Medically, the effects of inactivity can be most accurately studied in depressed subjects (680–81).[13] Since inactivity substitutes discourse for action, the expression of inactivity is a powerful witness and symptom in itself: its discourse is a long and repetitive lamentation of the self (682–83). Thus inactivity appears for Le Senne to be a drive, the Freudian death drive. Both melancholy and boredom are its consequences. The most inactive melancholics suffer from boredom. He explains, "It is among the most inactive of the sentimental [melancholics] that we find the most pathetic testimonies of boredom (*ennui*)—if the word pathetic is acceptable in the case of a disposition whose essence is the exclusion of any passion for the sake of passivity" (266). Le Senne observes that the nature of boredom is conditioned by the constitutive property of inactivity. The being-in-the-moment of the nervous melancholic prevents the condition of boredom from becoming a deadly disease: it is more superficial and less continuous over time.

It is only with the retrospective melancholic that boredom comes into its own. Retrospection, the tendency to ruminative reflection, enhances inactivity and seriously aggravates the inability to act. It achieves this paralyzing effect since it both introduces the past and encourages reflection, thereby enlarging the horizon of suspension in the possible indefinitely, as in the case of Kierkegaard's aesthetic personality. The hesitation and indecision provoked by the indefinite proliferation of mutually exclusive motives and possibilities renders impossible the already difficult act (261). Acts become indecisive, inchoate, virtual. The ensuing exacerbation of inactivity creates the ground for boredom, is boredom itself, whose essence is, Le Senne remarks, "the absence of all passion in favor of pure passivity" (266). He confirms the Pascalian boredom as "inner void" with a special negative relation to time and desire, and interprets the condition as the "incapacity to give birth to desire, to move from desire to activity, from the virtual to the actual" (267). It is dense inactivity as utter passivity that is experienced as boredom.

But Le Senne observes that boredom does not grow out of the total absence of desire—for the one who does not desire anything does not get bored, he is content to be what he is. Nor does it spring out of a strong desire that action can actualize. Boredom is the atmosphere surrounding desires that are refused entrance into history; it is the ghostly atmosphere hovering about the cemetery of stillborn desires. Man gets bored when desires awake in him—of love, of unknown countries, of glory—and then are condemned to die of inanition, too weak to conquer innate passivity. The essence of boredom is absolute futility, the lamentation of Ecclesiastes. In solitude and idleness, the inner void of boredom expands uninhibited. It engulfs the self completely until nothing is left but this void, absorbing abysmally the life of the self, since "boredom has cleaned out the self of all the determinations created by desire and left it naked and void" (268). Both Ficino and Hegel knew that age contributes to the aggravation of boredom by smoothing out emotions and dissolving interests. The temptation to withdraw in solitude and idleness is to be resisted vigorously since the external void, by mirroring the inner void, is prone to exacerbate the latter and deepen the gravity of the condition. This remedy proves false since, once again, it deepens the malignity of the melancholy.

THE DEMON OF PERVERSITY AS
THERAPEUTIC STRATEGY

Le Senne does not offer remedies but rather, like Binswanger, observes and notes the strategies used by the self to cope with its painful suffering. These strategies are presented as the psycho-dialectics of melancholic consciousness. In this light, the remedy is the instinctive method of the self to ease itself from the burden by enlivening its emotions and desires. The principal strategy is to awaken what Le Senne calls, using a term borrowed from Edgar Allen Poe, the *demon of perversity*. The *demon of perversity* is the self that in the fight against deadening passivity appeals to of the negative as a stimulus for action. The representation of the negative is the only stimulant sufficiently powerful to spur the passive self into action—by what Le Senne calls a monstrous reversal (195). Horror, dread, disgust, all the negative sentiments, all the modes of suffering become the springs of a propulsion that substitutes for an absent activity (196). This observation is seminal. Le Senne lists the melancholic fascination with the horrible, the cruel, the macabre, the forbidden, the obscene, the false, the absurd, and the void or nothing as forming the substance of aesthetic Satanism (200). He mentions Baudelaire, Poe, Dante, Auguste Comte de Villiers de l'Isle Adam, Alfred de Musset, Byron, Heine, and Oscar Wilde as the melancholic poets who expressed it.

But poetry and art are not the exclusive domains of the *demon of perversity*'s manifestation. According to Le Senne, philosophy itself bears its mark:

> In the sphere of philosophy too the spirit skillful in procuring stimulants can find them in all that opposes the exigency of unity, the need for order, truth, and being. Whatever breaks logical continuity, negates the positive, discredits candor, becomes a privileged object of attention. The paradoxical, the absurd are searched for, not as problems to be solved but rather as negativities to be privileged by a spirit whose secret often admitted intentionality is the identification of the absolute with the negative because such identification provides the most stimulation to a consciousness which, as analytic as intelligence may make, remains a nervous [melancholic] consciousness. (199)

The negative has the function of a titillation of emotion that, once reawakened, can regain its force and impulsivity and feel alive. Kierkegaard's aesthete is Neronian, Le Senne remarks. He is the artist par excellence, the Romantic poet, the ultra refined aesthete. His intuition of the powerfully creative stimulus exercised by repellent boredom is a rediscovery of Pascal's melancholic reflections on the misery of the human condition without God, prone to the constant double threat of despair or boredom, and an unreflective refuge in diversion.

The case of the sentimental melancholic consciousness is slightly different. While it is true that the self's strategy against passivity is still a mode of the *demon of perversity*, the demon has a different character. This time the activating forces are anxiety toward the future, fear of boredom, repugnance to indignity (279). The sentimental melancholic consciousness bears the mark of reflexivity that annuls impulsiveness, restrains emotion, and develops self-reflection. It is the sentimental melancholic who is menaced by a deep disquieting boredom, for whom the future is anguish provoking, who ruminates about the past and the passage of time.

PRESCRIPTIONS FOR A HYGIENE OF MELANCHOLY

This psychic metaphysics also articulates the dialectics involved in the sin of melancholy. Le Senne goes so far in covering the territory of melancholy that he develops a regimen for the relief from inactivity, which he calls a hygiene of melancholy (281). He even insists that the most important truth about melancholy is the danger—the sin—of indulgence. Le Senne offers several indications concerning the hygiene of melancholy:

> The spirit can break the habit of letting itself go down that slope if it takes care to control the spontaneous movements of an intelligence that is slave to excitability: if it assumes the energy included in all happy and tonic experiences, if it watches the dialectical steps by which its intelligence spontaneously inclines toward criticism, favoring the negative aspects of things, then it will access joy and happiness whose source is a positive conception of the world. (283)

The hygiene of melancholy for the sentimental melancholic psyche is an object of serious consideration. This temperament constitutionally inhabits an insecure place; one slip along the downward slope makes the subsequent fall into pathology difficult to avert. Le Senne understands this danger, and his preventive or therapeutic suggestions sanction the pertinent intuitions in the literature on melancholy and its remedial possibilities. The golden rule in the hygiene of melancholy is resistance to the temptation to indulge in inactivity, unlearning the habit of letting oneself go into a careless free fall— or, in Ricoeur's terms, avoiding the slide from fallibility to sin. The metaphor of the fall reverts to its original, literal, nonmetaphoric sense and signifies the state of absolute passivity toward the other qua the nonself. As Hegel observed, even standing is a matter of the will; certainly, this act demands self-awareness, vigilant self-observation, firm lucidity, and familiarity with the condition—all of which are grounded in the melancholic gift of rumination.

MELANCHOLY AND SUBJECTIVITY

To recapitulate, inactivity generates melancholy and boredom when it is aggravated by retrospective reflexivity against a background of delicate sensibility. That is the reason why the melancholic condition is the most fragile condition of all. Awareness of the painful hiatus between being and essence already lamented by Paul the Apostle, personalized as the difference between what one is and what one wishes to be, belongs to the melancholic soul. The melancholic is aware of his own inactivity as a fundamental weakness and impotence toward the other as obstacle. This intimate experience of the divided self is grounded in emotional vulnerability and colors the entire melancholic existence.[14] At the same time, Le Senne remarks, it is precisely the melancholic self that reminds us of what it means to be a human being. Having in mind Maine de Biran, he observes that the melancholic "brought the attention of philosophy to the primitive fact of inner sense" (217). Like Ficino, Burton, Pascal, Kierkegaard, and other great melancholics, Le Senne explains, Biran makes a conscious effort to understand himself and discover the truth about the world, a truth that would account for his own predicament of being bound by his melancholic modes, and a truth that would set him free. In his *journal intime*, there occurs the birth of philosophical thought out of the personal struggle with the melancholic condition. Like Ficino previously, Le Senne considers the melancholic as the privileged locus of the "individual human subject" since, he writes, "The quality of the mental individual human subject, capable of enjoying and suffering . . . absorbing himself in joy and especially in sorrow, is the privilege and the burden of the melancholic. Among all temperaments, it is the melancholic who reinforces for us all the sentiment of affective interiority" (231). In other words, the melancholic is the center of diffusion for subjectivity, and the rest of humanity is human to the extent to which it participates in melancholic subjectivity:

> Rumination prolongs an emotion and its echo far beyond its cause, even when another cause is opposing it. The sentimental [melancholic] opposes to the objectivity of these successive causes the subjectivity of persisting emotion.

Properly speaking, without this retrospection there would not be any subjectivity: ultimately there is no subjectivity except for the melancholic [subjectivity] since the other temperaments know it only to the extent to which they resemble him. Eliminate Rousseau, Biran, Amiel, do we have the same lively and sharp consciousness of the I? When Biran says "only the sick feel that they exist," he expresses the curse and blessing of melancholic consciousness that acquires, through painful and profound emotions, the right to defend in the world the reality of the I qua subject. What interests them, the object of their passionate and tireless curiosity, is man; not man the way one sees him, not man as animal or citizen, man for and in the others, but rather man made I, the way he sees, knows, perceives himself in inner analysis. (230–31)

Le Senne's metaphysics of the psyche thus mediates between the traditional discourse of melancholy and the contemporary phenomenology of subjectivity, especially as articulated in Michel Henry's understanding of immanent self-affection.

NOTES

1. Robert Burton, *The Anatomy of Melancholy*, ed. Holbrook Jackson; with an introduction by William Gass (New York: New York Review Books, 2001).

2. René Pascal, *Pensées*, trans. W. F. Trotter (Mineola: Dover, 2003), §131. Pascal's *Pensées* are hereafter cited in the text by section number (§).

3. Raposa, *Boredom and the Religious Imagination*, 45; see also 142.

4. Arthur Schopenhauer, *The World as Will and Idea*, trans. Jill Berman (London: Dent, 1995), 226.

5. Schopenhauer, *The World as Will:* "For where else did Dante get the material for his hell if not from our real world?" (205).

6. René Le Senne, *Traité de caracterologie: suivi de Précis d'idiologie*, a commentary by Édouard Morot-Sir (Paris: Presses Universitaires de France, 1973). Le Senne (1882–1954), French philosopher and psychologist, developed a philosophy of values and founded the French school of characterology. All translations of *Traité de caracterologie* are mine.

7. I choose to use the term temperament instead of character, which in English has different and, in the present case, misleading denotations.

8. Le Senne terms *emotivité*, the "capacity and readiness to be moved." This term could be translated as "excitability," "affectivity," "receptivity," "sensibility," and "sensitivity." Although "affective" or "emotional sensitivity" or "excitability" would be closer to Le Senne's intention, I will use "sensibility" with qualifying adjectives. By *activité* Le Senne means readiness for action, spontaneity, dynamism; for the sake of simplicity, I will use Le Senne's "activity versus inactivity." Le Senne's term *retentissement des représentations*, translated literally, gives the "resounding"

or "echoing of representations," propensity for reflection, representational retention, retrospection. What he means by this is the capacity of the psyche to allow representations to return, echo, ring, and resound in one's consciousness. Therefore I choose a term designating an attribute of the consciousness that would allow events to resound and return: *retro-spection* or *re-flection*.

9. Édouard Morot-Sir, in his commentary in the 1973 edition of Le Senne's treatise, wrote, "Le Senne goes a little further on the road of epistemological reform when he gives the character a unique source, that is, affective sensitivity (*emotivité*), and makes activity derive from this original energy" (746; my translation).

10. I will use the term *melancholic* with Le Senne's distinctive qualifications to refer to different temperamental dispositions defined by melancholy and boredom.

11. Friedrich Nietzsche, "On the Uses and Disadvantages of History for Life," in *Untimely Meditations*, trans. R. J. Hollingdale (Cambridge: Cambridge University Press, 1996), 60–61.

12. Here we take a step away from Le Senne's treatise toward his earlier more philosophical work *Obstacle et valeur* (1934), published in English as *Obstacle and Value*, trans. Bernard P. Dauenhauer (Evanston: Northwestern University Press, 1972). It seems that Le Senne's thought is a search for understanding, interpreting, remedying, and redeeming inactivity qua difficulty, innate or acquired inability to confront the Other qua obstacle, whether immanent or transcendent.

13. Le Senne agrees with Marcel Montassut's theory presented in *La dépression constitutionnelle* (Constitutional depression) published in 1931. The subjective manifestations of the depressed subject are fatigability, impressionability and sense of impotence, insecurity, and difficult effort. The one who is depressed has difficulty in preventing the degradation of his energy, is always ready to capitulate, turns away from social life toward inner life, succeeds in professions that do not demand enterprising vigor. Le Senne recognizes in this sketch the portrait of the *sentimental melancholic*. If the depressed condition deteriorates, it causes psychoses, withdrawal in the politics of malady, crises of anxiety, psychosis of exhaustion. The morphological signs are a long sad face, the effect of lassitude, and functional problems with digestion, hepatic function, hypotension, glandular instability, neuro-vegetative disequilibrium, suprarenal and thyroid insufficiency.

14. Here I follow the argument of J. Melvin Woody, "Mood Indigo: Darkling World Echoes of Affective-Cognitive Dissonance," an unpublished paper presented at the Annual Conference of the Association for the Advancement of Philosophy and Psychiatry, New Orleans, May 2001.

Chapter 5

Infinite Will, Skepticism, and Sublime Terror

A work among Descartes's juvenilia contains the highly enigmatic phrase *Larvatus prodeo*, "Like an actor wearing a mask, I come forward masked on the stage of the world." Jacques Maritain attempts to justify this phrase by arguing that Cartesian philosophy is a philosophy behind a mask.[1] Descartes's enigmatic phrase has been variously interpreted, but critical agreement on its definitive meaning has not been reached. It is disturbing and paradoxical, though, that three dreams and a masked persona are present at the foundations of modern rationalism. Could *tristesse* be Descartes's shameful other that his rationalism and desire of infinite will are pursued to transcend and mask?

DESCARTES: *TRISTESSE* OR THE SOUL'S ENCOUNTER WITH EVIL

Although Descartes's later treatise on *The Passions of the Soul* (1649) is a syncretic work, a conglomeration of several traditions, its great novelty resides in the fact that the anthropological exploration is undertaken within the limits of his self-designed idealism and rationalism. In it, Descartes identifies six primitive passions: admiration, love, hatred, desire, joy, and sadness. He defines the latter: "Sadness is an unpleasant languor, wherein consists the distress which the soul receives from the evil of defect which the impressions of the brain represent to it as belonging to it."[2] As Freud would later maintain, Cartesian sadness is introduced as an unfinished, indefinite mourning after the lost object of desire. It is caused when loss, absence, or death leave a void in the soul and it manifests all the bodily symptoms of death. Affected by sadness, the body slows down its operation and is marked by a weak pulse. One feels all the ties tightening around the heart, while an icy cold freezes it, spreading through the entire body. Thus, "in sadness [I observe] that the pulse is weak and slow; that one feels as it were bonds around the heart, which constrict it, and pieces of ice, which freeze it, and communicate their coldness to the rest of the body."[3] Like frigid air, sadness makes one pale, emaciated, cold, shrinking the orifices of the heart, making the blood cold, thick, withdrawn, and sluggish. All forms of sadness such as languor, disgust, regret, repentance, pity, remorse, worry, dread, despair, indecision, cowardice, and fear, have similar negative effects on the victim of the condition.

Indeed, in the life of the body, according to Descartes, sadness is a harbinger of death manifesting all the signs of extinction: coldness, pale-blueness, constriction, narrowing of the vessels, inertia, low pulse. Sadness of soul corresponds to the declining life of the body. It stands in opposition to the true nature of the soul that, according to Descartes, is disembodied transparent intellectual joy and tranquility. In sadness the soul lives out its tragic condition of embodiment and mortality ignoring or forgetting itself and its intrinsic potentiality. Descartes's theory of the passions has unmistakably Stoic features, enlivened by elements deriving from the ancient and Renaissance humoral tradition according to which Fire is the principle of embodied Life. The "body-machine" is thus constituted by four elements or humors; it can function like a clock without the intervention of the soul. In the interaction with the soul, the body plays an active part: although the passions are movements within the soul, they originate in actions of the body. In relation to the body, the soul can live passively according to the body, or actively according to its own nature. Thus Cartesian dualism implies a constant battle for supremacy between the will of the soul and the body-machine.

The frigid and blue passions are taken to be the unavoidable consequence of the soul's link to the body. Descartes dreams of the possibility of a joy unimpeded by the contingency of embodiment. He cherishes a Gnostic anti-natura, acosmic longing for disembodiment, for the reversal of incarnation, and for an impersonal rationality. A pale, blue, bloodless, frozen, paralyzing sadness is the soul's experience of the evil of incarnation and temporality: sadness is the soul's experience of evil par excellence. The soul must habituate itself to virtue, knowledge of the good, and guard itself against the onslaught of sadness, since joy and peace are the only convenient emotions for the soul. Significantly, sadness is more primordial than joy, it appears as the first experience of hunger, lack, or loss and is more necessary than joy to the extent that the soul is linked to the body. Through the use of imagination the soul can retrain the body and control it perfectly on the basis of clear and distinct knowledge, maintain a will to virtue, and create attractive representations that induce the body to change its course.

With Descartes, the passions form a territory of ambiguity, of the in-between, where body and soul paradoxically and mysteriously intertwine as completely heterogeneous principles. This is a domain of confusion where the would-be detached cogito of a Stoic modernity suffers the pathos of embodiment. Their ambiguous ontological status is inexplicable according to Cartesian classical dualism and reveals its radical vulnerability. For Descartes, the passions—especially sadness and its species—represent the *other* of the perfectly bodiless mind and infinite will—an other that must be transcended. The perfect ontological separation of the mind from the body is the docetic dream of Gnostic modernity, while *apatheia* is the Stoic ideal state of self-mastery and control over the passions. Modernity is essentially defined by Descartes's ideal of absolute freedom from contingency and finitude, an ideal that presupposes relinquishing our humanity and surpassing it—perhaps as a sort of premonition of Nietzsche's *Übermensch*. Except that for Nietzsche the *Übermensch* is fully embodied and impassionate, while Descartes's ideal human has a purely spiritual ontology. The process of achieving these states is one of progressive withdrawal from the body through proper knowledge, firm will, and appropriate imagination. It presupposes a rigorous self-discipline that is not unlike Evagrius's regimen or Ficino's celestial becoming. The ideal of all these programs of self-transcendence is intellectual joy and tranquility, but here the modern philosopher parts ways with these theological forerunners: for Descartes the journey is completed with a state of absolute reign over the body and its passions, a state sufficient to make man godlike; for Evagrius or Ficino it was only an initial stage of purification.

While preserving several previous attitudes and ideals, Descartes ushers the treatment of the passions into modernity, a modernity that fulfills the Gnostic acosmic ideal: the telos of the human soul is absolute freedom of the will that can be gained by relinquishing all ancient and Renaissance ties to cosmos and nature. If sadness displays many of the traits already familiar, these are studied in vitro, classified as objects of modern science, a new approach replacing the Renaissance networks of meaning and corresponding *magia*. Indeed, Descartes is the dialectical other of Jakob Böhme in replacing *magia universalis* with *mathesis universalis*. The mathematization of nature, human nature included, is intended to control and subject all being without remainder, to eliminate contingency and finitude while liberating reason for the infinite.

Descartes views sadness as the embarrassing locus where evil is encountered. Sadness emerges as the main obstacle in fulfilling superhuman perfection; it preserves an element of the primordial, the natural, the unsettling, the untamable. Thus, as the principal and indelible mark and consequence of pathetic finitude, sadness is alien to our eternal being, an *otherness* that has the creative power of the negative. Poe conceived of it as the *demon of perversity*, while Pascal and Kierkegaard attempt to unravel the enigma of uncanny creativity that the negative generates. It is sadness's negativity and otherness that provoke Descartes's desire for self-transcendence, which, at the threshold of modernity, generated utopian antinatural tendencies that vilified and demonized the pale blue evil.

DESCARTES'S ERROR AND UTOPIAN PROGRAMS

Utopian, modern projects to eliminate *otherness* have never subsided. In his study *Melancholy and Society* (1992), Wolf Lepenies discusses the socio-logical construction of melancholy as a disorder or *anomia* and its relation to social utopias.[4] He adduces Robert Burton's preface to his *Anatomy of Melancholy*, "Democritus to the Reader," as exemplifying an antimelancholy utopia. Although there have been numerous visions of such utopias and dys-topias, those of Thomas Morus and Tommaso Campanella to Edward Bel-lamy's nineteenth-century Boston 2000 fantasy, to the more recent Aldous Huxley's *Brave New World*, George Orwell's *1984*, and Jean-Luc Goddard's political-satirical film *Alphaville*, Burton's text retains its unique significance since, as an introduction to the study of melancholy, it makes transparent the dialectics between melancholy and utopia. Lepenies marshals abundant evidence to demonstrate the questionable merits of utopian alternatives to melancholy. As he reviews the most illustrious utopias from Plato to Orwell, there emerges an antimelancholic utopian impulse informing vast regions of human thought, ranging from realistic medical praxis to fantasist epistemol-ogy. Can or should melancholy be made to completely disappear in the ver-tigo of utopian rationalist enthusiasm? Modern technological possibilities of actualizing what used to be limited to metaphorical imagination are pressing this question with new urgency. Unreflective attitudes of ignoring or denying melancholy are, as Pascal already warned, misguided. But so too are radi-cal scientific and psychiatric intrusions, excisions, manipulations, as well as melancholy-demonizing social and political attitudes; let us not forget that the extraction of the stone of melancholy was an accepted therapeutic interven-tion throughout the Renaissance (as we saw in chapter 3), while melancholics and criminals have, as Foucault discovered, suffered indiscriminate impris-onment until disquietingly recent times. Centuries before Burton vilified melancholy, there was Plato's even more sweeping ban exiling all passions from the ideal political or intellectual state. Considered in this universal-ized significance, the horizon of anti-melancholy utopian programs could be extended to encompass the entire philosophical and theological tradition of Stoic *apatheia*, the Christian kingdom of God, Cartesian rationalism, and Hegelian idealism on the one hand, and forms of eudemonism and pragmatism on the other; or alternatively, it could be narrowed down to social utopias, communist, technological, and otherwise, with their secular version of the kingdom of God on earth and a corresponding ban of acedia-melancholy.

The data made available by contemporary neuroscience can be adduced to argue the *primordiality* of the pathetic subjective body. Indeed, Antonio Damasio's discussion of background feeling mounts such an argument.[5] As a moderately reductive neuroscientist, Damasio classifies feelings into three groupings: first, basic universal emotions, such as happiness, sadness, anger, fear, disgust; second, subtle universal emotions, which are variations of the former, such as euphoria, ecstasy, melancholy, wistfulness, panic, shyness; and third, background feelings. The order of this classification is misleading since background feelings actually precede the others in evolution: the first variety, based on universal "preorganized," "Jamesian" emotions, only seems to be first ontogenetically. The notion of background feeling is the core of Damasio's argument: it reveals the primordiality and tarrying presence of the sense of the body in the most elaborate process of feeling and thinking. Background feeling is the feeling of the body rather than of emotion, the "body state or image of the body landscape prevailing between emotions"; neither the "Verdi of grand emotion" nor the "Stravinsky of intellectualized emotion," rather the emotion of a "minimalist in tone and beat, the feeling of life itself, the sense of being," "neither too positive nor too negative, although [it] can be perceived as mostly pleasant or unpleasant" (150). If it persists without change, as thought contents ebb and flow, background feeling becomes a mood—good, bad, or indifferent.

Background feeling is, Damasio argues, the "feeling of life itself, the sense of being," as well as the "very core of your representation of self" that persists undisturbed, often unnoticed and unknown, throughout individual existence. Although the background body-sense is continuous, more flamboyant events are constantly superposing on it, distracting our attention from it (152). This obscure sense of being plays an essential role in the life of the self, and especially in the thinking process. Damasio maintains that in the absence of this background feeling the integrity of the self cannot be maintained and deteriorates progressively. In support of his affirmation Damasio adduces the condition of *anosognosia*, which he defines as a pathological condition of "a view of a mind deprived of the possibility of sensing current body state especially as it concerns background feeling," that obscure feeling of Life, the sense of being (154). Discussing famous cases of frontal lobe damage, such as that of Phineas Gage, he observes that anosognosic patients "know" but do not feel, specifically, they do not feel themselves in their diseased condition, although they preserve the memory of a personal identity that is no longer valid.[6] Spurred on by the desire to solve the case of Phineas Gage, neurobiological research indicates that prefrontal damage is responsible for this loss of feeling and the constitution of a "disembodied mind"—the cherished dream of rationalism.

The actual documentation of anosognosic cases, as well as "mind in a vat" thinking experiments, prove the rationalist dream to be a nightmare. Once deprived of background feelings, the "purified" mind, the "washed" brain loses itself: in the absence of background feelings—the ground for emotions, feelings, and thinking—the mind becomes irrational. Damasio retorts to Descartes, Kant, and their present day heirs: "Reason is nowhere pure" (246), nor should it be, he contends, since a mind that is bodiless and passionless, reduced to formal logic, is ultimately impotent to exercise itself. The consequences of Cartesian rationalism are still rampant today, and more influential than ever. Damasio laments the dismembering of the wholeness of the living person that followed the Cartesian declaration of war on the reality and mystery of embodiment. His own intention as a humanist and a scientist is, arguably, to reintegrate the disparate pieces together. He thus inscribes himself in the tradition of premodern precartesian scientist-philosophers, a tradition spanning from Hippocrates to the Renaissance. Healing the diremption at the root of being is a matter of urgency in a time when Cartesian dichotomies are reified in scientific reductionisms: mind as mental software, body reduced to a mere appendix and viewed as eventually disposable by "mind in the vat" science; or vice versa, the mind viewed as epiphenomenon to body and brain. His warning endorses prophetic apocalypticism:

> How intriguing to think that Descartes did contribute to modifying the course of medicine, did help it veer from the organismic mind-in-the-body approach which prevailed from Hippocrates to the Renaissance. How annoyed Aristotle would have been with Descartes, had he known. Versions of Descartes' error obscure the roots of the human mind in a biologically complex but fragile, finite, and unique organism; they obscure the tragedy implicit in the knowledge of that fragility, finiteness, uniqueness. And where humans fail to see the inherent tragedy of conscious existence, they feel far less called upon to do something about minimizing it, and may have less respect for the value of life. (251)

The background feeling as the feeling of the body and of Life is primordial, permanent, and indispensable for rational thinking. Its reality validates Heidegger's notion of fundamental ontological mood or attunement, as well as Henry's notion of the primordiality of the immanent subjectivity of the pathetic body (to be discussed in chapter 7).

HUME: MELANCHOLIC IMAGINATION, SKEPTICISM, AND PHILOSOPHICAL EMPIRICISM

In his *Treatise on Human Nature*, between his discourse on understanding and his discourse on the passions, Hume took advantage of an interlude to ponder himself and his existential situation.[7] He recalled past errors, considered present failings, and anticipated future difficulties. He had an attack of melancholy and suffered the temptation to despair. He confesses:

> My memory of past errors and perplexities makes me diffident for the future. The wretched condition, weakness and disorder of the faculties, I must employ in my enquiries, increase my apprehensions. And the impossibility of amending or correcting these faculties reduces me almost to despair, and makes me resolve to perish on the barren rock, on which I am at present, rather than venture myself upon that boundless ocean, which runs out into immensity. This sudden view of my danger strikes me with melancholy; and as 'tis usual for that passion, above all others, to indulge itself, I cannot forbear feeding my despair, with all those desponding reflections, which the present subject furnishes me with in such abundance. (311)

Hume displays his mental workings in the text. He appears to be familiar with the theology of sin and the wiles of melancholic temptation to indulge itself and deepen into despair. Like Evagrius, he lucidly observes his thoughts and related moods, or "passionate thought." He reflects on the causes of his dejection, on its effects, on the immediate instinctive temptation to flee his task and indulge in despair. Hume is the victim of a secularized philosophical form of the sin of melancholy.

Hume's melancholy seems to accompany a crisis of meaning provoked by his metaphysical skepticism. The meaning of life itself and his own philosophical attempt at understanding are questioned. The threat is that of meaninglessness, of discovering a void of meaning of cosmic proportions that contaminates existence itself, one that Paul Tillich viewed as the cause of an anxiety of meaninglessness. Hume falls into metaphysical despair, feels lost and confounded, thus deepening his mood and becoming paralyzed by the deepest darkness. He laments in Pascalian tones:

> Where am I or what? From what causes do I derive my existence, and to what condition shall I return? Whose favor shall I court and whose anger must I dread? What being surrounds me? And on whom have I any influence or who has any influence on me? I am confounded with all these questions and begin to fancy myself in the most deplorable condition imaginable inviron'd with the deepest darkness and utterly deprived of the use of every member and faculty. (316)

A *vox clamantis in deserto*, the voice of the religious skeptic who has renounced God, the individual abandoned to himself, the voice of one in search of certainty as a ground on which to stand, and who is trapped within the immediate and the finite. Hume suffers from Pascalian ennui without the appeal to faith or the will to believe. For him, philosophy does not begin in wonder but rather in the despair of uncertainty, dread, darkness, and acedic paralysis. For Hume, philosophy begins with painful existential questions without immediate answer.

Although he proposes to bring his meditation on human nature to a happy conclusion, when he evaluates the immense depths of philosophy and his own situation—that of a sea voyager on a leaky weather-beaten vessel attempting to compass the globe—he is overwhelmed by the enormity of the task and confounded by solitude, exiled from society, disconsolate. He imagines himself "a hated and insulted monster." He finds nothing inside but doubt and ignorance. He hesitates and doubts his reasoning. What brought on this crisis? Hume explains that in his search for truth he took leave of all established opinions, without having a criterion for truth. Interestingly, for empirical Hume, man's primordial labor qua man, "our aim in all our studies and reflections," is the search for the "original and ultimate principle" (314). This fundamental inquiry ends in total disappointment and hopelessness with the discovery that this principle is not something that resides in the external object, but "merely in ourselves and is nothing but that determination of the mind which is acquired by custom and causes us to make a transition from an object to its usual attendant" (314). Thus, he continues:

> Nothing is more curiously enquired after by the mind of man than the causes of every phenomenon; nor are we content with knowing the immediate causes, but push on our enquiries till we arrive at the original and ultimate principle. . . . This is our aim in all our studies and reflections. And how must we be disappointed when we learn that this connexion, tie or energy lies merely in ourselves and is nothing but that determination of the mind which is acquired by custom and causes us to make a transition from an object to its usual attendant and from the impression of one to the lively idea of the other? Such a discovery not only cuts off all hope of ever attaining satisfaction, but even prevents our very wishes; since it appears that when we say we desire to know the ultimate and operating principle as something which resides in the external object, we either contradict ourselves, or talk without a meaning. (314)

Hume faces the unsettling realization that certainty and stability are merely products of imagination. Sadly, imagination is an inconstant, fallacious, and contradictory principle that accounts for the reasoning from cause to effect and the belief in the continued existence of matter. This effect of the imagination is not "compensated by any degree of solidity and satisfaction in the other parts of our reasoning" (313). He finds only his own conglomeration of ideas, idleness, and carelessness filling out the space of an empty self and an absent God. Hume looks for God with his senses, for the existence of an objective transcendence lovingly and wisely preserving the world, but finds only subjective need and ungrounded faith. Reason, if honest to its own principles, cannot avoid aporias.[8] Hume reiterates the dilemma: either total skepticism that would "cut off entirely all science and philosophy" and would make ordinary life impossible, or fanciful reasoning, "no choice left but betwixt a false reason and none at all" (315). He experiences the discomfort of an "intense view of these manifold contradictions and imperfections in human reason," whose effect is a crisis of knowing and meaning, a total chaos and confusion. It is not reason but rather nature itself, by relaxing the mental tension or by impressing the senses, that cures "philosophical melancholy and delirium" (316).

Thus Hume presents a symptomatic view of his "spleen and indolence" (317). Like Pascal, he has a glimpse into the nothing left by the absence of God and vacuousness of the self; he flees the melancholic delirium provoked by this vision and takes refuge in distraction, letting "nature" take over and "obliterating all these chimeras." He allows himself to be distracted and to forget, "I dine, I play a game of backgammon, I converse, and am merry with my friends. . . . I find myself absolutely and necessarily determined to live and talk and act like other people in the common affairs of life. . . . my natural propensity and the course of my animal spirits and passions reduce me to this indolent belief in the general maxims of the world" (316). He recognizes splenetic humor and indolence by its passivity and receptivity to the "general maxims of the world," the decision never to renounce the pleasures of life for the sake of reasoning and philosophy," nor "strive against the current of nature which leads [me] to indolence and pleasure," nor "seclude myself in some measure from the commerce and society of men which is so agreeable," nor "torture my brain with subtilities and sophistries" (317). "Under what obligation do I lie of making such an abuse of time?"—he asks, under the influence of the noontime demon that was attacking the desert monastic. Like the latter, while in the grip of the splenetic humor, Hume decides that renouncing the pleasures of life for the sake of reasoning and philosophy without any "tolerable prospect of arriving . . . at truth and certainty" is "an abuse of time" (317).

He continues reasoning with himself under this same influence and decides against secluding himself and striving against the current of nature, torturing his brain with sophistries. Hume watches over the inner agonic struggle between himself and the other that, as Evagrius explains, takes the form of oneself and tempts one to destruction. He admits that philosophy, as the "force of reasoning and conviction," has nothing to oppose to his sentiments of spleen and indolence. This state of mind will be defeated instead by "the returns of a serious good-humored disposition." What helps bring his mood around back to the pleasures of reflection and reasoning is "amusement and company, a reverie indulged in his chamber or in a solitary walk by the riverside." After this pastime, he feels the "mind all collected within itself" and naturally inclined to the pleasures of philosophical reflection. Any distraction and diversion would be unwelcome at this moment. And Hume declares this natural pleasure of reflection to be the "origin of his philosophy" (318). His hope to contribute to bringing the science of man more into fashion recomposes his temper from spleen and reinvigorates it from indolence (320).

Hume presents his emotions in relation to his thoughts and actions in the world. Spleen and indolence are moods in which he became inclined to live according to general maxims without questioning, accepting superstition rather than true philosophy, in other words, living unphilosophically a life of dispersion and distraction. This interlude confession places him in the same family with Evagrius and Pascal, as well as Heidegger: thinkers who confront the temptation of the demon of acedia, evasion of the anxiety of meaninglessness that is induced by the absence of God. What is distinctive in Hume's case as compared with Pascal is his approach to existential despair, which indicates a new stage in the process of maturing consciousness. Hume agrees that the most important human endeavor is the metaphysical search for ultimate principles; since he searches for them empirically, instead of finding God or substantial self he finds nothing, a nothing veiled by thoughts and imaginations. Disillusioned, he falls victim to the demon of acedia and indulges in distraction. He does not lose himself completely in distraction, however, but patiently watches his inner trajectory as it carries him to the other side, where he resumes his silent and solitary philosophical investigation. Now facing the absence of God, lost in but not frightened by infinite spaces, he continues his existence with new deliberation and lucidity.

There is another significant element in Humean melancholy that is related to both his empiricism and his skepticism. His condition seems to be a case of what Cornelius Agrippa von Nettesheim termed "imaginative melancholy" and Henry of Ghent understood as the melancholy caused by a metaphysical incapacity to transcend the immediate.[9] The individual inclined to imaginative melancholy suffers from being imprisoned in empirical imagination. Indeed, Hume has taken empiricism seriously and pushed it to a logical dead end: substance, causality, God, and self cannot be known or demonstrated to exist since they can never be encountered as matters of fact in empirical experience. Thus his empiricism brought theology to ridicule and bankruptcy: all arguments for the existence of God, faith in miracles, belief in immortality, when brought into the light of reason, are seen as figments of diseased imagination and misplaced hope or intellectual sloth. This absolute failure of his melancholic imagination to access supersensible realms imprisoned Hume in empiricism and skepticism. It is significant that with Kant, as we shall see, it is precisely the shattering of imagination in the experience of the sublime that will make possible the realization of our supersensible vocation.

BURKE: THERAPEUTICS OF DELIGHTFUL HORROR

Edmund Burke's insights on the aesthetic and psychological categories of the sublime in *A Philosophical Inquiry into the Origin of our Ideas of the Sublime and Beautiful* (1757) provided the empirical ground for Kant's later theory of the sublime and melancholy, as articulated in his analytic of the sublime in the *Critique of Judgment*, and deserve attention in themselves.[10] Kant acknowledges his debt only toward the end of his exposition, when he refers to Burke as the foremost author of a psychological treatment of the sublime appropriate for an empirical anthropology (138–39, §29). Burke's main thesis is that the melancholic requires an awakening or quickening through work and terror—both belonging, according to him, to the category of the stimulating agency of the sublime. He presents the feeling of the sublime as being grounded in the impulse toward self-preservation in the fear and pain that agitate and awaken the entire being, thus clearing it of dangerous obstructions and producing pleasure, thrill, tranquility mixed with terror. In *A Philosophical Inquiry*, under the heading "How can pain be a cause of delight," Burke discusses the discomforts of a state of prolonged rest and inaction:

> Providence has so ordered it, that a state of rest and inaction, however it may flatter our indolence, should be productive of many inconveniences; that it should generate such disorders as may force us to have recourse to some labor, as a thing absolutely requisite to make us pass our lives with tolerable satisfaction; for the nature of rest is to suffer all the parts of our bodies to fall into a relaxation, that not only disables the members from performing their functions, but takes away the vigorous tone of fiber which is requisite for carrying on the natural and necessary secretions. . . . Melancholy, dejection, despair, and often self-murder is the consequence of the gloomy view we take of things in this relaxed state of body. The best remedy for all these evils is exercise or labor; and labor is the surmounting of difficulties, an exertion of the contracting power of the muscles; and as such resembles pain that consists in tension or contraction. (122)

Like Burton before him, Burke singles out idleness or rest as the ultimate cause of melancholy and even suicide. But his explanation of the condition is made in the new jargon of the organic dichotomy of contraction and relaxation prevalent in the eighteenth century, retrieving Hippocratic intuitions.

The remedy for unhealthy relaxation produced by inactivity and rest must be a mode of tension or contraction, in other words, work as pain for the body and terror for the mind: paradoxically, he maintains, painful labor and terror within limits are also pleasurable and healthy leading to "delightful horror," the strongest of all passions whose object is the sublime.

> As common labor which is a mode of pain, is the exercise of the grosser, a mode of terror is the exercise of the finer parts of the system. . . . Pain and terror [if not noxious, provoke] a sort of delightful horror, a sort of tranquility tinged with terror; which as it belongs to self-preservation is one of the strongest of all passions. Its object is the sublime. Its highest degree I call astonishment; the subordinate degrees are awe, reverence, and respect. (123)

Hippocrates, Cassian, Ficino, and Burton, all prescribed work as a therapeutic exercise. Pascal, on the other hand, insisted on contemplating the terrible nothing, the dark abyss; its repelling force would spur one toward God and another kind of labor, the labor of faith and love. It is Le Senne who will endorse Burke's insight and maintain that in the case of melancholic philosophers, only the *demon of perversity* understood as a propensity for and fascination with the negative can invigorate an apathetic sensibility: it becomes manifest as their predilection for metaphysical negation and otherness. What Burke proposes for the first time is the role of work as pain and terror in awakening by tension and contraction a languid organism and psyche. At the same time he initiates a unique interpretation of the sublime as the dialectics of terror and delight.

Burke specifies what he means by the sublime. Bodily pain and mental anguish, he argues, are productive of the sublime that belongs to self-preservation as our strongest emotion: "Of feeling little more can be said than that the idea of bodily pain in all its modes and degrees of labour, pain, anguish, torment is productive of the sublime; . . . the sublime is an idea belonging to self-preservation. . . . It is therefore one of the most affecting we have. . . . Its strongest emotion is an emotion of distress and that no pleasure from a positive cause belongs to it" (79). When the sublime is provoked, the acedic mood is transcended or temporarily abated by terror, obscurity, mystery, power, privation (vacuity, darkness, solitude, silence), vastness, infinity, difficulty, magnificence, blackness, shock, or pain (53–79). He explains the contribution of each such an object productive of the sublime as a "modification of pain or terror." The moment common to all is the mental arrest caused by a form of shock; ideas of eternity or infinity are "most affecting" as the "mind is struck" or "thrown out of itself." The idea of infinity itself provokes self-transcendence. It is not difficult to recognize Burke as the source of the Kantian, and via Kant, of the Romantic aesthetic in its ramifications into philosophical and theological constructions. More recently such therapeutics appealed to Rudolf Otto, for example, whose philosophical reflections on religion were substantially indebted to Burke and Kant, as well as to Böhme and Schelling; his symbol of the holy, the *mysterium tremendum et fascinans*, bears the mark of the melancholic sublime.

KANT: MELANCHOLIC ATTUNEMENT TO THE SUBLIMITY OF MORAL VOCATION

With Burke as a background for the Kantian discussion of the sublime and the melancholic, three different texts in which Kant reflects on the subject will be adduced: the precritical *Observations on the Feeling of the Beautiful and Sublime* (1764), the postcritical late collection of lectures on *Anthropology* (1798), which contains overt references to the melancholic and phlegmatic temperaments; and lastly the *Critique of Judgment* (1790), in which the problematic of the categories of the beautiful and the sublime are taken up.[11] Neither the *Observations* nor the *Anthropology* contribute substantially to the analytic of the sublime as it appears in Kant's *Critique of Judgment* (97–140, §23–29). Both instead belong to empirical anthropology and contain reflections on the four temperaments and their correlations with corresponding dispositions, aesthetic and moral feelings, epistemological and critical attitudes.[12] In *Observations*, Kant considers the melancholic frame of mind to be most fitted to the sublime and the moral due to its specific mental attunement (*Stimmung*)—a notion that will be adopted and adapted by Heidegger in his Dasein analysis.

Kant notes that the finer feelings of the sublime and the beautiful are apt to conjoin more easily with certain of these temperaments than with the others. Kant excludes from the investigation the exceptional extremes, both the melancholic's characteristic high intellectual insights, such as the "thrill that was possible to a Kepler" (*Observations* 46), and the phlegmatic's great deficiency of moral feeling, "with no ingredients of the sublime or beautiful" (*Observations* 62, 70). Hence, of the four temperaments, only three are considered, in the order of importance that Kant assigns them: the melancholic, the sanguine, and the choleric. The reason for the preeminence of the melancholic temperament is Kant's high appreciation for the quality of the moral dispositions that, he believes, can be actualized by this temperament. Kant writes:

> A profound feeling for the beauty and dignity of human nature and a firmness and determination of the mind to refer all one's actions to this as to a universal ground is earnest, and does not at all join with a changeable gaiety nor with the inconstancy of a frivolous person. It even approaches *melancholy*, a gentle and noble feeling so far as it is grounded upon the awe that a hard pressed-soul feels

when, full of some great purpose, he sees the danger he will have to overcome, and has before his eyes the difficult but great victory of self-conquest. Thus genuine virtue based on principles has something about it which seems to harmonize most with the *melancholy* frame of mind in the moderated understanding. (*Observations* 62–63)

The Kantian melancholic is a remarkable individual, to be added to Pseudo-Aristotle's list, a worthy inhabitant of the Saturnine seventh sphere in Dante's *Paradise*, a perfect child of Saturn in Ficino's *De Vita*. His defining characteristic is the paradoxical high ground. This "high ground," an oxymoron perfectly expressing the *coincidentia oppositorum* that characterizes melancholy, is responsible both for the elevation and depth of the principles it fosters. The Kantian melancholic knows himself; he is insightful, thoughtful, and silent, not easily moved, indifferent to changeable times and modes, truthful, reliable, respectful of secrets, a lover of freedom, and justified in becoming weary of himself and the world. He is particularly sensitive to the dignity of being human; he is wise and gives the impression of unadorned majesty, simplicity, sobriety, nobility, poise. He lives at higher altitudes than the common mortals, unmoved by contingencies; he disdains death perhaps because in a way he is already philosophically dead to mundane life. He is superior and aloof, a law onto himself, transcendent; morals, metaphysics, and mathematics are his domains, each bearing the traces of supersensible existence. He has the allure of an ancient god. Indeed, Kant's melancholic is the perfect embodiment of Ficino's symbol of Saturn in exaltation and of *melancolia gloriosa*. True, Kant admits, there is a risk of deterioration, a risk of dejection, fanaticism, enthusiasm, a risk of fearsome anger, of adventurous or grotesque inclination toward the visionary and the miraculous. It is as if Kant had carefully selected the aspects of the Aristotelian *Problem* and of the Saturnine symbol according to his own hierarchy of value. His emphasis on the melancholic's reason and understanding privileges the moral aspect to the detriment of the occult: inspirations, visions, meaningful dreams, presentiments, and miraculous portents indicate the deterioration of melancholic nature.

Kant's disparagement of divine frenzy and madness is even sterner than Plato's because it is a sign of the abasement of mental acumen: madness, miracle, vision, inspirations, prophecy; for Kant they belong to the illegitimate region outside the limits of reason. Thus the negative aspects of melancholy for the Kantian, the Scylla and Charybdis of dejection and prophetic frenzy—in which we may recognize Ficino's notions of excessive phlegm and black choler—are omitted from his analysis. With this warning in mind, melancholy as a temperament and a frame of mind is the mode of attunement favorable to the feeling of human sublimity. The portrait of the melancholic sketched in *Observations* emphasizes qualities meant to promote the sublimity of genuine virtue based on moral principles that will later become the ground for Kant's categorical moral imperative in his *Groundwork of the Metaphysics of Morals* (1785). The principal attribute of the melancholic that recommends this temperament as exceptional is its consciousness of the feeling of the beauty and dignity of human nature.[13] Melancholic nature attuned to the sublime is related to the faculty of understanding and the age of wisdom; it exerts the powers of the soul, has a tragic dimension, and actualizes the dignity of human nature. Thus it is the melancholic who hears both the call to the moral categorical imperative and to the sublime. While all temperaments have a share in melancholy, hence also in genuine virtue and sublimity, the person of melancholic temperament is the Kantian "man of principles" par excellence (*Observations* 65).

Kant's *Anthropology* presents a radically opposed interpretation of melancholy. Whereas the earlier treatise mentioned the phlegmatic temperament only to discard it as below the level of moral feeling and therefore of philosophical interest, the *Anthropology* gives it a place of eminence, thus reversing the significance of the melancholic and the phlegmatic. In order to further the understanding of temperament, its rapport with intellect and passion in the dialectics of freedom and necessity, Kant adduces the problematic of passions and emotions. Following Descartes, Kant declares emotion and passion to be pathological conditions suffered by reason; they are forms of blindness and symptoms of a diseased mind that incapacitate the perfectly pure function of reason. Emotion escapes the control of reason by being an unexpected reaction to a sudden event that disturbs the predictable and controllable course of events. Meanwhile, passion is a chronic emotion.[14] Passion presupposes a maxim of the subject and, thus, is disquietingly associated with the purposes of reason. This association of passion with reason circumscribes the domain of fault and is to be Stoically excised. The practical ideal is for Kant, as for Evagrius or Descartes, a Stoic *apatheia*, the "happy self-possession of the moral self." This Stoic principle is morally sublime, "The principle of apathy, that is, that the prudent man must at no time be in a state of emotion, not even in that of sympathy with the woes of his best friend, is an entirely correct and sublime moral precept of the Stoic school because emotion makes one more or less blind" (*Anthropology* 158, §75). Thus, for Kant, all passions are, "without exception, bad." His moral judgment condemns even virtue or charity qua passion. It is human nature per se, situated in between beast and pure reason that is abhorred. Whether beautiful or ugly, good or bad, the atmosphere of the soul must be sterilized. Only in this vacuum can universal reason function unimpeded by either love or hate.

Reflecting the Stoic emphasis that defines the Enlightenment, Kant's position toward melancholy undergoes a radical change in his *Anthropology*. Melancholy is here no longer related to the sublime but is considered in its negative dimension as a weakness of the mind, an illness of the soul together with mania, and is identified as hypochondria. Both melancholic hypochondria and mania affect cognition.[15] The melancholic is a self-tormentor with no control over his thoughts or affects, and is especially prone to delusions of misery (the melancholic delirium of loss and guilt to which Binswanger and Tellenbach refer). "Melancholy (*melancholia*) can also be a mere delusion of misery," Kant writes, "which the low-spirited self-tormentor (inclined toward feeling wretched) creates for himself. In itself it is not yet a mental disorder, but may easily lead to it. In other respects it is a mistaken but frequently used expression to speak of a melancholic mathematician (for example Professor Hausen) when one means only a profoundly thoughtful person" (*Anthropology* 110, §49).

Melancholy or hypochondria and mania, as mental illnesses or illnesses of the soul, are characterized by irrationality. In hypochondria, the self-affecting self suffers from centering its attention on certain negative impressions. The common feature here is the negativity of the imaginings that the victim-agent creates and imposes on himself. Kant argues:

> The defects of the faculty of cognition are either mental weaknesses or mental illnesses. The illnesses of the soul with regard to the cognitive faculty can be listed under two main types. The one is melancholia (hypochondria) and the other is mental disorder (mania). A melancholic man is well aware that the train of his thought does not move properly, but he has not sufficient control over himself to direct, restrain or control the course of his thought. Unjustified joy and grief whimsically change in such a person like the weather which one has to accept as it comes. (*Anthropology* 97, §45)

The source of this malady, Kant notes, is "anxious fear, childish in character, of the thought of death." Suicide can be the effect of this "disorganization" and "irregularity" of the "sudden change of moods." This disturbing dimension of melancholy determines Kant to look for another temperament more suitable for philosophizing and he reconsiders the previously excluded, the phlegmatic.

Kant's description of the phlegmatic temperament opens up in ambiguity, as it can be either a weakness or a strength, and he acknowledges this interpretative ambiguity. He explains that phlegm signifies *apatheia*, the Stoic ideal state, rather than the apathy of idleness or acedia—thus *apatheia*'s ambiguity comes forth once again. What is common to both is insensitivity to stimuli, indifference, and consequently a slow and deliberate reaction. In opposition to his earlier view expressed in the *Observations*, here it is the phlegmatic mental disposition that Kant considers most fortunate, since it has the potential to substitute for wisdom. The cold-blooded phlegmatic, whose vital power is low, has a correspondingly diminished instinctual nature. Hence his reactions will proceed from reason's principles rather than from instincts that are comparatively weak; the phlegmatic is a philosopher *in potentia*. The negative aspects of this temperament—inactivity, indolence, inertia, lethargy, insensitivity to stimuli, voluntary uselessness, and minimal motivation—are the negative extremes of the Stoic ideal of *apatheia*.

Thus Kant hesitates between two hypostases of the condition, the phlegmatic and the melancholic proper, and reverses his interpretation of them in relation to the ideal of philosophy and the high demands of human supersensible destiny. The early Kant, more romantic in inclination and closer to Burke's influence, favors the élan and inspiration associated with the melancholic; an aging Kant celebrates separation from nature, with its disturbing passions and instincts, and elevates the diminished vitality of the phlegmatic who is free for the life of the mind. Stoic *apatheia* as the ground for morality and philosophy seems accessible only to the phlegmatic. Kant's hesitation between the melancholic and the phlegmatic temperaments is interesting for clarifying the problematics of acedia and melancholy; his contrastive valorization of the two temperaments indicates Kant's hesitation between Romantic aesthetics and Enlightenment rationalism. In *Observations* and the *Critique of Judgment* the melancholic fulfills the morally sublime task, while in the *Anthropology* Kant inclines to consider the phlegmatic, with its propensity for Stoic *apatheia* (in both negative and positive modes), better fitted to the philosophical and moral calling.

The Kantian tragic-sublime complex dialectically counterbalances the idleness-boredom complex. It belongs to the melancholic rather than the phlegmatic (acedic) humor and supports the elevated notion of melancholy as the mark of the exceptional individual, the genius, who will figure prominently in the *Critique of Judgment*. In the latter text, the sublime results from a tension between the cognitive powers of imagination and reason that is experienced as a paradoxical *coincidentia oppositorum* of pain and pleasure (pace Burke). Kant explains that the experience of the sublime is not caused by "products of art . . . where both form and magnitude are determined by human purpose, nor in natural things *whose very concept carries with it a determinate purpose* . . . , but rather in crude nature." (*Judgment* 109, §26). "Crude nature" is the privileged object capable of provoking the feeling of the sublime because of the physically overwhelming magnitude and might it displays, provoking the mathematical and the dynamical sublime, respectively. At a safe distance from the natural display of overwhelming magnitude and might, the spectator is "seized by amazement bordering on terror." Kant explains:

Thus any spectator who beholds massive mountains, climbing skyways, deep gorges with raging streams in them, wastelands lying in deep shadow and inviting melancholy meditation . . . is indeed seized by *amazement* bordering on terror, by horror and a sacred thrill; but since he knows he is safe, this is not actual fear; it is our attempt to incur it with our imagination in order that we may feel that very power's might and connect the mental agitation this arouses with the mind's state of rest. In this we feel our superiority to nature within ourselves and hence also to nature outside us. (*Judgment* 129, §29)

The overwhelming display brings into conflict the two powers of cognition, namely, imagination and reason; the conflict will be resolved through the sacrifice of the imagination. Faced with the magnitude and might that evoke ideas of infinity, imagination is inadequate for the task of unity and totality imposed by reason, since as a power of sensibility it cannot produce the required images of totality and the absolute; whence the negative feeling of displeasure. Nevertheless, it is precisely in experiencing the inadequacy and defeat of the imagination that the mind comes to feel the sublimity that lies in its own supersensible and moral vocation; whence the feeling of pleasure (*Judgment* 121, §28). Kant writes, "We are dealing only with nature as appearance. . . . We cannot determine the idea of the supersensible any further, and hence we cannot *cognize* but can only *think* nature as an exhibition of it. But it is this idea that is aroused in us, when, as we judge an object aesthetically, this judging strains the imagination to its limit, whether of expansion (mathematically) or of its might over the mind (dynamically). The judging strains the imagination because it is based on a feeling that the mind has a vocation that wholly transcends the domain of nature, namely, moral feeling (*Judgment* 128, §29). Thus the feeling of the sublime is a figure of struggle involved in the moral triumph of reason over the finitude of imagination and sensibility. It is only through this inner struggle and triumph, stretching the limits of the imagination and finally overcoming its resistance, that the individual comes to a full sense of the sublime supersensible vocation that is the essence of human dignity. It is not the exterior object that is sublime, but the mind, or rather the melancholic mind, and only by "a strange subreption" is sublimity attributed to the object (*Judgment* 114, §27).

Kant's mathematically and dynamically sublime is the absolutely large, the absolutely powerful. Both absolute magnitude and absolute might provoke terror, "raise the soul's fortitude above its usual middle," allowing us to discover in ourselves an ability to resist that is of a different order, giving us the courage to believe that we are a match for nature's seeming omnipotence. The sublime calls forth affects of the vigorous kind which make us "conscious that we have forces to overcome any resistance, i.e., make us conscious of our *animus strenuus*)": enthusiasm, *apatheia*, amazement, admiration, anger, indignant desperation, voluntary isolation, sublime madness, calm, "*interesting* sadness," vigorous not dejected grief, moral control, belligerence (*Judgment* 132–37, §29). These affects of *sublime mental attunement* push the self to the brink of physical annihilation and open the mind onto the realm of the supersensible: they are affects sine qua non of self-conquering and self-transcendence that, according to both Pseudo-Aristotle and Kant, form the makeup of the melancholic exceptional individual (*Judgment* 134–37, §29).

Richard Kearney argues in *Strangers, Gods, and Monsters* that the postmodern understanding of its own aesthetic misreads and distorts the Kantian analysis.[16] To wit, the correlation of sublimity, the monstrous, and terror suggests to Julia Kristeva, and more particularly to Jean-François Lyotard and Slavoj Žižek, a cult of the monstrous—aesthetical, theological, and political—that informs the postmodern paradigm. Most disquieting to Kearney is the postmodern predilection of placing of the sublime—the noumenal or God according to Žižek's reading of Kant—outside the ethical and in close proximity to radical evil. Indeed, Kearney writes, with Žižek "we discover that 'Sade is the truth of Kant,' since Kant is compelled to formulate the 'hypothesis of a perverse, diabolical God' and to make 'the ethical God and Evil indistinguishable'" (96). Kearney acknowledges that the sublime for Kant involves a 'representation of limitlessness' and provokes a negative pleasure, combining fascination with repulsion (128). The experience discloses an encounter with metaphysical *otherness*, the absolutely other, the ground of the order and proportion revealed in the beautiful. Diverging from the postmodern monstrous sublime, Kearney argues for a more faithful reading of Kantian analysis. Sublime otherness "challenges our capacity both to know and to represent"; it is that which "arises on the ashes of presentation (conceptual or sensible)" (128). But why is the melancholic temperament prone to the experience of sublimity, as Kant maintained? Is it because it is attuned to this *otherness* to which it deeply responds? Kearney's analysis suggests an alternate explanation for the relation between melancholy and the sublime.

> With the sublime the mind is incited to abandon sensibility and admit that there is no adequate presentation for the event in question. . . . In fact, it is the experience of the annihilation of the external world (what Kant calls nature) and the threat which this poses to us as perceivers, which excites the sublime as an experience of our own subjectivity. We become more aware of our freedom—and therefore our superiority to nature—at the very moment when nature threatens to humiliate our sensible faculties. . . . We negate the negation, as it were. And the name for this double negation is freedom. The sublime, in sum, expresses our freedom from nature. Freed from objective reality, we become free for our own subjectivity.[17]

The experience of the sublime entails the anguish of physical annihilation and the joy of overcoming. It is the inner triumph of subjectivity and the spirit over the threat of natural apocalypse, a triumph precisely over the malignity and monstrosity of otherness, and one that is liberating and exhilarating. The experience is of the tragic, and thus, the cathartic. While Burke provided the scandal and paradox of the notion of "delightful horror," Kant clarified and explained it in rational and ethical terms that illumined the illustrious hermeneutics of *melancolia gloriosa*. The postmodern sublime seems to revert to Burke, while overlooking Kant. As such, the Kantian sublime represents the fundamental therapeutic for the melancholic individual who is bound by his own "mathematical imagination," the type referred to by the medieval scholastic Henry of Ghent as a "good mathematician but poor metaphysician."[18] Perseus's victory over Medusa is the mythical illustration of this triumph. At the same time, the connection postulated by Pseudo-Aristotle between melancholy and the abnormal or exceptionally gifted individual is validated by and fulfilled in the Kantian theory of the genius; the melancholic genius will be the center of dawning Romantic philosophy.

NOTES

1. Jacques Maritain, *The Dream of Descartes* (New York: Philosophical Library, 1944), 41.
2. Descartes, *The Passions of the Soul*, trans. Stephen Voss (Indianapolis: Hackett, 1989), 70 (art. 92).
3. Descartes, *Passions of the Soul*, 73 (art. 100).
4. Wolf Lepenies, *Melancholy and Society* (introduction, n. 2). Lepenies (b. 1941), a German sociologist and political scientist, is professor of sociology at the Free University of Berlin and a guest researcher at Princeton University.
5. Antonio R. Damasio, *Descartes' Error* (New York: Avon, 1994), 150–51.
6. Damasio, "Unpleasantness in Vermont" and "A Modern Phineas Gage," in *Descartes' Error*, 3–51. Phineas Gage, an employee at Rutland & Burlington Railroad, Vermont, in the mid-nineteenth-century survived serious damage to the frontal lobe of his brain and suffered a complete change of personality. His case became famous and helped advance neurological research.
7. David Hume, "Conclusion of this book," in *A Treatise on Human Nature* (New York: Penguin, 1985), 311–21.
8. Hume, *Treatise on Human Nature*: "The understanding, when it acts alone and according to its most general principles, entirely subverts itself and leaves not the lowest degree of evidence in any proposition, either in philosophy or common life. We save ourselves from this total skepticism only by means of that singular and seemingly trivial property of the fancy" (315).
9. Cornelius Agrippa von Nettesheim, *Three Books of Occult Philosophy*, trans. James Freake (St. Paul: Llewellyin, 2000), 188–92. We will revisit Agrippa and Henry of Ghent in chapter 10.

10. Edmund Burke, *A Philosophical Enquiry into the Origin of our Ideas of the Sublime and Beautiful* (Oxford and New York: Oxford University Press, 1990).

11. Immanuel Kant, *Observations on the Feeling of the Beautiful and Sublime*, trans. John T. Goldthwait (Berkeley: University of California Press, 1960; reprint, 1991); *Anthropology from a Pragmatic Point of View*, trans. Victor Lyle Dowdell (Carbondale: Southern Illinois University Press, 1978; reprint, 1996), and *Critique of Judgment*, trans. Werner S. Pluhar (Indianapolis and Cambridge: Hackett, 1987). Hereafter these works will be abbreviated parenthetically in the text as *Observations, Anthropology* (citing page number, section number), and *Judgment* (citing page number, original German page number), respectively.

12. This is how Kant introduces the correlation between disposition and temperament in *Observations* (62).

13. The pertinence of this concealed or forgotten grounding in feeling and subjectivity of the Kantian architectonic will reemerge in our discussion of Heidegger's emphasis on this aspect.

14. Kant, *Anthropology*: "The inclination which can hardly or not at all be controlled by reason is passion. On the other hand, emotion is the feeling of a pleasure or displeasure at a particular moment, which does not give rise to reflection" (155, §73).

15. Kant, *Anthropology*: "The *hypochondriac* is a capricious fellow (a visionary) of the most pitiful sort, obstinately unable to come to grips with his imaginings, always running to the physician" (109, §50).

16. Richard Kearney, "Evil, Monstrosity, and the Sublime," in *Strangers, Gods, and Monsters*, 83–109.

17. Kearney, "On Terror," in *Strangers, Gods, and Monsters*, 128–31.

18. Cited in Hubertus Tellenbach, *Melancholy, History of the Problem: Endogeneity, Typology, Pathogenesis, and Clinical Considerations*, trans. Erling Eng (Pittsburgh: Duquesne University Press, 1980), 13.

Chapter 6

On God's Otherness

Melancholy is present in Hegel's anthropology as the painful experience of the soul undergoing the critical transformation from immediacy and total union with Nature to freedom.[1] Hegel introduces the subject matter of his anthropology, namely the dialectical unfolding of the soul or basis of man:

> We must begin our treatment with immediate mind; but this is natural mind, soul. . . . We must start therefore from mind which is still in the grip of Nature and connected with its corporeity, mind which is not as yet in communion with itself, not yet free. This basis of man is the subject-matter of *Anthropology*. The first stage in *Anthropology* is the qualitatively determined soul which is tied to its natural forms (racial differences for example belong here). Out of this immediate oneness with its natural aspect, soul enters into opposition and conflict with it (this embraces the states of insanity and somnambulism). The outcome of this conflict is the triumph of the soul over its corporeity, the process of reducing, and the accomplished reduction of this corporeity to a sign, to the representation of the soul. In *Phenomenology*, the soul by the negation of its corporeity, raises itself to purely ideal self-identity, becomes consciousness, becomes "I," is for itself over against its Other. (*Mind* 26–28, §387)

In its original immediacy, indeterminacy, and universality the soul "compresses" universal Nature. The proximity to Nature, the indistinctness from it, makes the soul vulnerable to all the idiosyncracies of the former. At this stage of unfreedom and distinctionless unity with planetary life, the soul is dependent and bound, receptive to the latter's influences (*Mind* 36, §391). In one sweeping gesture, Hegel justifies and leaves behind the ancient and Renaissance anthropological ideal of attunement between the human individual and the universe. Certainly attunement or mood is discounted as axiologically inferior since it does not manifest the human according to its Notion (*Begriff*). Hegel explains the ontologically inferior indeterminate nature of mood:

> What we have to consider at this stage is simply and solely the *unconscious* relationship between outer sensation and mental or spiritual inwardness. Through this connection there originates in us what we call *mood*; this is a manifestation of mind of which, admittedly, we find analogue in animals . . . but which at the same time has a peculiarly human character and further, acquires an anthropological significance in our stricter sense of the word, by the fact that it is something not yet known by the subject with full consciousness. . . . At the stage we have now reached in following out the development of the soul, it is outer sensation itself which provokes the mood. But this effect is produced by outer sensation in so far as an inner meaning is immediately— that means without the intervention of conscious intelligence—associated with it. By this meaning, the outer sensation becomes something *symbolical*. We must observe, however, that what we have here is not yet a symbol in the proper meaning of the word; for in its strict meaning a symbol is an external object distinct from us in which we are conscious of an inner quality, or which we generally connect with such a quality. In a mood provoked by an outer sensation we are not as yet in relation with an external object distinct from us, we are not yet Consciousness. (*Mind* 80–81, §401)

In the economy of the dialectic of the Idea (*Idee*), mood is a presymbolic state of blurred self-consciousness antecedent to the genesis of the self; the primordial stage of passivity toward the organic from which, according to Maine de Biran, the self emerges through effort. It is only with Heidegger that mood or state of mind—and more precisely boredom—undergoes a radical hermeneutical transformation by which it becomes a "fundamental ontological attunement" (to be discussed in chapter 7). The unity and harmony with nature that was dear to the ancients and Renaissance thinkers alike indicates a natural level of immediate being that is very rarely prone to strain and mental disturbance.[2] According to Hegel, mental strain and disturbance are already symptoms of a superior stage in the evolution of the Idea, a stage of crisis pregnant with possibilities that are inaccessible at the natural stage. Indeed, as the soul evolves it begins to oppose its own past natural life of harmony with and integration in Nature, thus entering a state of self-contradiction and self-division. In this state, the soul is in an intermediary condition between Nature and the world of ethical freedom, one of conflict between unfreedom and freedom: between substantiality and naturalness on the one hand, and objective free consciousness on the other (*Mind* 36, § 391). In order to become adequate to its Notion, the soul as unfree mind struggles for its liberation from its own immediacy and substantiality (*Mind* 91, §402). Hegel explains:

The soul opposes itself to its substantiality, stands over against itself, and in its determinate sensations at the same time attains to the consciousness of its totality, but a consciousness which is not as yet objective but only subjective. . . . In this part, because the soul here appears as divided against itself, we shall have to consider it in its *diseased* state. In this sphere there prevails a conflict between the freedom and unfreedom of the soul; for, on the one hand, soul is still fettered to its substantiality, conditioned by its naturalness, while, on the other hand, it is beginning to separate itself from its substance, from its naturalness, and is thus raising itself to the intermediate stage between its immediate, natural life, and objective, free consciousness. (*Mind* 89, §402)

This intermediary stage of self-contradiction constitutes the key moment in the evolution of the Idea, the stage when the synthesis as qualitative leap occurs. This stage, posing the identity of being and feeling, is for Hegel that of the Romantic Weltanschauung and represents a necessary but inferior or rather immature stage in the evolution of the soul toward its maturity and fulfillment as Mind and Concept (*Mind* 89–90, §402); the soul at this stage occupies a middle ground between ideational consciousness and immediate sensation, when the universal and the individual, the subjective and the objective, have not yet separated (*Mind* 73, §400).

This "world of concrete content with an infinite periphery" is the locus of disproportion par excellence—the disproportion that Pascal viewed as the mark of the human fallen condition, while Ricoeur considered it defining for the human condition per se (*Mind* 90, §402; cf. 124–25, §408). It is this disproportion as *faille* that is the condition for the possibility of fault and sin. Hegel refers to this condition of the soul, or unfree mind, as diseased, a reversion to mere nature; it is a condition that allows for the insertion of personal passions and for the irruption of evil, always latent in the natural and selfish heart. Hegel therefore classifies mental distress, melancholy, or disgust with life as forms of insanity, even though insanity too is an essential stage in the development of the soul. He maintains that crime and insanity are extremes of the condition of distress that the soul in its evolution has to overcome. The distress does not commonly manifest itself in these extreme forms, however, but rather in limitations, errors, follies, and offenses (*Mind* 124–25, §408). While the pain of self-contradiction characteristic of the metaxic stage between immediacy and freedom is a necessary stage in the evolution of the soul, madness and idiocy are pathological states that manifest the failure of the soul to transcend its immediacy, distinctionlessness, and unfreedom.

Hegel identifies several forms of madness and idiocy; they all represent the fall of the soul, which can be described either as sinking back into itself as immediate subjectivity or as reverting to nature, returning to a prior stage of evolution. For Hegel the melancholic is the mad. Indeed, Hegel's description of madness can be read as a description of melancholy, its contingent causality manifesting itself as disgust for life and a pronounced suicidal impulse.[3] Meanwhile, idiocy can be read as acedia, an apathy in the form of a generalized indifference toward oneself and the other (*Mind* 131–32, §408). As Alan M. Olson perceptively notes, Hegel was obliquely reflecting on Hölderlin's melancholic madness, though without any direct reference.[4] Hegel, for whom philosophy is pneumatology, as both Olson and Cyril O'Regan argue, must have been profoundly disturbed and embarrassed by his friend's fall.[5] This embarrassment and disquiet must explain Hegel's ridicule of melancholics— all of them English since, he explains, the English in particular are not able to rise above their "subjective particularity."

Thus madness in the form of acute melancholy and idiocy in the form of acedia are forms of soul sickness caused by the soul's failure to transcend its nature; they make impossible the spontaneity and freedom proper to the mind. As such, they allow the evil present in the heart to manifest itself through the medium of the passions—those that have since Evagrius been enumerated as mortal sins. Hegel refers to the medical theory of the temperaments only to discard it, reasoning that temperament is not a locus of freedom since it manifests an excessive proximity to nature.[6] Character, by contrast, is an expression of freedom (*Mind* 51–54, §395).

According to Hegel, boredom refuses self-transcendence and reverses evolution and time; its cause is the absence of a resistant inner and outer other. The moment of pain that occurs in an encounter with a resistant other is absolutely necessary for the birth of self-consciousness. The resistant other that inhabits the self, and the dialectical necessity of overcoming it echoes the intuitions and visions of Jakob Böhme, whom both Hegel and Schelling valued highly. Maine de Biran had already experimented with Böhmian intuition as a mode of coming to terms with his own pronounced condition of acedic melancholy. In the absence of this encounter, sleep, boredom, and death take over.[7] Indeed, Hegel maintains that "our mind only feels fully awake when it is presented with something interesting, something both new and meaningful, something with a differentiated and coherent content" since the mind needs to recognize itself, to mirror itself in the object, to find itself again (*Mind* 69, §398). If the condition of self-reflection is not satisfied, the mind "withdraws . . . into its distinctionless unity, is bored, and falls asleep." The Hippocratic and Ficinean correlation of boredom, sleep, old age, and death resurfaces in Hegel's anthropological study in which he gives the original medico-humoral paradigm an explanation befitting his system.

Hegel posits two alternate states of the mind, corresponding to its two hypostases as soul and as mind proper: namely, sleep and wakefulness. These two states parallel what Nietzsche will refer to as the Apollonian and the

Dionysian forms of consciousness. Sleep is a return to the soul's Dionysian modality, while wakefulness is the Apollonian mode par excellence (*Mind* 67, §398). It even seems that boredom is the immediate cause of old age and death, for boredom means extinction of vitality and abandonment of hope, uniformity of habit and loss of resistance, disappearance of opposition, general dulling; all these phenomena, Hegel explains, "change the man into an old man." In the absence of boredom and its causes, man would neither age nor die (*Mind* 63–64, §396).

INFINITE ANGUISH AND THE OTHERNESS OF GOD

The moment of negation in the evolution of individual mind discussed in *Anthropology* is taken up at the level of historical self-consciousness in *Phenomenology of Spirit* as the moment of unhappy consciousness (*das unglückliche Bewusstsein*).[8] The immediately prior moments are Stoicism and Skepticism, which follow the Master-Slave stage. The Master-Slave stage is the first stage in the history of self-consciousness in which the possibility of the encounter of another self, an encounter that is absolutely necessary for the genesis of self-consciousness, is posited. The confrontation with another self occurs in the dialectical Master-Slave struggle for mutual recognition. The outcome is not successful precisely because the Slave is denied selfhood and so the necessary mutual recognition is not reached; the abstract dialectical development of consciousness played out in the Master-Slave relationship is taken over in historical consciousness, namely, in Stoic consciousness. Here the contradictions of the prior stage are not overcome but rather circumvented by a withdrawal into interiority and an exaltation of inner freedom and self-sufficiency. Stoic rejection of the concrete and external is deepened by Skeptical consciousness, for which the self alone abides while all else is subject to doubt and negation. The Skeptic fails to eliminate natural consciousness, however, and therefore enters into self-contradiction, becoming Unhappy Consciousness.

This consciousness, *unglückliche Bewusstsein*, finding itself in self-contradiction, agonizes over its own nothingness—what Ludwig Binswanger and Hubertus Tellenbach call the "delirium of loss." This is how Hegel introduces it: "Consciousness takes its own reality to be immediately a nothingness, its actual doing thus becomes a doing of nothing, its enjoyment a feeling of its wretchedness. Work and enjoyment thus lose all universal content and significance. Both withdraw into their mere particularity, which consciousness is set upon reducing to nothingness" (*Spirit* 135, §225). Unhappy Consciousness is the consciousness divided and self-alienated: torn between finitude and the infinite, between the fallen and the ideal, between the human self and transcendent God. The contradictions intrinsic to Hegel's Unhappy Consciousness are overcome only in religious consciousness, which is aware of the immanence of God in all selves; the imperfect actual self becomes aware that the true self lives within and manifests itself through its finite operations. "The Unhappy Consciousness [as contrasted with Comic Consciousness] is the tragic fate of the certainty of the self that aims to be absolute. It is the consciousness of the loss of all essential being in this certainty of itself and of the loss even of this knowledge about itself—the loss of substance as well as of the Self, it is the Grief which expresses itself in the hard saying that 'God is dead'" (*Spirit* 455, §752).

Consciousness becomes Unhappy Consciousness only when it hubristically desires to be absolute as God. Imprisoned in itself, in the depths of the night that no longer distinguishes or knows anything outside of itself, the Unhappy Consciousness undergoes the death of God. This moment of darkness is the sine qua non condition for the new moment of liberation of Spirit and actualization of subjectivity. The death of God is a "hard saying" only for picture-thinking (*Vorstellung*), the term Hegel uses to refer to religion. The death of the picture-thought of the Mediator only means:

> The death of the abstraction of the divine Being which is not posited as a Self. That death is the painful feeling of the Unhappy Consciousness that God himself is dead. This hard saying is the expression of innermost simple self-knowledge, the return of consciousness into the depths of the night in which I = I, a night which no longer distinguishes or knows anything outside of it. . . . This knowing is the inbreathing of the Spirit, whereby Substance becomes Subject, by which its abstraction and lifelessness have died, and Substance therefore has become actual and simple and universal Self-consciousness. (*Spirit* 476, §785)

According to conceptual knowledge, good and evil are moments of the life of divine Being, while evil is not alien to God. In order to understand the meaning of the death of God in Hegel's system and the relation between the death of God and the Unhappy Consciousness, we will appeal to Hegel's *Lectures on the Philosophy of Religion.*[9] The moment of Unhappy Consciousness reemerges throughout the history of consciousness as the moment of negation or evil inhabiting an affirmation, the element of negativity in the affirmative, "meaning that, within itself, the affirmative is self-contradictory and wounded," defined by anguish or unhappiness.

Hegel explains the two sides of the cleavage or antithesis that inhabits humanity itself: the antithesis vis-à-vis God, which results in infinite anguish, and the antithesis vis-à-vis the world, the fact that humanity lives in a state of rupture from the world, which is the cause of unhappiness or misery, the "universal unhappiness of the world." Historically, the first corresponds to the Stoic consciousness and the Jewish religion; the second to the Skeptical consciousness and Roman religion. Infinite anguish is the experience of evil at the heart of the good:

> This anguish is thus one moment of evil. Evil merely on its own account is an abstraction; it *is* only in antithesis to the good, and since it is present in the unity of the subject, the latter is split, and this cleavage is infinite anguish. If the consciousness of the good, the infinite demand of the good, is not likewise present in the subject itself, in its innermost being, then no anguish is present and evil itself is only an empty nothingness, for it *is* only in this antithesis. (*Religion* 448 [229])

It is the cleavage at the heart of the self between one's own natural being, perceived as nothingness and evil, and the ideal of the good or God that produces infinite anguish. For Heidegger, *Angst* becomes the existential mood par excellence, the mood of the finite being temporalizing itself toward its death, which nevertheless is also the condition for the possibility of authentic existence and vision.

It is the Spirit, human and divine, that undergoes anguish, in the absence of which it would cease to be Spirit. Hegel refers to the necessary process of self-differentiating and positing of distinctions suffered by the Spirit, "The incongruity is [there], resides in spirituality. Spirit is the process of self-differentiating, the positing of distinction. . . . This incongruity cannot disappear, for otherwise the judgment of spirit, its vitality, would disappear, and it would cease to be spirit" (*Religion* 453 [235]). God's self-othering is reflected in the cleavage, antithesis, negation, contradiction that manifest as infinite anguish, unhappy consciousness, and the misery of the human individual: it is a sine qua non moment of the Spirit, both in God and in the human, one that eternally arises and sublates itself, "The antithesis arises eternally and just as eternally sublates itself; there is at the same time eternal reconciliation. That this is the truth may be seen in the eternal divine idea: God is the one who as living spirit distinguishes himself from himself, posits an other and in this other remains identical with himself" (*Religion* 453 [234]). The notion of Infinite Grief is the translation of the feeling that God himself is dead into speculative philosophy. Hegel explains, "Formerly, the Infinite Grief only existed historically in the formative process of culture. It existed as the feeling that "God himself is dead," upon which the religion of more recent times rests."[10] He explains that Pascal expresses this feeling when he writes that nature indicates a lost God both within and outside of man. Infinite Grief for God's death is a moment of the supreme Idea: the pure concept or infinity as the abyss of nothingness in which all being is engulfed signifies the Infinite Grief of the finite. The pure concept gives philosophical expression to the sacrifice of empirical being for the sake of the moral precept, and thus enters ethical freedom of the spirit.

In his superb study *The Heterodox Hegel*, Cyril O'Regan discusses in detail Hegel's complex relation to Christian theological traditions, including Patristic, Lutheran, mystical, and Gnostic.[11] Most relevant for an understanding of Hegel's deipassionist element, according to O'Regan, is the notion of speculative Good Friday and the announcement of the death of God at the end of the early text *Faith and Knowledge*; thereafter the theme of the death of God will be present throughout the *Lectures on the Philosophy of Religion* and *The Phenomenology of Spirit*. Although Hegel seems to adopt Luther's vision of the *Deus patibilis*, O'Regan argues convincingly that Hegel's divergences from Luther are profoundly significant and indicate the influence of the speculative-mysticism of Jakob Böhme. He adduces Thomas J. J. Altizer's suggestion that Hegel's deipassionism subverts the theological tradition generally, and the Lutheran tradition specifically. O'Regan maintains that central to Hegel's theological vision is the "divestment of the divine splendor, the descent of the divine infinite into the nadir of the finite and human"; moreover, his existential-ontotheological vision refers both to a "particular experience of God and to an actual change of form by divine-infinite reality" (211).

Thus death can be predicated of the divine. O'Regan explains that the Lutheran theme of the death of God (*Gott selbst ist tot*) centers around a "double divestment or kenosis (*Entausserung*), namely, the divestment of finitude and the divestment of the eternally complete, invulnerable, apathetic divine." O'Regan emphasizes that for Hegel the assertion that "God himself is dead" has radical implications of "predicating pathos and death of the divine itself." In most disquieting but unequivocal terms, Hegel pronounces and justifies the death of God as the absolute crux of his philosophical system, thus explicitly acknowledging God's intrinsic otherness, "God himself is dead" it says in a Lutheran hymn, expressing an awareness that:

> the human, the finite, the fragile (*das Gebrechliche*), the weak (*die Schwache*), the negative are themselves a moment of the divine (*gottliches Moment selbst sind*), that they are within God himself (*dass es in Gott selbst ist*), that finitude, negativity, otherness are not outside of God (*nicht ausser Gott*) and do not, as otherness (*als Anderssein*), hinder unity with God. Otherness, the negative, is known to be a moment of the divine nature itself. This involves the highest idea of spirit. (206)

The otherness of God as the negative, the human, as pathos, finitude, fragility, weakness, is an ineluctable moment in the life of God and involves the highest idea of spirit. It also implies, O'Regan notes, a redefinition of divine agapeic love that can occur only through the milieu of otherness, "Truly real, that is, truly effective agape is predicated upon the union of genuine contraries and this can only take place in the milieu of otherness (*Anderssein*), or more accurately, through the milieu of otherness" (207).

The otherness may be outside the immanent Trinity, but not outside the narrative Trinitarian explication of the divine as such. Hegel reconsiders two prevalent theological interpretations of the passion and death of Christ: the theory of satisfaction, with its juridical emphasis, and the theory of sacrifice. Regarding the former, O'Regan argues that Hegel subverts the theory of satisfaction as at-onement between the divine and the human by suggesting at-onement *within* the divine itself, since for Hegel oneness is not a given but an agonic process. Hegel's theological position becomes clearer in his subversion of Irenaeus's classical theory of sacrifice as at-onement. Sacrifice emerges not only as the condition for salvation but also as an intradivine ontological mode. Thus a theogonical process of self-differentiation and self-determination becomes the explanation of the genesis of evil as well as of reconciliation: it is a theogony that reveals for O'Regan the influence of Böhmian Gnosticism and determines Hegel's principal departure from the Lutheran *theologia crucis* (209).

Thus for Hegel the correlation between Infinite Grief and the death of God is established as a moment of the Idea that manifests itself within the psyche, history, culture, religion, and speculative philosophy. If we recognize melancholy in Hegel's Infinite Grief and Unhappy Consciousness, then melancholy can vanish only with the death of the Spirit. To understand its metaphysical ground, we must acknowledge that melancholic human suffering and God's pathos and death inhabit the same moment in the dialectic of the Spirit, and reflect one another. Both require sublation by the Spirit and reconciliation in the form of a sacrificial death by love that gives birth to a new consciousness. Subsequently the death of God will be declared by Nietzsche and resurface with new vigor in Altizer's theology, where it becomes radicalized. Recently the theme of God's otherness has returned in different variants that inform a spirited intercultural debate.

HEGELIAN THERAPEUTICS: WORK
AND SELF-CONSCIOUSNESS

Hegel's justification for a therapeutic in the form of work is elaborated in the *Phenomenology of Spirit*. The breakthrough in the Master-Slave relationship occurs through work: it is work that transforms the Slave into an independent being, "Through work however the bondsman becomes conscious of what he truly is. . . . Work is desire held in check, fleetingness staved off; in other words, work forms and shapes the thing. . . . Consciousness, *qua* worker, comes to see in the independent being [of the object] its *own* independence" (*Spirit* 118, §95). Work generates self-consciousness, identity, and freedom, and most importantly, it transforms the initial negative fear of the Slave, who realizes that only "in his work wherein he seems to have only an alienated existence . . . he acquires a mind of his own." It transforms the self's original absolute fear by externalizing it and giving it a voice, a possibility to become manifest. Thus Hegel writes, "Without the formative activity [of work] fear remains inward and mute, and consciousness does not become explicitly *for itself.* . . . If it has not experienced absolute fear but only some lesser dread, the negative being has remained for it something external, its substance had not been infected by it through and through" (*Spirit* 119, §196).

Whereas imposed work has the potential to provoke a transfiguration of the self by transmuting the absolute fear that engulfs the natural being of the worker into the relative freedom from nature of a mind of one's own and self-will, work chosen deliberately in the Deed gives the self its actual identity since, Hegel writes, the "true being of a man is rather his Deed." It is the Deed that brings to end the spurious infinity of the merely meant of unfulfilled desire or intention" (*Spirit* 194, §322). Thus, since consciousness gives reality to itself through the work produced, the individual is explicitly for himself what he is implicitly in himself (*Spirit* 242–43, §404–5). Hegel's view of the transforming and self-generating significance of work illuminates the work-therapeutic traditionally recommended in cases of melancholy, whether secular or religious, from Cassian to Kant.

Intrinsic to the system, however, there is a higher therapeutic accessible only to the individual consciousness that has reached a stage closer to the actualization of Spirit. That therapeutic involves the ultimate transmutation as the sacrifice of the natural and empirical for the sake of the Spirit. The model is God's sacrifice for love in the Passion. Absolute freedom and absolute passion—the "Golgotha of Absolute Spirit"—are inseparable and are acknowledged as such by speculative philosophy and true religion. The highest totality can achieve resurrection, Hegel insists, only through this consciousness of total loss, encompassing everything, and ascending out of this deepest ground of abnegation to the most serene freedom. The speculative Good Friday will be seen in its harsh truth as God-forsakenness.[12] In light of Hegel's speculation, it becomes clear that the only possible freedom from melancholy involves the descent into the abyss with the consciousness of total loss and forsakenness. Arising out of darkness into the Spirit amounts to a resurrection.

SCHELLING: THE METAPHYSICAL GROUND
OF ACEDIA AND MELANCHOLY

A hermeneutics of melancholy must hesitate between two ontological modes—or rather, two meontological moods—which correspond to two distinct metaphysical principles in Schelling's thought respectively: the first principle is Schelling's *Ungrund*, antecedent to the opposition of *Grund* and existence; the second is Schelling's primordial nought, both negation and ground of existence. While the latter, the primordial nought, is the metaphysical principle grounding the interior mood of melancholy proper, the former, absolute indifference, is the metaphysical principle grounding *acedia*. Our concern here is to understand acedia and melancholy in relation to Schelling's metaphysics articulated in the treatise *Philosophical Investigations of the Essence of Human Freedom* (1809) and *The Ages of the World* (1815).

Schelling argues philosophically and justifies metaphysically the mystical theology of *via negativa*, which involves the paradoxical denial of God's existence. He constructs an elaborate theogony that presupposes a complex dialectical becoming; the first moment of this becoming necessarily manifests God's self-negation, "for the beginning really only lies in the negation."[13] At all its levels of manifestation and in all its hypostases, this self-negation is perceived as divine pathos. This, Schelling believes, explains the ground of melancholy in all creation. For the human individual, melancholy is the reflection of the pathos of God's self-negation. This self-negation can never be dispensed with since divine revelation occurs only in and through the struggle against it. God manifested as nonbeing is the metaphysical ground for God's being. By extension, melancholy or melancholic madness forms the ultimate ground of the life of the self; the self is always in the process of becoming itself by conquering it, that is, by conquering the pathos of the agony of self and God.

Schelling's dialectics of God in labor with himself unfolds in several critical scenes. Interestingly, he discovers what Heidegger was later in search of, "a more originary beginning," and thus the first scene is the scene prior to the beginning. Schelling postulates a primordial indifferent groundless totality outside all categories of being and nonbeing, of nature and existence, an absolute indifference. This groundless indifference cannot be conceived either as being or nonbeing; it is outside the time-eternity dichotomy since time is not yet born. This indivisible primordial essence is one and the same, the unity of all antitheses, without contradiction and therefore without life or progress, only an eternal immobility, "without its being nought or a non-entity." Schelling speculates "there must be a being *before* all basis and before all existence, that is, before any duality at all; how can we designate it except as 'primal ground' or, rather, as the 'groundless'?"[14]

The beginning properly so called is the second scene. A break in the primordial Indifference can only occur with the positing of the negative, the power of nonbeing. This primordial negation is the ground of both God and the entire creation. It is in reaction to this negation that God comes to be and to know himself. Thus in God the eternal beginning is this contraction, denial, darkness, or evil, since in creation the power of the nought will constitute the power of sin:

> God is only negating force with respect to Being in order to make a ground for Itself as eternal Love. But this negating force does not know itself and hence, also does not know its own relationship. It does not know the freedom of the decision, by virtue of which it alone is what is active. It had to be so. So that there would be a true beginning, this higher life had to sink back into unconsciousness of itself. (*Ages* 85 [314–15])

Schelling explains his conception of God as the divine dialectics between God's nature or basis of existence—the paradoxical God but not God, the God of necessity and wrath—and God's existence or God himself, the God of freedom and love. The first, God's nature, is the will of the depths, not fully conscious, therefore not free; the second is the will of love altogether conscious and free (*Freedom* 74–75 [395]). The basis of God's existence is an eternally dark basis, defined as a "longing which the eternal One feels to give birth to itself" and "prescient will" (*Freedom* 34 [359]). It is this that permeates the entire creation and constitutes "the incomprehensible basis of reality in things," "the unruly," and "irreducible remainder which cannot be resolved into reason by the greatest exertion but always remains in the depths" (*Freedom* 34 [360]).

The eternal dallying of the two principles, with an emphasis on the absolute necessity of the dark, unruly, unreasonable one, is one of the crucial junctures at which Schelling and Hegel part ways. For both, reason is born out of the unreasonable, as light out of darkness, for without this preceding gloom, creation would lack ground, reality, and freedom. Schelling insists, "The negating, contracting will must precede into revelation so that there is something that shores up and carries upward the grace of the divine being, without which grace would not be capable of revealing itself. There must be Might before there is Leniency and Stringency before Gentleness. There is first Wrath, then Love. Only with Love does the wrathful actually become God" (*Ages* 83 [311–12]). But for Schelling in contradistinction to Hegel, this alien ground is never to be sublated; it lingers as the "irreducible remainder" (*Freedom* 34 [360]).

The analogy Schelling uses to explain the relation between God and his dark basis is the necessary relation between gravitation and light (*Freedom* 32 [358]). The precedence of gravitation over light is neither temporal nor essential. The dark basis and God, like gravitation and light, are involved in an eternal circular movement in which each is cogenerating the other, "There is here no first and no last, since everything mutually implies everything else, nothing being the 'other' and yet no being being without the other. God contains himself in an inner basis of his existence [which] precedes him as to his existence, but similarly God is prior to the basis as this basis, as such, could not be if God did not exist in actuality" (*Freedom* 33 [358]).

NATURE, THE *UNGRUND*, AND *CHORA*

John Sallis emphasizes the significance of Schelling's appropriation of Plato's chorology for the construction of his metaphysical dialectics, as well as for later modern philosophy.[15] Sallis notes Schelling's sustained interest in the "divine" philosopher Plato generally, and in the *Timaeus* particularly. Schelling's essay on *Timaeus* discusses precisely the two beginnings that bring into play the three ontological categories—being, becoming, and the enigmatic metaxic *chora*, mediatrix between the two—which according to Sallis became with Kant the categories, appearances, and the transcendental schema (154–55). Primordial nature, the third ontological kind in *Timaeus*, provides Schelling with an answer to his lifelong quest for a true explanation of absolute beginning and a philosophy of nature to complement transcendental idealism, especially that of Fichte.

To unravel the mystery of the beginning, Schelling posits a dialectical opposition between nature or ground and existence, in which nature, Sallis maintains, reappropriates Timaeus's *chora*: this primordial nature is "the unruly (*Regellose*) that precedes the establishment of rule, order, form, and that even in ordered nature still persists as capable of breaking through again" (157–58). Like *chora*, the "pregenetic nature" is "an enduring but invisible substance" or substratum, one that receives all bodies, prior to all generation. Sallis remarks that Schelling refers to this nature in poetic and metaphorical terms that recall Plato's bastard discourse on *chora*: the dark nature is likened to an "originary longing" ("moving like an undulating surging sea"), which he refers to as "Plato's matter" (165). Sallis advances the further claim that it is the thinking of *chora* that prompted Schelling to conceive the *Ungrund*. He explains that Schelling looks beyond the distinction of ground and existence, but instead of dissolving the opposition in the earlier notion of absolute identity, he posits a more originary ground or unground, an absolute indifference. Sallis comments:

> The move beyond the opposition of ground and existence is not such as to dissolve the opposition into an antecedent unity. The move beyond to absolute indifference does not, then, dissolve the opposition opened up in the *Timaeus* between νουϛ

and αναγκη, the opposition that Schelling reinscribes as that of existence and ground. Rather, the move is an initiative toward thinking this opposition in a way that forestalls its recoiling destructively on that thinking, its recoiling in such a way as to produce the self-laceration and despair of reason. (165–66)

It seems that Schelling hesitates in his interpretation between two reappropriations of chorology, the unruly ground of existence and the abysmal *Ungrund* underneath both ground and existence, which cannot be thought or spoken of. These two primordial beginnings live in the present as past, and reverberate throughout creation. Sallis's conclusion suggests the restructuring of consciousness prompted by Schelling that will be actualized in the new thinking of existence in Kierkegaard and Nietzsche, twentieth-century existentialism, and postmodernism. This precosmic, pregenetic dimension "proves indeed so radical, in Schelling's reinscription of it, as to threaten reason as such with self-laceration and despair and thus to require of it a perhaps unprecedented initiative" (166). The primordial choratic nature is never sublated, Sallis maintains; though cosmicized by God's creation, it ominously remains the permanent threat of the abyss ready to resurface, "Secluded nature is originary (*ursprunglich*) not only in the sense that it precedes order and form (creation consisting, then, in bringing the unruly to order), but also in the sense that it remains as the irreducible ground always capable of breaking through the order brought by creation" (158).

Schelling justifies the necessity, dialectics, and metamorphoses of the irreducible remainder across all ontological levels. The omnipresence of the dark principle, ground of all there is, explains both individuality or selfhood and the "premonitions of evil" in nature, beyond their human relevance (*Freedom* 53 [377]). Universal evil is in a state of potentiality and conceal-ment until it is aroused by God's love. The dark, the deep, the sorrowful, the arousal of passion and selfhood—all these hypostases of the primordial nought ensure life's intensity. In their absence there would be the "complete death, goodness slumbering; for where there is no battle, there is no life"; "thence the veil of sadness which is spread over all nature, the deep, unap-peasable melancholy of all life" (*Freedom* 80, 79 [400]). In *The Ages of the World* Schelling deepens the connection between this primordial nought and melancholy or melancholic madness whose destiny can retrospectively be traced back to the metaphysical beginnings of both God and the stars, the works of God's wrath (*Ages* 96–99 [329–333]). Melancholic madness is the human actualization of the primordial positing of the theogonic and cosmogonic drama. The melancholic other to reason corresponds to its meta-physical ground of chaos and the eclipse of God. Reason cannot encompass or dissolve it:

Philosophy that would explain everything found nothing more difficult than to provide an explanation for precisely this Being [opposed to thought]. They had to explain this incomprehensibility, this active opposition toward all thought, this dynamic darkness, this positive inclination to obscurity. But it would have preferred to do away altogether with the inconvenient, to dissolve the unintelligible entirely into reason or (like Leibniz) into representation. (*Ages* 7 [212])

There are two main hypostases of the condition detectable in this unfolding; the first corresponds to *acedia*, the second to melancholy proper. The acedic hypostasis is indifference, literally acedia, carelessness, the hesitation before being. This hypostasis implies the temptation to reverse creation and time, to uncreate oneself and withdraw into the primordial deathly slumber of all powers, into the abyss of absolute indifference. The experience of empty time in boredom and apathy is perhaps the most significant mark of this hypostasis. Indeed, according to Heidegger, this depressed or fallen state of consciousness, to which he refers as the fundamental ontological attunement of boredom, manifests the nought in the experience of being left empty, entranced in time and held in limbo.[16] Ultimately boredom seems to be a reflection in the abyss of individual being of the primordial absolute indifference, the unground. Indulgence in it, the mortal sin of acedia as carelessness or self-forgetting, is a withdrawal from being, or in Kierkegaardian terms, a refusal to choose oneself. The indifferent hears the call of the nothing and is caught between contrary impulses: to lose itself in sleep and withdraw from time or lose itself in the world. The two impulses, perceived in their complex dialectics, constitute what is known theologically as the sin of acedia, the dreaded monastic temptation.

The melancholic hypostasis, by contrast, reflects the primordial negation, the angry otherness of God, initiator of the beginning. Melancholy is a trace of the melancholy that God himself suffers during the primordial eclipse and self-negation; it is a remainder of God's dark nature and ground, the negative potency, the past in God, the wrath of the Father, God according to necessity and not freedom.[17] It is a figure of the power that must be negated subsequently by the second potency, the power of expansion, the love of the Son. Since this power is unconscious of itself as God's beginning, the absolute absence of God may be erroneously posited.[18] If man's melancholia reflects God's melancholia, only then is it revealed why the sin of melancholy is also a mortal sin: melancholic delirium manifests the first negative potency in which the God of wrath denies the God of love, or more simply, in which God denies himself. At the end of *The Ages of the World*, Schelling refers to Pseudo-Aristotle's treatise on melancholy, *Problem 30.1*, "Since Aristotle it is even customary to say of people that nothing great can be accomplished without a touch of madness. In place of this, we would like to say: nothing great can be accomplished without a constant solicitation of madness, which should always be overcome, but should never be utterly lacking" (*Ages* 103 [338–39]).

Indeed, Schelling's *The Ages* is a metaphysical reflection on melancholic madness in response to Pseudo-Aristotle's question. The treatise is meant to identify the metaphysical source of this madness, in the absence of whose solicitation there is no life, no intelligence, and no creativity. Madness must be constantly conquered by reason but never eliminated entirely. This solicitation of madness as the threat of nonbeing preserves the life and freedom of God, world, and self; it presupposes the continual labor of overcoming the Other of being and reason, calling the self back from delusion and delirium; it is the ground of individuality and freedom. Schelling concludes, "That the self-lacerating madness is still now what is innermost in all things is the greatest attestation of this description. Only when it is governed and, so to speak, verified [*zugutgesprochen*], through the light of a higher intellect, is it the real force of nature and of all its products" (*Ages* 103 [338–39]).

The main philosophical concern that has informed Schelling's thought throughout his entire work is the conception a truly living and free God that would solve the theodicean problem of God, freedom, and evil. The dark nature of God that is posited as the primordial nought, ground of negation and revelation, represents Schelling's metaphysical solution to this conundrum. In the absence of his dark nature as ground, God would remain a Spinozist God, lifeless and incorporeal. According to Böhme and Schelling, following the Platonic intuition of the value of limit and also the decisive Christian commitment to Incarnation, corporeality is the ultimate telos of both God and creation.

NOTES

1. G. W. F. Hegel, "Anthropology," in *Philosophy of Mind*, trans. A. V. Miller (Oxford and New York: Oxford University Press, 1971; reprint, 1992); hereafter cited as *Mind*, followed by page number and section number.

2. Hegel, *Philosophy of Mind*: "While still a substance (i.e., a physical soul) the mind takes part in the general planetary life, feels the difference of climates, the changes of the seasons, and the periods of the day, etc. This life of nature for the main shows itself only in occasional strain or disturbance of mental tone. In recent times a good deal has been said of the cosmical, sidereal and telluric life of man. In such a sympathy with nature the animals essentially live. . . . In the case of man these points of dependence lose importance, just in proportion to his civilization, and the more his whole frame of soul is based upon a substructure of mental freedom" (36–37, §392).

3. Hegel, *Philosophy of Mind:* "In the English, this disgust with life is manifested mainly as *melancholy*, the state in which mind constantly broods over its unhappy idea and is unable to rise to spontaneous thought and action. Not infrequently this psychical state develops into an uncontrollable impulse to commit suicide" (134, §408).

4. Alan M. Olson, "Madness," in his *Hegel and the Spirit: Philosophy as Pneumatology* (Princeton: Princeton University Press, 1992), 84–106.

5. Cyril O'Regan, *The Heterodox Hegel* (Albany: State University of New York Press, 1994).

6. Hegel, *Philosophy of Mind*: "Just as four cardinal virtues were distinguished, so too, as we know, four temperaments were assumed: the choleric, the sanguine, the phlegmatic and the melancholic. Kant has a great deal to say about them" (52–53, §395).

7. Hegel, *Philosophy of Mind*: "The substance of mind is freedom, i.e., the absence of dependence on an Other, the relating of self to self. . . . But the freedom of mind or spirit is not merely an absence of dependence on an Other won outside of the Other, but won in it; it attains actuality not by fleeing from the Other but by overcoming it. Mind can step out of its abstract, self-existent universality, out of its simple self-relation, can posit within itself a determinate, actual difference, something other than the simple 'I,' and hence a negative; and this relation to the Other is, for mind, not merely possible but necessary, because it is through the Other and by the triumph over it, that mind comes to authenticate itself and to be in fact what it ought to be according to its Notion, namely, the ideality of the external, the Idea which returns to itself out of its otherness. . . . The Other, the negative, contradiction, disunity, therefore also belongs to the nature of mind. In this disunity lies the possibility of pain. Pain has therefore not reached mind from the outside as is supposed when it is asked in what manner pain entered into the world. Nor does evil, the negative of absolutely self-existent infinite mind, any more than pain, reach mind from the outside; on the contrary, evil is nothing else than mind which puts its separate individuality before all else. . . . But mind has power to preserve itself in contradiction, and, therefore, in pain; power over evil, as well as over misfortune. . . . This power over every content present in it forms the basis of the freedom of mind" (15–16, §382).

8. G. W. F. Hegel, *Phenomenology of Spirit*, trans. A. V. Miller (Oxford and New York: Oxford University Press, 1977); hereafter cited in the text as *Spirit*, with page number and section number.

9. G. W. F. Hegel, *Lectures on the Philosophy of Religion: One-Volume Edition, The Lectures of 1827*, trans. R. F. Brown, P. C. Hodgson, J. M. Stewart and H. S. Harris (Berkeley: University of California Press, 1988); hereafter cited in the text as *Religion*, followed by page numbers for the English translation and the original German edition, respectively.

10. G. W. F. Hegel, *Faith and Knowledge*, trans. Walter Cerf and H. S. Harris (Albany: State University of New York Press, 1977), 190.

11. Cyril O'Regan, *The Heterodox Hegel* (Albany: State University of New York Press, 1994).

12. Hegel, *Faith and Knowledge*, 191.

13. F. W. J. Schelling, *The Ages of the World*, trans. Jason M. Wirth (Albany: State University of New York Press, 2000): "Precisely that which negates all revelation

must be made the ground of revelation" (16 [223–24]). Hereafter this work is cited as *Ages,* followed by page numbers for the English translation and the original German edition, respectively.

14. F. W. J. Schelling, *Philosophical Inquiries into the Nature of Human Freedom,* trans. James Gutmann (Chicago: Open Court, 1936), 87; hereafter cited in the text as *Freedom* followed by page numbers for the English translation and the original German edition, respectively.

15. John Sallis, "Appropriation," in *Chorology* (chapter 1, n. 2), 154–67.

16. Heidegger, *Fundamental Concepts of Metaphysics* (introduction, n. 1), 145–67.

17. Schelling, *Ages*: "God, in accordance with the necessity of its nature, is an eternal No, the highest Being-in-itself, an eternal withdrawal of its being into itself, a withdrawal within which no creature would be capable of living. But the same God, with equal necessity of its nature, although not in accord with the same principle, but in accord with a principle that is completely different from the first principle, is the eternal Yes, an eternal outstretching, giving, and communicating of its being. . . . But, in an equally eternal manner, God is the third term or the unity of the Yes and the No" (11 [218]).

18. Schelling, *Ages*: "Hence perhaps some people will say that so long as this is the case, there is no God whatsoever. Certainly not! For God is already the whole God with respect to the possibility (of becoming manifest)" (86 [315]).

Chapter 7

Boredom, Time, and the Self

Augustine's fundamental thinking of time was perhaps the philosophical-theological ground for all later Western fascination with temporality. In fact, Augustine's reflections on time can be construed as the ground for both Kant's theory of pure intuition and Heidegger's phenomenology of temporalized Dasein.[1] He realizes that time is not a matter of movement—human or heavenly—and understands that time is a matter of the mind. Both the past and the future, the whole life of the individual and of humanity, exist only in our mind as memory or expectation, respectively. Time is not a substance existing or unfolding outside man's consciousness, but exists only inside it; it is man's consciousness itself, or as Kant will appropriately qualify, it is pure intuition, the frame, the space of man's consciousness, an all-encompassing space that informs the substance of difference and being. Augustine's reflections on time and consciousness are rethought by Kant who elaborates the concept of time in his transcendental aesthetic.[2]

KANT ON THE NOTHING OF TIME

According to Kant, time is "a pure form of the sensuous intuition," the formal a priori subjective condition of our perception of internal and external objects (*Reason* 28). Although time and space are both a priori conditions for receiving internal and external objects respectively, to the extent to which all objects received in intuition cannot be but received in internal perception as internal phenomena, time is more primordial than space, is even a foundation for the subjective condition of space.[3] In other words, time is the space in which all phenomena can be received, from inner volatile states to external heavy objects; it is a space receiving, organizing, and ordering our sense perceptions without which there would be no sensibility, hence no understanding either. Kantian time is transcendental *chora*, the mysterious Platonic receptacle-nurse or divine milieu discussed above (in chapter 1).[4] Although time is a sine qua non for human self-consciousness, independently of the mind, time in itself is nothing.

> If we abstract our internal intuition of ourselves, and all external intuitions, possible only by virtue of this internal intuition, and presented to us by our faculty of representation, and consequently take objects as they are in themselves, then time is nothing. It is only of objective validity in regard to phenomena, because these are things which we regard as objects of our senses. It is no longer objective, if we make abstraction of the sensuousness of our intuition, in other words, of that mode of representation which is peculiar to us, and speaks of things in general. Time is therefore merely a subjective condition of our human intuition (which is always sensuous, that is so far as we are affected by objects), and in itself, independently of the mind or subject, is nothing. (*Reason* 31)

Neither Augustinian nor Kantian time has an objective existence outside the mind; it neither inheres in external objects, nor remains in the mind when phenomena are removed. As "a subjective condition of our human intuition," time has only a potential existence that requires actualization by our encounter with phenomena that are given only through the medium of time. In the absence of phenomena, time is indistinguishable from the self.[5] As for the noumena, they cannot be received by time or space since the domain of the latter is only that of sensuous phenomena; the unknowability of the things-in-themselves (*Dinge an sich*) is predicated upon time's incapacity to receive them.[6] Kant explains that not even an absolutely clear empirical intuition would make visible and knowable the things-in-themselves. Such a clear empirical intuition though would allow for the cognition of our sensibility, our mode of intuition under the conditions of time and space.[7] Thus it is possible to see pure time, time void of phenomena, since "with regard to phenomena in general, we cannot think away time from them, and represent them to ourselves as out of and unconnected to time, but we can quite well represent to ourselves time void of phenomena" (*Reason* 28). Time void of phenomena is pure a priori time, the empty receptacle of all our representations of both ourselves and of external objects.

Evidently, the implications of Kant's theory of time for our discussion, given that melancholy that has a special relation to time, are of seminal importance. Applying this intuition to the context of desert monasticism, one could speculate that, in Kantian terms, the monastic is testing the human capacity for knowing God as the absolute thing-in-itself. The monastic is clearing his empirical intuition by a rigorous *askesis* imposed on the senses, imagination, and reason. He voids his environment of external objects: the desert becomes a figura of pure space; he empties his sensibility of phenomena in order to create space for God, the absolute thing-in-itself. According to Kant, in spite of this clearness, the monastic would never encounter God, not because, as Hume concluded, God does not exist, but because God transcends our transcendental schemata. At noon, under the blinding light of the sun, the monastic encounters the nothing of time, the void of phenomena. The effect of this encounter is acedia—that is, boredom or ennui—or in Tillich's terms the "anxiety of emptiness." The immediate natural reaction is to take refuge in Pascalian distraction or Heideggerian everydayness; in other words, to fill the void with phenomena or to give the mind an object in which to recognize itself, as Hegel would recommend.

The concept of time in the *Critique of Pure Reason*'s transcendental aesthetic supports the later brief notations by Kant, in his *Anthropology*, on boredom and inactivity as "passing time" and "killing time."[8] Kant provides the familiar phenomenology of boredom already present in Burton and Pascal, as well as in the theology of the sin of acedia. We know that boredom is caused by inactivity, which in turn is the consequence of the post-Adamic self-deceiving belief that ultimate contentment means doing nothing. According to pietistic Kant, as was the case with the progressive social thinker Burton, involvement with fine arts and social life are just modes of passing or—if even pointless amusement is absent—killing time. Kant distinguishes between the natural need for rest after effort and the weariness that grows out of inactivity, in which one "does nothing," just killing time. In the emptiness of the bored mind, the nothing of time appears. These various moments and depths of the experience of time are thought further by Heidegger.

HEIDEGGER: AN INVITATION TO PROFOUND BOREDOM

Heidegger's analysis of boredom is in ambiguous rapport with the tradition of the hermeneutics of acedia-melancholy. By his response, which addresses the problem of the two major complexes of hypostases of boredom and sublimity, Heidegger inscribes himself as a descendent of both Pascal and Kant, while his call of the bored back to boredom can even be viewed as a form of Evagrian courageous resistance to acedia. Indeed, if the theology of sin condemns the soul's turn toward the world or its withdrawal into sleep and recalls it to the contemplation of God, similarly Dasein is called to resist the eccentric temptation to self-forgetfulness and inauthentic existence. But contrary to tradition, in Heidegger this call is not to God but to boredom. In order to decipher the meaning of this counterintuitive move, a deeper understanding of both boredom and God is necessary. According to Heidegger, boredom is a fundamental ontological "attunement" (*Stimmung*) of Dasein and therefore the space and time that appear in boredom are revelatory of Dasein's essence.

What marks all forms of boredom is interpreted as a condition of *suspension* and *entrancement in limbo* whose cause is the indifference of the world and the unification of the three temporal horizons. Voided of phenomena by the loss of world, time appears as time itself, a time that, as Kant argued, is nothing. Through the transparency of time and the vanished world, the self sees itself as a nothing. The theological intuition of the tradition of acedic melancholy interpreted as a sin appears to be finally vindicated: the demonic temptation to boredom is mortal since it is the deadly embrace of the nothing. But Heidegger goes further: he adopts Schelling's quest for a more originary origination that identifies nonbeing or nothing as the groundless ground of Being itself. In the depth of boredom one encounters the primordial nothing at the heart of Being itself. The Heideggerian call to the nothing of boredom is therefore a call to Being itself, or God, but to that in God that is not God or Being. Here Heidegger articulates existentially Schelling's metaphysical intuition and, though apparently diverging from the theology of sin, he paradoxically fulfills it and even deepens it.

In *Fundamental Concepts of Metaphysics* (1929) Heidegger engages in a reflection on mood, attunement, boredom, time, and the self.[9] For Heidegger mood is no longer an inferior manifestation of nature to be overcome by the Spirit as for Hegel, but rather a fundamental mode of being since understanding and state of mind are the two constitutive equiprimordial ways of being-there (*Da-sein*), of finite being. State of mind is our mood or attunement and emerges as an ontic mode, one of the fundamental existential(e)s.[10] As a fundamental mode of being, mood is a locus of disclosure of the essence of Dasein and must not be evaded, although evasion itself is also meaningfully disclosive.[11] What qualifies boredom to be a perfect case for Dasein analysis? This is how Heidegger justifies his interest in boredom:

> Philosophizing is a comprehensive questioning arising out of Dasein being gripped in its essence. Such being gripped is possible only from out of and within a fundamental attunement of Dasein. This fundamental attunement itself cannot be some arbitrary one but must permeate our Dasein in the ground of its essence. Such a fundamental attunement cannot be ascertained as something present at hand that we can appeal to or as something firm upon which we might stand but must be awakened—awakened in the sense that we must let it become awake.

This fundamental attunement properly attunes us only if we do not oppose it, but rather give it space and freedom. . . . We can only ever encounter such a fundamental attunement of our Dasein in a question, in a questioning attitude. This is why we asked whether perhaps contemporary man has become bored with himself and whether a profound boredom is a fundamental attunement of contemporary Dasein. (*Fundamental* 132)

Profound boredom (*tiefe Langeweile*) appears as a fundamental attunement, permeating contemporary Dasein in the ground of its essence. Since philosophizing is a questioning that arises out of a fundamental attunement of Dasein, and since profound boredom is such, philosophizing must begin with and arise out of Dasein's profound boredom. Heidegger initiates the questioning of the relation of boredom, time, and the ground of Dasein:

Boredom, *Langeweile*—whatever its ultimate essence may be—shows particularly in our German word, an almost obvious relation to time, a way in which we stand with respect to time, a feeling of time. Boredom and the question of boredom thus leads us to the problem of time. Or . . . does boredom first lead us to time, to an understanding of how time resonates in the ground of Da-sein. (*Fundamental* 80)

Boredom reveals our feeling of time, and leads to an understanding of time in relation to the self. Since in boredom time stands in a relation to us, boredom is a fundamental attunement of our philosophizing in which we develop the three metaphysical questions of world, finitude, and individuation. The attunement to boredom, as the ground of mood that gives us the possibility of "grasping" time and the being-there of man, offers the possibility of answering the three questions (*Fundamental* 81). For the first time in the history of Western consciousness boredom undergoes, with Heidegger, a radical hermeneutical transformation: no longer an evil coming from the outside—whether as noontime demon or absent God—or from the inside—as idle passivity or the curse of our fallen condition—boredom emerges as our own fundamental attunement. This attunement must be lucidly cultivated not as a spur toward attaining God's grace and recovering our initial fullness, but because its relation to time grants it an exceptional insight into world, finitude, and individuation.

Following Kant's brief exposition of the distinctive levels of boredom, Heidegger identifies three forms of boredom of increasing depth. The first one is *becoming bored by something* and *killing time*:

We are sitting for example, in the tasteless station of some lonely minor railway. It is four hours until the next train arrives. The district is uninspiring. We do have a book in our rucksack, though—shall we read? No. Or think through a problem or some question? We are unable to. We read the timetables or study the table giving the various distances from this station to other places we are not otherwise acquainted with at all. We look at the clock—only a quarter of an hour has gone by. Then we go out onto the local road. We walk up and down, just to have something to do. But it is no use. Then we count the trees along the road, look at our watch again—exactly five minutes since we last looked at it. Fed up with walking back and forth, we sit down on a stone, draw all kinds of figures in the sand, and in so doing catch ourselves looking at our watch again. (*Fundamental* 83)

I have quoted the entire passage with the description of the first level of boredom, *being bored by* something and *killing time*, for its striking resemblance to Evagrius's description of acedia. Heidegger refers to it as the first form of boredom, which develops two moments, "being held in limbo by time as it drags" and "being left empty by the refusal of things" (*Fundamental* 99–101).

Heidegger then exemplifies the second form of boredom, *being bored with oneself* and the *passing of time* belonging to it:

We have been invited out somewhere for the evening. We do not need to go along. Still we have been tense all day, and we have time in the evening. So we go along. There we find the usual food and the usual table conversation, everything is not only very tasty but tasteful as well. Afterward people sit together having a lively discussion, as they say, perhaps listening to music, having a chat, and things are witty and amusing. And already it is time to leave. . . . There is nothing at all to be found that might have been boring about this evening, neither the conversation, nor the people, nor the rooms. Thus we come home quite satisfied. We cast a quick glance at the work we have interrupted that evening, make a rough assessment of things, and look ahead to the next day—and then it comes: I was bored after all this evening, on the occasion of this invitation. (*Fundamental* 109)

The second type of boredom, *being bored with oneself* and *passing the time*, is no longer superficial or naïve, projecting itself on the world and blaming its lack, as in *being bored by* while waiting in the train station. Self-consciousness deepens and this fundamental attunement is let to appear and recognized as one's own: the boring arises out of Dasein itself. Heidegger remarks that an ever deepening understanding of boredom occurs through which the temporality of Dasein, and thus Dasein itself in its ground, emerges.

The third form of boredom is profound boredom, *it is boring for one*, as in "it is boring for one to walk through the streets of a large city on a Sunday afternoon" (*Fundamental* 135). *It is boring for one* recalls the Pascalian ennui, that is, the experience of the groundless ground inside the self, the nothing as essence of the human condition, one that is subverted by distraction, and from which only God can redeem. The three instances offer access to deepening degrees of boredom and consciousness: determinate boredom, or *being bored with this or that*; indeterminate boredom, or *being bored with nothing in particular except oneself*; impersonal boredom, or *it is boring for one*. In determinate boredom, waiting for the train in an unfamiliar setting creates an inner sense of being trapped in spatio-temporal vacuity. Empty time is killed by filling it with meaningless activities: counting the trees, looking at one's watch. In indeterminate boredom, one passes the time by filling the empty time with company, and being alone with others. It is only in impersonal boredom that boredom cannot be resisted and is allowed to appear in its essence and depths as a fundamental attunement: it is let occur on a Sunday afternoon while strolling through the streets of a big city.

Profound boredom transforms Dasein, who only now understands that the mood is irresistible and cannot be avoided by killing or passing the time, and is compelled to listen to what it wishes to say. To "no longer permit any passing the time means to let this boredom be overpowering." We are compelled to listen by a "kind of compelling force which everything properly authentic about Dasein possesses and which accordingly is related to Dasein's innermost freedom" (*Fundamental* 136). Tarrying in the nothing of boredom leads to authentic being since it is the clearing (*Lichtung*) of profound boredom in which Dasein has access to innermost freedom that opens up the possibility of vision. But is not this indulgence in profound boredom the deadly sin of acedia? Before we can answer this question we must follow Heidegger further in his analysis of boredom.

Within all three forms of boredom, Heidegger identifies two structural moments: *emptiness* and *entrancement* or *suspension in limbo*; both are related to time. Dasein is suspended in limbo and trapped in its emptiness. The condition for the possibility of boredom is the complete indifference of the world. It is this indifference of the world that leaves time, the bearer of beings, empty of its content of beings. Dasein is left as the self that is there. Bearers of beings, the three temporal horizons of past, present, future conjoin into a horizon of the whole time of Dasein, a perfect moment of empty totality in which Dasein encounters itself in its temporal essence. This unified horizon entrances Dasein and calls it to its possibility, the moment of vision.

With Heidegger, boredom springs from the temporality of Dasein; it is Dasein itself in the depths of its ground. In order to see Dasein in its essence, boredom must be let to appear and must be listened to through conscious attunement. Boredom calls for an ontology of both time and being, of being in relation to time. Two fully adequate illustrations of this suspended entrancement in a time that is empty of beings are Evagrius's monastic in the desert at noontime and Pascal's man left alone in an empty chamber. In the absence of distractions, that is, in a time voided of beings, one faces the abyss of one's being, suspended between infinities. There are significant similarities between Heidegger's phenomenology of the first form of boredom, on the one hand, and the phenomenology of the sin of acedia and Pascalian distraction, intended to cover up the abysmal nothing at the heart of being, on the other. Unreflective boredom expels one into the world, leads to everydayness and the falling of Dasein signaled by idle talk, curiosity, ambiguity, falling, and thrownness—all forms of the "they" (*das Man*) consciousness, the sin of acedia. This flight from boredom makes one eccentric to oneself and deaf to the call of God or conscience. Both Evagrius and Pascal emphasize the evil of distraction generated by boredom: immersion in the world leading to abandonment of monastic life, for Evagrius, and concealing the void of one's condition, for Pascal. The sin of acedic boredom deepens into forgetfulness. It is only Heidegger's first form of boredom that is akin to this condition: killing time while waiting for a delayed train, where killing time means filling the emptiness of waiting with meaningless activities, such as counting the trees. For Heidegger, as for Pascal, the sin is distraction from what boredom reveals, the unreflective evasion of it, which is not a remedy but the deepening of the "sin."

In the third degree of depth, in profound boredom, Heidegger interrupts the kenosis of the acedic mood into its sinful effects, the eccentric killing or passing the time. At the profound level, he preserves the attunement to boredom and contemplates the mood itself in its purity: the experience in consciousness of *the nothing* (*das Nichts*) as the essence of Dasein's being. True, the remedy recommended by Evagrius, Pascal, and Heidegger is recognition, resistance to the impulse of flight, silence, and return to authenticity. But for Evagrius and Pascal, authenticity means return to God, while for Heidegger it calls forth attention to what the attunement to profound boredom discloses. Heidegger's analysis invites the deepening of consciousness by cultivation of mindful attending to or indulging in the mood: the experience progresses from a passing discomfort to an experience of nonbeing or the otherness of Being. Heidegger undertakes two radical and disturbing unveilings. First the call back to boredom that can be understood through a shift in Dasein's consciousness, since only a deepening and maturing of consciousness is able to welcome attunement to profound boredom as the ground of Dasein's own depths. Second, the ground of Dasein in its depths, the Pascalian nothing, is Being itself in its otherness. The attunement to boredom as the depths of Dasein thus discloses a more originary origination, a Schellingian *Ungrund* more primordial than Being, whose contemplation offers the possibility of freedom for a new beginning, a renewed self-creation.

Thus Heidegger's call to boredom is a twofold paradoxical departure from the tradition of the hermeneutics of melancholy. It is a call to remembering Being itself which is no longer a transcendent absolute object and can be reached only in one's own depths being-here. At the same time, Being reveals its ultimate groundless ground or *Ungrund*—the absolute indifference, in theological terms, or God's otherness as the ground of God. Existentially, boredom must be followed into its abysmal depths with the care and the lucidity of an Athena-inspired Perseus in order for Dasein to open up in freedom.

CARE AND ANXIETY

A brief excursion into *Being and Time* (1927) is needed in order to pose the question: how do the Heideggerian existential moods par excellence— care (*Sorge*) and anxiety (*Angst*)—relate to boredom as the fundamental ontological attunement?[12] All three have traditionally been identified as hypostases of melancholy. The first step toward an answer is to find out what each of these attunements discloses about Dasein, since it is in the context of Dasein analysis that Heidegger associates existential anxiety and care. While *Fundamental Concepts of Metaphysics* is an analysis of boredom, time, and the self, *Being and Time* provides an existential-phenomenological interpretation of the Augustinian-Kantian intuition of time and rethinks Husserl's phenomenology of temporal subjectivity. In anxiety, care appears as the being of Dasein. Like boredom, anxiety is unreflectively avoided through flight into the inauthentic existence of everydayness and of *das Man* consciousness. If listened to, anxiety shows Dasein as the being of care, care that may take either authentic or inauthentic forms. Anxiety is the existential condition of a being defined by care for itself, one whose horizon is death.

In "Melancholy: Between Gods and Monsters," Richard Kearney introduces the existentialist account of melancholy and adduces Heidegger's "allusion to melancholy—or what he prefers to call *angst*—in the ancient myth of Saturn" in section 42 of *Being and Time*.[13] He notes that Heidegger justifies Dasein's being of care by appealing to a myth whose main protagonist is the god of time, so let us turn for a moment to *Being and Time*, §39–42. In order to make clear that his "existential interpretation [of man as a being of care (*cura*)] is not a mere fabrication, but that as an ontological construction it is well grounded and has been sketched out beforehand in elemental ways," Heidegger adduces a "document which is pre-ontological in character, even though its demonstrative force is 'merely historical.'" In this document "Dasein is expressing itself 'primordially' unaffected by any theoretical interpretation" as "'historical' in the very depths of its Being" (*Being* 241–42, §42). According to the myth, once Care gave shape to a piece of clay, Jupiter gave it spirit. Together with Earth they begin to argue over whose nature and name the new being should bear. They ask Saturn to mediate. Saturn deliberates that at death the soul of the creature will return to Jupiter, its body to Earth, but during its life it belongs to Care; the creature's name will be *homo.*[14]

As Kearney remarks, for Heidegger the myth indicates that each human being is a creature cleft between its terrestrial genesis and celestial longing, and the split accounts for the Saturnine quality of finite existence. For Heidegger, Saturn is an emblem of both melancholy and time, the melancholy that the passing of time produces in a being that temporalizes itself, "Being in the world has the stamp of Care which accords with its Being. It gets the name *homo* not in consideration of its Being but in relation to that of which it consists (*humus*). The decision as to wherein the primordial Being of this creature is to be seen, is left to Saturn, Time" (*Being* 243, §42). He understands care in its essentially twofold structure: it becomes manifest as thrownness (*Geworfenheit*), or care for inauthentic being, surrendered to the world of its concern, and also as care for its own authentic being, through which man's perfection is accomplished, his transformation into being free for his ownmost possibilities. Kearney explains that Saturn, the god of time, connects our being to our temporality, a "connection which Heidegger identifies with our experience of (a) dread (*Angst*) as a facing up to our own inner nothingness, and (b) care (*Sorge*) as a being-free for one's own possibilities, that is, for one's own authentic future which is not yet." Kearney continues, "In melancholic dread we experience 'nothing' and 'nowhere.' Or to be more precise we encounter ourselves as a free temporal projection of possibilities culminating in our death. . . . But it is, strangely, this very experience which individualizes us and makes us authentic (*eigentlich*)" (167). The fact that the experience of nothing is a condition for authenticity should not surprise one familiar with the hermeneutics of melancholy. Kearney remarks that the existentialist view of melancholy as a "precondition for authentic insight" was already intimated by Aristotle, Ficino, and Kant (168). He notes the tradition of Saturnine ambivalence, which subsumes both anxiety and care into the concept of melancholy, thus bringing clarification to the otherwise confusing separation between the two. He also emphasizes that melancholy escapes the nets of scientific reason, that ultimately only indirect discourse of symbol and myth does justice to this infinitely complex experience.

If we return to profound boredom as a fundamental ontological attunement, we begin to understand the intricate interrelation among the different hypostases of melancholy. Profound boredom lets finite being see within the depths of its own emptiness—this is the acedic hypothesis of melancholy. Care emerges as the background nature of Dasein in its authentic and inauthentic forms: it is care that leads to existential anxiety as a response to the encounter in boredom with the nothing. In acedia—literally a lack of care (*a-kedos*)—which is logically the negation of Dasein's ground of being, care disintegrates into cares and the acedic becomes careless about its very ground of being. Indeed, Heidegger's analysis endorses the traditional theology of sin according to which acedia is the gravest of mortal sins—the sin against the spirit that cannot be forgiven.

HEIDEGGER'S LAST GOD

Most significant at this juncture is Kearney's discussion of Heidegger's thinking of the "last God" (*der letzte Gott*) in three texts of Heidegger's so-called turning (*Kehre*), written in the late 1930s and published posthumously.[15] Kearney indicates that Heidegger referred to the last God as radically different from the gods of the past, available only to an elite, and subordinate to the destiny of being; inaccessible in personal or interpersonal experience, appearing only in the "abysmal space (*abgrundigen Raum*) of Being itself" and whose "terrifying destitution . . . petrifies us" (218). The last God is experienced as nothing, alien (*befremdend*), indigence (*Durftigeit*), disturbing (*entsetzlich*), inhuman (*unmenschlich*), and godless (*gottlos*), since it is only when the elect encounter the godlessness of the abyss of being that they again become *capax dei* (*gottfahig*) (219). Kearney paraphrases Heidegger's meaning: "Paradoxically then, it is by facing down the de-divinization (*Entgotterung*) of divinity (*Gottschaft*), marked by our present age of fake sacralization (*Vergotterung*), that we can once again embark, in apocalyptic dismay and distress, upon a new divinization (*Gotterung*)."[16]

Kearney observes that Heidegger's last God, arguably of Nietzschean descent, implies a new initiation and beginning arising out of the emptiness and dereliction, the void left by the vanishing of the old gods. God-less and abysmal, removed from the religious God of transcendence, eschatological hope, kenotic giving, and theophanic redemption, the last God resembles Plato's *chora*, Kearney remarks—and we would add, resembles as well that inauspicious Saturn whose sacred malignity emerges in the medieval *Prayer to Saturn* (in chapter 3, above). Kearney notes that the last God's indigence (a symbolic feature of Saturn) provokes terror, anxiety, and fear—moods that, for Heidegger, accompany the experience of the nothing. Such experience of the nothing is the condition for authentic thinking since wonder, and thinking itself, begin with the revelation of the nothing, "Only because the nothing is manifest in the ground of Dasein can the total strangeness of beings overwhelm us," Heidegger writes. "Only when the strangeness of being oppresses us does it arouse and evoke wonder. Only on the ground of wonder—the revelation of the nothing—does the 'why?' loom before us."[17] The experience is one of pathos, endurance, suffering, although it comes either as shock or splendor, thus, as Kearney observes, recalling and qualifying Kant's sublime terror.

It is interesting to note the striking difference in attitudes between Heidegger and Levinas toward the strangeness of being: while Heidegger is titillated by the *tremendum*, Levinas is horrified by it. This distinction, Kearney remarks, significantly discloses Heidegger's blind spot: his emphasis on the poetic-ontological rather than the practical-ethical, thus the absence of clear ethical coordinates necessary for adequate world-transformation. It is this lack of an ethics of action, and the nonethical character of Heidegger's god, that has provoked the criticism of many Jewish and Christian thinkers, Kearney being one of them. At the same time, Kearney welcomes Heidegger's breaking through the ontotheological prejudice against the possible in favor of the actual. Heidegger has provoked a radical transformation in our thinking about God, one that has rediscovered the premodern mystical and heretical alternatives—the God beyond being and nonbeing and the God who may be—formerly obliterated by mainstream theologies. Kearney discovers the witness to a God "that may be" in Heidegger's Being as the "loving possible," a point of convergence with Kearney's own concept of God as *posse*, a loving may-be.[18]

An alternative hermeneutic strategy to decode the cipher of the last God is John D. Caputo's appeal to Heidegger's mystical sources, Meister Eckhart on the one hand, Schelling on the other.[19] Meister Eckhart's mystical theology and Schelling's theogonical dialectics (between the first and second potencies, and between these and primordial absolute indifference) may help illumine Heidegger's ambivalence between Being and God, ontology and theology, and his turn in *Contributions to Philosophy* (*Beiträge zur Philosophie*, 1936–38) from the first beginning to the other beginning.[20] In his *Schelling's Treatise*, Heidegger reaches a climactic point in unveiling Schelling's distinction between God's ground and his existence, distiguishing "that which in God is not God himself" but is the "terrible in God," from that which is God himself. Here Heidegger also unveils the absolute indifference that precedes the "duality of ground and existence."[21] According to Caputo, Schelling's primordial absolute indifference and his dialectics of the duality of God's ground and existence develop stages that are already present within Meister Eckhart, which can be translated as a progressive withdrawal from creation toward the primordial, or from the first beginning toward the other beginning. Heidegger's last God points away from God himself as God's existence, God according to love, toward "that which in God is not God himself," God's dark basis, God according to wrath; here Heidegger even seems to advance further toward the ground of the duality, toward absolute indifference.

Caputo argues that Heidegger's turn, in the language of mystical experience, moves away from God toward Godhead. Heidegger's last God appears to be the god of the groundless ground, who can only be reached by one who becomes poor in self and world, one who unbecomes. Certainly from the perspective of the world, this abandonment of beings is apocalyptic. If Heidegger's turning intends the primordial abyss of absolute indifference, the last God is also the first, the journey having reached its end in the point of a more originary beginning, for whom Saturn, the chaos of melancholy, and chora are appropriate emplems. In the clearing of profound boredom one can get a glimpse of the other beginning, the dark nature of God: the moment of vision through *Gelassenheit*—thus Meister Eckhart, thus Schelling and Heidegger.

LEVINAS: THE HORROR OF THE *IL Y A*

In his early "preparatory" study *Existence and Existents*, Levinas responds to Heidegger's Dasein analysis with a reflection on time, existence, and existents.[22] Starting with Heidegger's analysis of the temporality of Dasein as a being who, through anxiety, is disclosed as a being toward death, he proposes to take it one step further and in a different direction by rethinking the relation of the existent finite being to existence in time. Levinas departs from the concept of time as it appears both in classical understanding and in Heidegger. Whereas the former has conceived time as a continuous flow with past and future as its main contents, the present moment being evanescent, Levinas emphasizes precisely the present instant. The instant is not a unified temporal horizon but rather a moment devoid of past and future, a pure present moment, the moment that escaped Augustine. The present instant is the only time when the articulation of existent being to existence is renewed and can be observed. Since continuous and unhindered activity makes this renewal invisible, it is only in fatigue and indolence—the symptoms of melancholy that have been previously identified as sloth and idleness—that the articulation emerges. That is because indolence is a hesitation before Being.

Levinas does not subscribe to the Heideggerian notion of Being; rather, Being as such is for Levinas a neutral existence that gives rise to dread and is a Sisyphean burden to be continually assumed. The Heideggerian anxiety toward death is replaced by the horror of impersonal existence, of the *there is* (*il y a*). Levinas explains the *there is* as being in general, the "impersonal anonymous inextinguishable being, which murmurs in the depths of nothingness":

> Let us imagine all beings, things, and persons reverting to nothingness. One cannot put this return to nothingness outside of all events. But what of this nothingness itself? Something would happen if only night and the silence of nothingness. This indeterminateness of this "something is happening" is not the indeterminateness of a subject and does not refer to a substantive. . . . It designates not the uncertainly known author of the action, but the characteristic of this action itself which somehow has no author. The impersonal, anonymous, yet inextinguishable "consummation" of being, which murmurs in the depths of nothingness itself we shall designate by the term *there is* (*l'il y a*). The *there is* inasmuch as it resists a personal form is "being in general." (51–52)

The murmur of inextinguishable anonymous being in the depths of nothingness of *there is* seems to be closer to Heidegger's profound boredom—the "it is boring for one" on a Sunday afternoon—than it is to Dasein's anxiety before death. Meanwhile, Levinas's invitation to imagine the apocalypse of existents and residual nothingness as emptiness reminds one of the Heideggerian essential structural moments of boredom, emptiness, and entrancement or suspension in limbo. Levinas asks, Is not the dread of being even more originary than the anxiety of death? Indeed, the terms in which Levinas describes the phenomenology of *irremissible being* evoke the obscure menace of anonymous being:

> The disappearance of all things and of the I leaves what cannot disappear, the sheer fact of being in which one participates whether one wants to or not, without having taken the initiative. Anonymously. Being remains like a field of forces, like a heavy atmosphere, belonging to no one. . . . There is a nocturnal space, but it is no longer empty space. . . . Darkness fills it like a content; it is full, but full of the nothingness of everything. . . . Nothing approaches, nothing comes, nothing threatens; this silence, this tranquility, this void of sensations constitute a mute, absolutely indeterminate menace. In this ambiguity the menace of pure and simple presence of the *there is* takes form. (53–54)

The tragedy of existence is not finitude but Being itself in its neutrality and anonymity. Like the Pascalian silence of infinite spaces, Levinas notes, the experience of existence empty of existents, depriving the I of its own subjectivity, is profoundly frightening and provokes ontological horror: horror is not an anxiety about death, rather it is the horror of the undead, the Shakespearian specters that continue to haunt the living, or the Hegelian spurious infinite.

> The rustling of the *there is* . . . is horror. . . . Horror is in nowise an anxiety about death. In horror a subject is stripped of his subjectivity, of his power to have private existence. The subject is depersonalized. It is a participation in the *there is*, in the *there is* which returns in the heart of every negation, in the *there is* that has no exits. It is . . . the impossibility of death, the universality of existence even in its annihilation. (55–56)

Significantly, the relation between the experience of impersonal Being as horror and the absence of God is reaffirmed in Levinas's analysis. Just as Thomas Altizer's notion of the death of God implies resurrection of the dead God, Levinas's *there is* pertains to existence even in annihilation, the paradox of the presence of absence, the density of the void, in which "negation, annihilation, and nothingness" are the essential events that replace affirmation, creation, and subsistence (60). Referring to Levy-Bruhl's study of horror in primitive religion as similar to the horror of the *there is*, Levinas observes, "Rather than to a God, the notion of the *there is* leads us to the absence of God, the absence of any being" (55–56). The void of existence, the negation of beings echoes the Pascalian abyss of the human condition without God that emerges in the state of ennui. It is the return of presence in negation, the impossibility of escaping from an anonymous existence that, Levinas believes, is the essence of Shakespeare's tragedy and the tragedy of subjectivity and consciousness. Levinas emphasizes the distinction between his position and that of Heidegger: between the "horror of being and the anxiety over nothingness," "fear of being and not fear for being," horror of irremissible existence and anxiety of being toward death:

> The horror of the night as an experience of the *there is* does not then reveal to us a danger of death, nor even a danger of pain. That is what is essential in this analysis. The pure nothingness revealed by anxiety in Heidegger's analysis does not constitute the *there is*. There is horror of being and not anxiety over nothingness, fear of being and not fear for being. Horror carries out the condemnation to perpetual reality, to existence with no exits. We are opposing then the horror of the night, the silence and horror of the shades to Heideggerian anxiety, the fear of being to the fear of nothingness. While anxiety in Heidegger brings about being toward death, the horror of the night with no exits which does not answer is an *irremissible existence*. There is horror of immortality, perpetuity of the drama of existence, necessity of forever taking on its burden. (57–58)

The burden of *irremissible existence* must be constantly reassumed, Levinas observes, and being must be constantly conquered as if it must recommence with every instant, just as Malebranche intuited and designed in his occasionalism.

FATIGUE AND INDOLENCE

In this context, the struggle for existence becomes the birth that occurs every instant by which an existent takes over its existence. The labor of this birth is witnessed to by the efforts made in the prereflective phenomena of weariness, namely, fatigue and indolence, phenomena that have not been examined by philosophical analysis outside of moral theology. The weariness of the self is manifested in indolence as the aversion toward all effort to begin, to insert oneself into anonymous Being, and in the rigidity and ossification of this refusal. He writes:

> Indolence is an impossibility of beginning, or, it is the effecting of beginning. . . . And indolence as a recoil before action, is a hesitation before existence, an indolence about existing. . . . The trouble in acting from which the indolent one holds back is not some psychological content of pain, but a refusal to undertake, to possess, to take charge. Indolence is an impotent and joyless aversion to the burden of existence itself. It is a being afraid to live which is nevertheless a life, in which the fear of the unaccustomed, adventure, the unknown is a repugnance devolving from the aversion for the enterprise of existence. (13–17)

Indolence is holding back from the solitude of impersonal existence. In this analysis of indolence, while refusing Heidegger's experiment into the unfamiliar terrain of meontotheology and the metaphysical nought, Levinas retrieves and actualizes the poetics of Hell, demonology, and the haunting undead that is experienced in a melancholic delirium. For Levinas, salvation comes in the form of love of the other: in a gesture that echoes the theological tradition of sin and grace, the horror of existence from which the indolent recoils can be appeased only by love, the love of the other.

With fatigue, the articulation of the existent to existence deepens further (18–25). Levinas discards psychologistic and physiologistic interpretations of fatigue and instead examines the instant of fatigue phenomenologically as an event, a "numbness, an impossibility of following through, a constant and increasing lag between a being and itself," inscribed in the event of effort since "there is fatigue only in effort and labor" (19). The instant of effort reveals a condemnation; it is the fatigue and suffering of the instant. "Effort is hence a condemnation because it takes up an instant as an inevitable present. It is an impossibility of disengaging itself from the eternity upon which it has opened. . . . Effort involves pain because it is an event of subjection in its instant. The ancient curse of labor does not only lie in the necessity of working to feed oneself; it is already wholly to be found in the instant of effort" (23–24). Fatigue arises out of effort and is a condemnation to being while also a breaking with the sources of life. Levinas reverses the hermeneutic of effort and labor as *sublime horror* proposed by Burke and Kant, while also discarding Hegel's work-constituted self: both are a curse and generate simple fatigue or weariness of being itself. In its simple form, fatigue makes visible the lag in the upsurge of an existent into existence. But Levinas insists, to be means to take up being, the existence of an existent is by essence an activity.

The one who is indolent and fatigued hesitates before impersonal Being and withdraws into nonbeing. This hesitation is a postponement of the decision implied in the act of resuming existence. The apparent carelessness of the indolent and fatigued one, which might superficially appear as indifference (acedia, carelessness), is only a mask for an intense recoil from faceless existence: it is a prereflective ethical refusal. This refusal to enter an impersonal existence perceived as hostile ossifies into the dread of being. Thus Levinas's analysis revisits and implicitly questions the theology of the sin of sloth. Often an object of disparagement and ridicule, sloth has always been understood as a visible symptom of more serious conditions. The hesitation in front of Being as impersonal existence indicates a dark intimation about this Being and thus questions the truth of ontotheology: the ground of Being appears as an otherness, an other than Being that is evil and not simply nothing.

MAINE DE BIRAN: A THREE-STAGED EXPERIMENT IN THE THERAPEUTICS OF MELANCHOLY

The philosophical work of François-Pierre-Gonthier, known as Maine de Biran (1766–1824), emerges out of a natural attunement to melancholy, and the stages of his philosophy are experiments in living and thinking melancholy. At a time when Kant was "purifying" the faculties of reason, understanding, and imagination, Biran was inventing and verifying their adequacy as instruments of healing his melancholic being. His threefold philosophical experiment is proto-Hegelian: the shared impact on their thought of Jakob Böhme may explain the similarity in their respective trajectories of the self out of nature into freedom (though this filiation or influence is not documented with respect to Biran). He begins with a study of originary passivity and self-affection in which the self is immersed and conditioned by the body. During this moment the self and the organic are indistinguishably one; for Biran, this is understood as a pathetic or pathos-filled immanence. The second moment of coming to self-awareness articulates Biran's most properly original thought: the emergence of the self in its effort against the resistant inner other. In this primordial effort of the will, the self gives birth to itself. It is this philosophy of the will that has assured him the title of a French Jakob Böhme. The pathos of the melancholic self is never completely removed, as the effort must be constantly repeated to prevent a falling back into pathetic immanence. Fatigued by the relentless effort to be, melancholic Biran leaves behind the second moment in search of a different philosophical therapeutic. He undergoes a religious *metanoia* and accepts grace as the only salvific remedy. Thus the third moment of his confrontation with melancholy is the abandonment of the self to the divine, a gesture taken up in thought as a philosophy of grace.

BIRAN'S FIRST THINKING EXPERIMENT: ORIGINAL TRUTH AS IMMEDIATE SELF-PRESENCE

Michel Henry celebrates Maine de Biran, the mysterious thinker who wrote during the French Revolution as one of the "founders of a phenomenological science of human reality," and the only philosopher in the history of human reflection to think "our body" as a subjective body.[23] The fundamental intention that has informed Henry's thought is the study of human reality as one of contingency, corporality, finitude, the absurd, these "central phenomena" that have not been honored by either objective or subjective idealism.[24] In his quest to understand "what a human being is, this being whose existence is circumscribed by contingency, finitude, the absurd," Henry proposes Biran's answer, "a body that is already an I" (11). He explains that "our body is not primordially a biological body, neither a living body, nor a human body," and he endorses Biran's fundamental thesis that "our body is subjective, the self itself": our body belongs to a radically different region, which is that of absolute subjectivity (15).

Henry retraces Biran's steps in the discovery of the subjective body via a phenomenological ontology. In order to account for the life of the self, Biran introduces what Henry calls "ontological dualism," that is, two incommensurable orders of being: the being of nature and the being of the self (20). Both are given to us phenomenologically, the former in Baconian observation, the latter in inner experience. Biran's novelty resides in a departure from the established ways of traditional psychology; he considers that metaphysics is actually psychology and replaces classical reflection, given in inner transcendent experience, with an inner transcendental experience whose organ is not the eye of reflection but the transcendental inner sense (21–23). External nature and inner self stand for the two heterogeneous ontological orders, which are known by equally incommensurable organs and methods. While Biran's dichotomization of reality is as rigorous as that of Descartes or Pascal, the region of the self is circumscribed and defined quite differently—as *immanence*—and it is in this difference that Henry intends to ground his own phenomenological-existential undertaking. Biran labors his way through both idealism and materialism. The inner experience is not given in intellectual intuition, nor is it received by the intellect and reflected upon. At the same time, the self is not a pure, abstract thought thinking itself: the Cartesian ego is a creation of docetic imagination. The organ experiencing inner transcendental experience is the transcendental inner sense. Henry follows Biran toward a more originary source of the self, the ground of all intentionalities as well as all the faculties (22).

Since transcendental inner experience is the medium where truth originally emerges, subjectivity comes to be conceived as original truth. Original truth belongs to a sphere of absolute certainty that "belongs to the structure of experience itself to which its content is given in the absolute transparency, resulting from the absence of all distance, of immanence." He attests that Biran's entire work is "nothing but a vast phenomenological reduction" in which the primitive fact, given in absolute certainty, is the only one still standing (23). The Cartesian cogito is secondary, although first among intuitive judgments whose certitude is only a reflection of the absolute certitude of the primitive fact on which all the others are founded (29). Henry concludes that Biran's fundamental intuition is immediate self-presence: the essence of selfhood is the interiority of immediate self-presence (53). The absolute immanence of the self is not an abstraction, a generic term, but life itself, which in its immanent absolute certainty is also original truth (57).

BIRAN'S SECOND THINKING EXPERIMENT: GENESIS OF THE SELF IN EFFORT

For Biran this primordial state of immediacy and immanence emerges only in and through the experience of effort. The concomitant genesis of self and world in the experience of effort given through phenomenological transcendental reduction gives rise to Biran's original ontological dualism: the primordial fact is a primordial duality, a primordial opposition between the being of the world and the self as a being of effort, "the feeling of the self engaged in effort is the primitive fact of knowledge" and the condition for the possibility of all knowledge; the event of the genesis of the self as this self whose reality does not need to be proven, is the foundation of all proofs and factual truths (49, 52, 56). Biran is, Henry insists, the only philosopher to have conceived the ontology of subjectivity as an ontology of *effort*. By his ontology of subjectivity and his interpretation of original transcendental effort that knows itself as *subjective body*, Biran opposes both Cartesian rationalism and Humean empiricism (91). Whereas Descartes established the certainty of the being of pure, abstract thinking substance, Biran thinks the ontology of effort, the subject of which is the ego of the cogito (74). The Cartesian ego could think ideas and be modified therein, but actual movement belonged to a separate heterogeneous order of being. Descartes's dualism is thus the focus of Biran's critique.

In the attempt to understand the nature of movement, its intentionality, its relation to the idea of movement and to subjective agency, Biran thinks the subjective body that is phenomenologically given in transcendental inner experience. Movement is known in a primitive cognition that can explain the unreflective, instinctive use of the body, "Movement is us, we are these movements, the being of movement is the being of subjectivity itself" (75). This concrete subjectivity—neither abstract, nor intellectual, nor contemplative—is the body, a body that transforms the world. Henry explains:

> Thus the self acts directly on the world. It does not act through the intermediary of a body, it does not use in its movements any means; it is itself this body, this movement. Self, body, movement—they are only one and the same thing and this thing is very real; it does not dissolve in the night of the unconscious or in the void of nothingness, it is a being, and this being is all that is given to us in transcendental inner experience, it is the being of the self itself. (83)

Similarly, it is participation of the original subjective body in the sphere of absolute immanence that solves or rather dissolves Hume's conundrum of causality by changing the empirical ontological horizon (85). The main distinction between Biran and Hume is the opposed role of movement and body, hence also of effort. For Biran, "the being of subjective movement is the immediate revelation of the self to itself without the mediation of a phenomenological distance in the medium of transcendent being" (98). Movement becomes the locus where original truth occurs, being the most profound intentionality of the life of the self (99, 101). Since intentionality intends its object, movement and its transcendent object are phenomenologically coinstitutive. The transcendent object of original primordial movement is the being of the world, which emerges as a resistant other to our movement's effort. Henry notes Biran's existentialism avant la lettre, "What we think depends on what we are . . . the idea is not the fundament of the real; to the contrary, it could not even be affirmed except by a philosophy that conceives of a real capable of being at the origin of our ideas, since it is the place where truth originally realizes itself."[25] The original encounter of our body and movement with the object's resistance in effort is a *figura* for all possible encounters of our transcendental subjectivity with transcendent being. In the moment of encounter we gain certitude of both our self and the world.[26] The subjective being of effort, our embodied self, is thus the locus of all origins and the bearer of all our certitudes of the reality of self and world.

BIRAN'S MELANCHOLY

According to Henry, "Biran's personal experience is one of alienation. It is the experience of an affective life constantly changing, of a mood more often sad than joyful, whose modifications seem independent of the will of the self who suffers them. This servitude is doubly painful" (213–14). Indeed, Maine de Biran is an acedic melancholic whose philosophy represents successive attempts to come to terms with his condition and achieve self-transcendence. Fatigue, *taedium vitae*, ennui, profound boredom, discomfort, discouragement, despair—these moods make up his fundamental ontological attunement (214). They indicate, as Le Senne observed in the case of indolent melancholics, an *otherness* at the core of his being, a substantial evil as an original ground in which the self is rooted, and which may consume it.

Biran's relentless intellectual effort to save himself from annihilation in the chaos of inchoate affectivity and meontological mood, in effect translates his melancholy into a sui generis philosophical reflection. He experiences and describes the pathos of the "more originary" ontology, that of the passivity of the self toward the body and the organic; Henry identifies this original passivity as the foundation of subjectivity, one beneath and beyond the dichotomy of activity and passivity. In Biran's case, though, the movement out of original melancholic passivity into the active verticality of the self in effort must be understood as therapeutic. Hence, in Biran's phenomenological description of the genesis of the self, effort is the labor of the self to give birth to itself out of original acedic immanence. As such, it is always a tremendous primordial event, for just as Levinas affirmed, the triumph over morning indolence is a triumph over impersonal Being. Dualism is not, as Henry thinks, a "dead feature" of Biran's thought. On the contrary, for Biran the individual becomes himself precisely through the effort of the will, transcending the immanence of primordial melancholy and becoming receptive to organic life, instinct, and sensibility. He identifies self and effort because, in his case, they are coeval.

Henry questions Biran's distinction between the self, identified with active volition, and the passions, impressions, affections, imagination, which are relegated to an independent, more originary region. This "more originary" foundation is, for Henry, the "essence of life, the structure of the being of the ego, which should not be limited to the active modes of volition"(222). He concludes that "our experience of passivity is an original experience," and repeatedly laments the absence of a positive ontology of passivity in Biran. The most serious difficulty into which this absence pushes Biran's thought is: when not actively engaged in the effort of self-genesis, the self reverts to nothing (232). As a matter of fact, here Henry is right in the case of melancholic Biran, for in the absence of effort, the self's disintegration is a real threat. The self "unbecomes," becomes nothing: it experiences the Pascalian abysmal ennui or the Hegelian regression to nature.

BIRAN'S THIRD THINKING EXPERIMENT: THE THERAPEUTICS OF GRACE

Passivity returns in Biran's late philosophy as a phenomenology of grace. At this third and last stage, the self suffers a sublime pathos: the self is disburdened from itself by a heterogeneous reality, this time not organic but divine (240). Biran's self emerges from the originary passivity toward the organic, generates itself through willful effort, only to move into passivity toward the divine. Henry wonders how it is possible to reconcile an active philosophy of the will with the irruption of a transcendent absolute in which all personal reality dissolves (241). He concludes that Biranism is best understood as a single intuition that traverses all the stages and modes of the self, from the early philosophy of passivity through the organic to the last philosophy of passivity to grace. The ontological structure of absolute subjectivity ends up revealing an original ontological passivity.

HENRY: MELANCHOLY AS THE GROUND OF THE SELF

Immanent passivity as ultimate ground of being and of absolute knowing is Henry's own theme, which he finds implied in Biran's passive modes of sensible life, as well as in the passivity to grace (243). It is the intuition of this passivity to grace that Henry recognizes in both Biran and Meister Eckhart, wherein metaphysics is fused with psychology, and self-knowledge coincides with knowledge of God.

A philosophy that has risen to the concept of absolute subjectivity has thereby founded the possibility of absolute cognition. It is the implicit or explicit recognition of such cognition as an adequate possibility of the human being that brought Biran to the idea of a rapport, or perhaps even a unity, between knowledge of the self and knowledge of the divine. One finds in Eckhart an explicit theory of the identity of self-knowledge and divine knowledge. (250)

Henry announces his own philosophical quest for a new philosophy of life via an ontological elucidation of subjectivity and the body. Building on the Biranian intuition of the subjective body, Henry thinks further the pathos of self-affection. He opposes the agonistic dualism that defines Western cultural tradition, the origin of which he traces back to Hellenism, and traces of which he detects in classical philosophy, in Kantian and Hegelian idealism, and also in empiricism and naturalism. In its mainstream interpretations, Christian anthropology and common unreflective opinion alike partake of a Gnostic vision: the dichotomy of matter and spirit, body and mind, in which the former is to be subordinated or transcended qua inferior, is for Henry the origin of all iniquities toward the body. This infecting Gnosticism has been the basis of a distorted anthropological vision with dire effects in multiple domains, ranging from metaphysics to ethics.

Like Heidegger, Henry searches for a more originary beginning, in this case, for a more primordial ground of self-knowledge. He discovers this primordial ground in the subjectivity in and for itself, revealed to itself in the immanence of the subjective body. Thus Henry mediates between Maine de Biran and Johann Gottlieb Fichte: the body is already subjective and subjectivity is always embodied. In transcendental inner experience, subjectivity gives itself to itself in self-affection. Because the human reality is "I am my body" rather than "I have a body," ontological elucidation of the subjective nature of the body and of absolute subjectivity are intertwined. Subjectivity comes embodied, it is not known first as an impersonal universal entity, nor as a contentless abstract void, a nothing face to face with transcendent being. More primordially, subjectivity is life: the life of the subjective body, life revealed in a sphere of absolute immanence. The transcendent element is the "dead" element to be maintained in life by something more concrete, by life itself (258). As contrasted with the transcendent, the transcendental appears as an "ontological region perfectly determined and absolutely concrete rather than a pure nothing, the leftover remainder after withdrawal from reality" (257). Henry insists that subjectivity "has always already a primordial content which has not been constituted by transcendent being, that is, the content of the internal transcendental experience which gives life its irreducible primordial ontological density, a density that subsists even when life collapses in despair" (269).

This primordial immanence, lived in the body prior to any relation to the transcendent element, gives itself as the ground for the possibility of absolute knowing. This bodily self-knowing is a knowing of life and of subjectivity, a knowing that always involves the concrete individual, the "I," which cannot be given or received otherwise. This understanding of primordial embodied subjective life carries enormous importance for Henry because human nature itself is at stake. Understanding of human nature is profoundly altered by a Gnostic-Cartesian vision in which the body is a transcendent object confronting consciousness as its other. Within this vision, embodiment appears as a paradox, a "mysterious synthetic addition" that establishes an opposition between the "pure nothing of consciousness and being." The phenomenon of embodiment can be comprehended only in a vision in which "consciousness is not the void of nonbeing and the body is not an object." The being of the body is not a "being there," an objective determination whose finitude, contingency, and absurdity are revealed to man qua metaphysical being. For Hegel and for the entirety of classical philosophy, Henry notes, life is exterior to the self, is subjectivity's other, and is thus pure negation. This presupposition is an abomination: he maintains that life cannot be transcended, surpassed, overcome, sublated, since "human life emerges as a serious matter which no pure spirit has the right to overcome" (261).

HENRY: THE PATHETIC SUBJECTIVE BODY

Henry argues against the reductive interpretation of sin that assimilates sin with the body. Certainly, this is only a superficial reading of what the phrase "sin of the flesh" means. Sin and resurrection are for Henry existential historical modes or intentionalities, both belonging to the ontological corpus, the absolute subjective body. They correlate with two divergent metaphysical destinies of the subjective body—damnation and redemption—since, as Henry observes, "the bodies will be judged" (306). The body as a mode of life reveals a specific intentionality and therefore implies an existential perspective rather than an ontological one. Neither sin nor redemption is an ontological structure. Henry explains that "for Christianity the flesh and the spirit designate specific modes of existence: two intentionalities belonging to the same ontological sphere, that of absolute subjectivity" (288). Paradoxically, the imperfection of finitude and sin belongs to a life that is absolute, an existence that remains infinite. Ontologically existence belongs to a milieu of radical immanence (303). Henry's fundamental thesis as to the primordiality of immanence is thus justified, "More originary than the phenomenon of transcendence, prior to it in some way, is that of immanence in which transcendence ultimately finds its condition of ontological possibility" (304).

As a complement to Heidegger's search for a more originary beginning, which he finds in the Schellingian nought, Henry's project culminates with an alternate ontological reversal. For him the more originary beginning is the pathetic subjective body. This originary beginning has been hidden and forgotten, a forgetting that began with the Greeks and was subsequently deepened by modernity. The forgotten primordial ontological fact of subjective immanence implies the absoluteness of human existence lived as the life of the subjective body. Henry indicates Maine de Biran as the only philosopher whose thought has reached this far. Because the idea that corporeal existence is an absolute existence is opposed to the entire Western cultural tradition, once admitted it has the potential to modify an entire Weltanschauung. Modern naturalism, which maintains the naturalness of the body and its functions, misunderstands the essence of the human body as a first-person subjective body. Naturalism, idealism, empiricism are all distortions produced by a diremption at the heart of being, sundering the spirit from the natural impersonal body. Henry, by contrast, insists that the self and the body can never be separated: the bodies will be judged (306). He therefore elaborates his ontology of immanent pathetic affectivity as the more primordial beginning and as the original revelation of the absolute.

NOTES

1. Saint Augustine, *The Confessions of Saint Augustine*, trans. Rex Warner (New York: Pelican, 1963), book 11, chapters 1–31.

2. Immanuel Kant, *Critique of Pure Reason*, trans. J. M. D. Meiklejohn (Buffalo, N.Y.: Prometheus, 1990), 28–43; hereafter cited in the text as *Reason*.

3. Kant, *Critique of Pure Reason*: "Time is the formal condition a priori of all phenomena whatsoever. Space, as the pure form of external intuition, is limited as a condition a priori to external phenomena alone. On the other hand, because all representations, whether they have or not external things for their objects, still in themselves, as representations of the mind, belong to our internal state; and because this internal state is subject to the formal condition of the internal intuition, that is, to time—time is a condition a priori of all phenomena whatsoever—the immediate condition of all internal and thereby the mediate condition of all external phenomena" (30).

4. John Sallis notes in *Chorology* the Kantian appropriation of Plato's three ontological primordial kinds, and suggests that the transcendental schemata is a reinscription of *chora* (154–55).

5. Kant, *Critique of Pure Reason*: "*Time*, no doubt, is something real, that is, it is the real form of our internal intuition. It therefore has subjective reality, in reference to our internal experience, that is, I have really the representation of *time*, and of my determinations therein. *Time* therefore is not to be regarded as an object, but as a

mode of representation of myself as an object. The empirical reality of *time*, therefore, remains as the condition of all our experience" (32).

6. Kant, *Critique of Pure Reason*: "These sources of knowledge (i.e. Time and Space) being merely conditions of our sensibility do therefore and as such strictly determine their own range and purpose in that they do not and cannot present objects as things-in-themselves but are applicable to them solely in so far as they are considered as sensuous phenomena. The sphere of phenomena is the only sphere of their validity, and if we venture out of this, no further objective use can be made of them" (33).

7. Kant, *Critique of Pure Reason*: "Supposing that we should carry our empirical intuition even to the very highest degree of clearness, we should not thereby advance one step nearer to a knowledge of the constitution of objects as things-in-themselves. For we could only, at best, arrive at a complete cognition of our own mode of intuition, that is, of our sensibility, and this always under the conditions originally attaching to the subject, namely the conditions of space and time" (36).

8. Kant, *Anthropology* (chapter 5, n. 10): "There is a disgust of one's existence, which arises from the emptiness of mind toward the sensations for which the mind continually strives, that is caused by *boredom*. One grows weary of all inactivity, that is, the weariness of all occupation that could be called work, and which could drive away that disgust because it is associated with hardship, a highly contrary feeling, whose original cause is none other than a natural inclination toward being at ease (rest without preceding fatigue). This inclination, however, is deceptive even with regard to the purpose which the human reason ordains for man, namely, self-contentment, when *he does nothing at all* (when he vegetates without purpose), because he assumes that he can do nothing evil in this state. This inclination toward further self-deception (which can be achieved by concentrating one's attention on the fine arts or, more effectively, through social activities) is called *passing the time (Tempus fallere)*. Here indeed the expression signifies the intention, which is really an inclination to self-deception through lazy inactivity, when the mind amuses itself by dallying with the fine arts, or when at least a mental cultivation is effected by a peaceful effort, which is pointless in itself; otherwise it would be called *killing time*. Force accomplishes nothing in the struggle against sensuality in the inclinations; instead we must outwit these inclinations, and, as Swift says, in order to save the ship, we must fling an empty tub to a whale, so that he can play with it" (68).

9. Martin Heidegger, *Fundamental Concepts of Metaphysics* (introduction, n. 1); hereafter cited in the text as *Fundamental*.

10. Heidegger, *Being and Time*: "What we indicate ontologically by the term state of mind is ontically the most familiar and everyday sort of thing; our mood, our being attuned. Prior to all psychology of moods, a field which in any case still lies fallow, it is necessary to see this phenomenon as a fundamental existential(e) and to outline its structure" (173). For more on the meaning of the term *existential(e)*, see "Being in the World in General as the Basic State of Dasein," in *Being and Time*, part 1, division 1, §12.

11. Heidegger, *Being and Time*: "Dasein always has some mood. . . . A mood makes manifest how one is and how one is faring. In this how one is having a mood brings

Being to its there. The being of the there is disclosive moodwise in its that it is. In an ontico-existential sense, Dasein for the most part evades the Being which is disclosed in the mood. . . . In the evasion itself there is something disclosed" (173–77).

12. Martin Heidegger, *Being and Time*, trans. John Macquarrie and Edward Robinson (San Francisco: Harper & Row, 1962); hereafter cited in the text as *Being*.

13. Richard Kearney, "Melancholy: Between Gods and Monsters," in *Strangers, Gods, and Monsters*, 167–68.

14. Heidegger, *Being and Time:* "Once when Care was crossing a river, she saw some clay; she thoughtfully took up a piece and began to shape it. While she was meditating on what she had made, Jupiter came by. Care asked him to give it spirit and this he gladly granted. But when she wanted her name to be bestowed upon it, he forbade this, and demanded that it be given his name instead. While Care and Jupiter were disputing, Earth arose and desired that her own name be conferred on the creature since she had furnished it with part of her body. They asked Saturn to be their arbiter and he made the following decision which seemed a just one, "Since you, Jupiter have given its spirit, you shall receive its spirit at its death; and since you, Earth have given its body, you shall receive its body. But since Care first shaped this creature, she shall possess it as long as it lives. And because there is now a dispute among you as to its name, let it be called *homo* for it is made out of *humus* (earth)" (242 [198], §42).

15. Richard Kearney, "Last Gods and Final Things," in *Strangers, Gods, and Monsters*, 213–28, quote on 217 n. 14. The three texts are *Beiträge zur Philosophie* (1936–38; Gesamtausgabe 65, Frankfurt, 1989); *Besinnung* (1938–39; Gesamtausgabe 66, Frankfurt, 1997), and *Die Geschichte des Seyns* (1938–40; Gesamtausgabe 69, Frankfurt, 1998); the first two are published in English as *Contributions to Philosophy (From Enowning)* and *Mindfulness*, respectively; a translation of the third, *History of Being*, is in preparation. Kearney indicates his debt to Jean Greisch's analysis of the theme of the last God in several studies, one of them being "La pauvreté du dernier dieu de Heidegger," in *Post-Theism: Reframing the Judeo-Christian Tradition*, ed. H. Krop, A. Molenddijk, and H. de Vries (Leuven: Peeters, 2000).

16. Kearney, *Strangers, Gods, and Monsters*, 218–19, citing Heidegger, *Besinnung*, Gesamtausgabe 66 (n. 23 above), 239.

17. Martin Heidegger, "What is Metaphysics?" in *Basic writings*, ed. David F. Krell (San Francisco: Harper, 1977), 111, cited in Kearney, *Strangers, Gods, and Monsters*, 221.

18. Richard Kearney, *The God Who May Be: A Hermeneutics of Religion* (Bloomington: Indiana University Press, 2001).

19. John D. Caputo, *The Mystical Element in Heidegger's Thought* (New York: Fordham University Press, 1986).

20. Martin Heidegger, "From the First to the Other Beginning: Negation" in *Contributions to Philosophy (From Enowing)*, trans. Parvis Emad and Kenneth Maly (Bloomington: Indiana University Press, 1989), 124–31, §89–§92. As Sallis observes in *Chorology*, in Plato's *Timaeus*, due to the logic of narrative, the first beginning is the beginning of creation, the second beginning precedes creation and refers to *chora*. Schelling recasts Plato's beginnings as God's existence and God's nature or basis.

21. Martin Heidegger, *Schelling's Treatise on the Essence of Human Freedom*, trans. Joan Stambaugh (Athens: Ohio University Press, 1985), 106–110, 121, 124, 157, 161–63.

22. Emmanuel Levinas, *Existence and Existents* (introduction, n. 1). All further quotations of Levinas are from this work.

23. Michel Henry, *Philosophie et phénoménologie du corps* (introduction, n. 1), 12; all translations are mine. An English translation by Girard Etzkorn is available under the title, *Philosophy and Phenomenology of the Body* (The Hague: Nihhoff, 1975).

24. Henry, *Philosophie et phénoménologie du corps*: "The philosophy of subjectivity must give way to a realism and an existentialism that would begin with central phenomena such as 'situation,' 'corporality,' 'incarnation,' and that would have at least the courage to recognize and study human reality and what is implied by this condition, i.e., contingence, finitude, the absurd" (10).

25. Henry, *Philosophie et phénoménologie du corps*: "What we think depends on what we are . . . the idea is not the fundament of the real, on the contrary, it could not even be affirmed except by a philosophy that conceives of a real capable to be at the origin of our ideas, since it is the place where truth originally realizes itself" (102).

26. Henry, *Philosophie et phénoménologie du corps*: "Truth inhabits the interior man and in our case we must say that truth is the subjective being of the movement which carries in it our certitude of the reality of the world" (105).

Chapter 8

Psychic Pathos, Creativity, and Insight

The first generation of psychiatrists who introduced phenomenology into psychiatry—including Eugene Minkowski (1885–1972), Erwin W. Straus (1891–1975), Viktor Emil von Gebsattel (1883–1976), Ludwig Binswanger, and Hubertus Tellenbach (1914–1994)—were interested in time in relation to the melancholic self. Melancholic symptoms were interpreted in connection with the temporal distortion provoked by the fundamental depressive event and the alteration of the personality. In spite of methodological differences, the theme of time constituted their common interest. In 1922 Minkowski introduced the phenomenological method into psychiatry in his study of schizophrenic melancholy. His starting point was the vaguely defined Bergsonian notion of élan vital, analogous to Le Senne's sensibility that orients life toward the future, thus making time relevant for the study of the structure of human personality. Since this temporal orientation toward the future is of absolute importance for human life, the structures of personality and time were viewed as inseparable, such that any modification in the élan vital provokes structural modifications in both the perception of time and personality. Once the élan vital weakens, the future collapses and becomes a hostile power that provokes suffering: the cause of the melancholic delirium of guilt and persecution seemed to be connected with this modification of temporality. The closing of the future, which was also Le Senne's explanation of melancholy, is the first structural moment of mental malady: the melancholic comports himself as one without a future, condemned to death. Minkowski terms this modification of temporality the "hostile ground" or "power of the terrible" that is unleashed in melancholy (44). Straus focuses on the lived psychic sphere at the mundane level and considers the psychic and the biological as analogical spheres. Here again, the original moment is the phenomenon of inhibition that provokes the modification of inner temporality (45).

Binswanger (1881–1966), for whom Husserl and Heidegger are the two most significant influences, is considered one of the most interesting thinkers in the field of philosophical psychiatry for having developed a transcendental phenomenology of intentional consciousness, thereby complementing the descriptive naturalist studies that limit themselves to the content of lived experience, such as those of Jaspers, von Gebsattel, and Minkowski.[1] Heidegger's temporalization of profoundly bored Dasein finds a complement in Ludwig Binswanger's application of phenomenology to the psychiatric study of melancholy that he presents in *Melancholie und Manie* (1960).[2] Once he makes clear that pathological melancholy should be distinguished from existential anxiety, Binswanger engages in a careful analysis of the condition in the dialectics of the phenomenological selves in relation to temporality. In his contribution to psychiatric methodology he intends to describe mental diseases and their particular constitution of being. For him, phenomenology does not mean the descriptive phenomenology of subjective manifestations of psychic life, as is the case of Jaspers, but is rather to be understood in terms of pure transcendental Husserlian phenomenology. He refrains from using the term "depression" since, he explains, its vague multiple significations disqualify it as a starting point for phenomenological analysis. Nor will the term "black humor" (*Schwermut*) be used, since he considers that black humor has a wider semantic field as a Dasein's existentiel. His analysis involves both Husserlian phenomenological doctrine of intentionality and Heideggerian Dasein analysis.

BINSWANGER: MELANCHOLY AS NATURE'S SUI GENERIS CREATIVE THERAPEUTIC

According to Binswanger, psychoses are nature's experiments, and as such are phenomenologically significant since they make visible the otherwise inaccessible transcendental operations.[3] This enables the phenomenologist to discover the events responsible for the failure of Dasein in the melancholic malady. The guiding formula throughout the analysis is Husserl's statement that "the real world is nothing but the constantly restated presupposition that experience will continue to unfold in the same constitutive style."[4] Binswanger explains that this presupposition is a transcendental presupposition and that the phenomenological *epokhē* makes visible the constitutive moments of our world. This implies a return from consideration of the constituted world back to its constitutive structural moments; in other words, it implies sending each constituted "object"—temporal objects in the form of past, present, future, as well as psychic intentional objects in the form of joy, pain, judgments, desires, feelings—back to their essential form of intentionality. Binswanger insists that his method belongs to the science of transcendental phenomenology—which is neither "a psychology of inner experience," nor one of lived experience (*Erlebnispsychologie*), nor a phenomenology of lived time or space (23). He believes that the originality of his approach consists in observation of the specific transcendental modification in melancholy, that is, the dissolution of the constitutive connections inside the transcendental structural order. Thus he adopts a pure transcendental phenomenological position in opposition to any psychological, natural, naïve attitude. In adopting the transcendental attitude, Binswanger is not interested in clinical analysis of the structures of personality, nor in temperamental and hereditary morphological constitution, nor in the distinction between exogenous and endogenous malady (30–31). The only question that he poses is: What has happened to Dasein's transcendental occurring?

In order to answer this fundamental question, Binswanger appeals to Husserl. In Husserl's *On the Phenomenology of the Consciousness of Internal Time* (1928), time is understood through intentionality; that is, future, past, and present are understood through the intentional-structural moments that constitute them: *protentio, retention*, and *praesentatio*, respectively. Their normal interdependent functioning grounds the *Worüber* (*à propos de*), the "about what" or point of the present theme or context. In the case of melancholy, the three temporalized intentionalities and their interactions develop "deficient modes." Binswanger attempts to understand the alterations affecting the intentional structure of temporality without appealing to practical knowledge or causal and genetic derivation (32). This entitles him to affirm the primordiality of the transcendental dissolution of constitutive temporal articulation in melancholy.

> It is because melancholic dysthymia, as the "isolated capacity to suffer," represents the dissolution of the constitutive connections of the natural experience, that the particular melancholic theme can take over the entire psychic space and resist all reassurances and consolations. The melancholic inaccessibility to consolation and comfort can be understood as a consequence of the extended alteration of the transcendental constitution whose result is the isolation of the capacity for suffering detached from the totality of Dasein's possibilities of being. (24)

In melancholy, this dissolution provokes extreme pusillanimity and reaches a delirium of self-abnegation, suffering of being-in-the-world, withdrawal from the world, stagnation of thought and activity, interruption of all existential continuity. The alteration of futural intentionality disfigures both the continuity of temporalization and of thought, since alteration of the relation to the future affects one's relation to both the past and the present. Binswanger distances himself from the psychopathological attitude and explanations based on biological derivation and vital inhibition in order to discover the a priori structure of temporal intentionality. Thus melancholic confession is not understood as self-explanation but rather as the beginning of a hermeneutic of the melancholic mode of being, of what Dasein or Life tells about itself in melancholy (53).

Binswanger attempts to understand the a priori essence or eidos of the melancholic self-reproach, "if only . . . then," which can either take the form of particular delirious ideas of transgression, fault, and sin, or of melancholic delirium in general (41–42). The grammatical structure of self-reproach provides an important indication: the conditional form of "if only . . . then" can present only empty possibilities, "Here what is free possibility withdraws into the past. That means that the protentive constitutive acts must become empty intentions. Thereby, *protentio* becomes autonomous to the extent to which it has no longer a present relevance nor anything else to produce except the temporal objectivity of a void future" (33). What emerges in melancholy is a failure in the intentional operations that constitute temporal objectivity, a failure whose consequence is the loosening of the temporal texture and the emergence of defective regions within it (47). The result of this failure consists in empty intentions and lamentations that make up the melancholic style of loss (49, 51). Binswanger emphasizes that the theme of melancholic loss is independent of any specific or mundane content, and does not depend on or follow melancholic humor. On the contrary, melancholic humor is already an expression of experience according to the style of loss. What occurs in melancholy is a collapse of intentional acts constitutive of temporal synthesis, a collapse that limits the transcendental possibilities of the self. The subjective experience of this limitation becomes manifest in the threefold melancholic delirium of ruin, illness, and guilt as the fundamental melancholic theme of loss (52). What becomes visible in the melancholic mode of Dasein is "the narrowing of the great themes of Dasein in its reference to the I, unified in the fundamental melancholic theme of loss. This fundamental theme, in its turn, cannot be separated from the themes passionately described, of atrocious suffering, unbearable anguish, and irresistible suicidal drive" (54). The confusion occurring between *protentio, retentio*, and *praesentatio* is linked to suffering, anguish, and suicide. The melancholic conceives suicide not as a failure or withdrawal from life and resignation; on the contrary, suicide is the present *à propos de*, the final mode in which Dasein is able to constitute itself sufficiently to make an unequivocal decision. Suicide may be replaced by a spontaneously emergent present meaning (see Hegel's cases of surprising healing, or Le Senne's *demon of perversity*). The event confirms that as long as Dasein is able to find an object of feeling that can lighten up the future, it will grasp at this possibility, thus temporalizing itself, and will remain alive (59–60).

Thus Binswanger's original thesis is that melancholic anxiety, in loosening the weave of intentional threads constitutive of temporal objectivity, is not a vestigial phenomenon of the psyche but rather an experiment of nature in which nature creates something new, sui generis—as opposed to unearthing something primordial—in order to aid itself when the course of normal processes is altered (61). Melancholy is not the emergence of human primordial anxiety but precisely a relinquishing of the conditions constitutive of ordinary experience. Faced with the disintegration of normal constitutive links, human nature tries to create new connections in melancholic self-accusation, guilt, and loss in general. Binswanger finds that Husserl's doctrine of the pure ego provides the basis for comprehension of the essence of melancholy. In his phenomenological analysis, patterned after Husserl, it is in the functioning, or rather malfunctioning, of the three egos—empirical, transcendental, and pure—that Binswanger detects the melancholic disorder. The pure ego is the key to his analysis because it is the pure ego that is charged with the constitution of the ego totality. Binswanger made visible both the empirical "I" through case observation and the transcendental "I" in the turn toward the structural elements constitutive of consciousness; the element missing, he finds, is the pure ego, the sine qua non moment of Husserlian phenomenology, "The Pure Ego constitutes the unity of the mundane-empirical 'I' and the transcendental 'I,' as constitutive experience is the unity of mundane-empirical experience and transcendental experience" (117–18). In contrast to German idealism, particularly Fichte, Husserl's pure ego lives only in unity with the empirical I and the transcendental I. Hence Binswanger endeavors to characterize the place of melancholy within consciousness from the perspective of this doctrine of the pure ego. He begins by comparing melancholic with nonmelancholic experience. In the latter, unreflective and unproblematic, the pure ego performs its constitutive and unifying function with ease. In the melancholic mode, by contrast, the pure ego is distressed and constrained, its constitutive function is hindered and questioned. Binswanger believes that melancholy indicates an alteration in the constitution of the pure ego, its perplexity and despair as a result of failing to fulfill its task. He explains, "Since the inferior authorities of experience failed in their task, the superior authority is perplexed: it cannot but despair in the face of the troubles of empirical and transcendental experiences. In the totality of experience, this negative moment precipitates itself as 'dysthymie,' i.e., melancholic depression, anxiety, and torment, or manic withdrawal from the task of total control over self and world" (119).

If in melancholy, however, the function of the pure ego is jeopardized and questioned, it is never completely annulled; the pure ego, though weakened, makes an effort to fulfill its role in the totality of experience, since only the regulatory function is impaired, not "the function of constituting the belonging-to-me of the I am" (120–21). This belonging-to-me constitutes the critical aspect of melancholic distress, since the self in pain is mine, it is "I" myself. Binswanger emphasizes, "The empirical I, the individual, would not consume himself in suffering and torments . . . if in the fact of suffering and evasion, the 'I' would not maintain itself. When there is no longer a pure ego, no longer the constitution of 'belonging-to-me,' then there is no longer either any painful overwhelming (or joyous evasion from the I) of the I" (121). The belonging-to-me guarantees both the pain and the sense of self, and this is the crucial articulation of Binswanger's phenomenological analysis: melancholic suffering makes visible both the impotence and the power of the pure ego. Indeed, "this dead end for the pure ego is not understood only as lack or impotence but also as the power of affirming the I in the midst of the chaos of melancholic experience, a power of affirming the I in suffering that persists even in the decision of suicide" (121).

The possibility of healing resides in the preservation of the belonging-to-me assured by the distressed yet functioning pure ego, since "the pure ego is still awake above this writhing and breaking loose." Indeed, the melancholic delirium of loss is the expression of the pure ego's despair when confronted with its failure in the task of constituting the totality of experience. The empirical ego suffers from the pure ego's withdrawal. This suffering is a call back to the totality of experience under the guidance of the pure ego. Binswanger concludes that the economy of the triad of egos is circular, refusing to establish a causal relation among the events of melancholic consciousness, the only possible relation being one of cofunctioning among the three egos. As a mode of consciousness, melancholy operates in the absence of the control or guidance of the pure ego and its regulatory function. The pure ego's partial relinquishing of the regulatory function results in its withdrawal from the constitution of experience. Melancholy is not historically or biographically conditioned, in other words, it is not an existential condition; it is rather an ontological creation of Dasein.[5]

JASPERS: MELANCHOLY AS CONDITION
FOR ARTISTIC CREATIVITY

In contrast to Binswanger's approach, Karl Jaspers's theoretical presuppositions do not allow for a rigorous classification or definition of melancholy as a sui generis morbid entity. From the beginning of his impressive *General*

Psychopathology, Jaspers clarifies his theoretical and methodological positions: his existentialist respect for the mysterious and incomprehensible whole of the object of research that is the psyche, as well as for the uniqueness of the individual case—which cannot be the object of scientific approach in itself but only in its manifestations—makes any definition inadequate.[6] Indeed, Jaspers refrains on principle from presenting the main psychoses—epilepsy, manic-depression, and schizophrenia—as complete entities (or, as he writes, "classified plants in the botanical album"); in fact, aspects or hypostases of these pathologies will appear individually, since the whole will always be a unique and unclassifiable case. Melancholy and schizophrenia appear fragmented into their principal components— complexes or hypostases—that can form different morbid entities according to the contingent nature of the case. The essential disturbance in melancholy is the distorted experience of time and self, manifested in temporal stagnation and emptiness, inner vacuity and non-existence. The corresponding delusions are delusions of insignificance and guilt, of metaphysical sin, destitution, and nothingness that often result in abysmal despair. The abnormal feeling-states differ from the normal ones by arising endogenously as a psychological irreducible, thus lacking an understandable causal development. Explanations point to sources beyond consciousness, such as physical events, phases, periods. Jaspers notes that bodily feelings are part of the feeling-states and that the core of depression, especially the cyclothymic form, is a change in vital feeling. Depressive patients experience most commonly a feeling of insufficiency, incapacity, uselessness for the world; they feel incompetent and incapable of action, unconfident and wavering, clumsy, unable to make a decision, think, or understand anymore. This feeling is only partly objective and understandable; essentially, it is an unfounded primary feeling. Apathy or lack of feeling, indifference and abulia, the feeling of not having feeling, are common states in depressive patients. Jaspers mentions the existential anxiety and depression and monastic acedia that also has an element of restlessness and reluctance to work (65–114).

Jaspers discusses theory formation in psychopathology (534–46). Before developing his own critique, he puts forth a succinct presentation of the theories of Carl Wernicke (1848–1905) and Sigmund Freud, as well as the constructive-genetic theories of von Gebsattel and Straus that refer to the pathology of depression-melancholy. Jaspers explains that "constructive-genetic" is von Gebsattel's term for Straus's theoretical psychology, Hans Kunz's philosophical anthropology, Alfred Storch's existential analysis, and Binswanger's existential anthropology. They all refer to endogenous depression, compulsive illness, and delusions, and attempt to explain them through a "disturbance in the basic events": these are characterized as vital inhibition, a disturbance in becoming a person, an elementary obstruction of becoming, an inhibition of one's own inner timing, an inhibition of the personally molded urge to become (the urge toward self-realization), and a standstill in the flow of personal becoming. Vital inhibition will become manifest differently in different illnesses (540). The time-experience is that of time standing still, and thus of no future, one in which the past predominates; the delusions related to this stagnation are delusions of insignificance, poverty, and sin; thus the creation of a temporal vacuum, the absence of the future, and the incapacity to rise to a decision or make an end.

Gebsattel explains these symptoms by a disruption of the trend of basal happenings that instead of moving toward development, growth, increase, and self-realization, is turned toward reduction, downfall, and dissolution of the particular life form. This modification in the trend of basal happenings fills the psyche with negative significance symbolized by death, corpses, rot, contamination, images of poison, feces, ugliness. The morbid basic events within color the patient's interpretation of the world. Gebsattel establishes the connection between disturbance in becoming and contamination: as Burton warned, he who rests, rusts, standing water stagnates. Guilt and contamination are variants of the same condition: the patient experiences the guilt of not fulfilling his life by a purifying movement into the future; in Gebsattel's forward moving life, form-developing is opposed by a hostile formlessness of a self-distorted past. Negative meanings dominate as forces of dissolution of form. Straus explains the tedium of depression and melancholy by the absence of the patient's awareness of power combined with the presence of an urge to development: the impossibility of filling the passing time with content is the result—the symptomatic of boredom discussed by Le Senne. Absence of a future empties the past of meaning as well.

According to Jaspers's own interpretation of psychic life as an "infinite whole, a totality that resists systematization," which cannot be reduced to a few principles and psychological laws but rather allows only tentative hypotheses, his overall intention in *General Psychopathology* is to engage in the pure appreciation of facts and "make every possible approach to psychic reality using all methods," without prejudice, but with detachment and sympathy (17, 20–22). It is on this presupposition that Jaspers constructs his critique of Gebsattel and Straus. He argues that both Gebsattel and Straus display perceptive intuition and accurate observation of psychological fact, but their theories originate in the psychiatrist's encounter with the "inexplicable other" and apply to phenomena that, Jaspers believes, are ultimately rooted in the "phenomenon Man" as "unconfined freedom which lies beyond the reach of empirical inquiry" (30). "Man" is "the great question that stands at the margins of all our knowledge" (31). The vital substrate replaces existence itself and, while both are impenetrable and incomprehensible, only existence is, Jaspers reflects, capable of an infinite illumination. Jaspers laments the fatal leap of thought from a meaningful psychology lit by illumination of existence itself into the world of biology that requires a method appropriate to somatic fact. Jaspers does not deny validity to the latter, what he regrets is the confusion of the two that leads to a nonphilosophical philosophizing and a pseudo-knowledge respectively. From a scientific perspective, the theology of the eclipse or loss of God is as empty an hypothesis as is "a disturbance in vitality"; knowledge of life should not attempt to simulate scientific knowledge.

Nevertheless, Gebsattel and Straus, unlike Freud and Wernicke, do not harbor a fanatical theoretical attitude; they exhibit the desire to give meaning, thus helping patients toward self-understanding, and offer the skeptical-humanistic permissiveness of interpretations as both more and less than scientific theories (545–46). But Gebsattel develops a metaphysics of human existence rather than a psychopathology of depression. Jaspers explains that, although nothing can be said against his basic plan and aim, "the totality of human life and its ultimate origin cannot be the object of any scientific research. [Gebsattel's] theory refers to human life as a whole. This, however, is the proper theme of philosophy, whereas science is only concerned with particular aspects of the whole" (543). It is with this philosophical reflection, the seed of Jaspers's mature thought on the possibilities concealed in boundary situations for the illumination of Existenz, that he concludes his critique of theories of depressive-melancholy.

What is significant for Jaspers's critique of psychiatric theories of depression-melancholy is his insistence on the fact that depressive-melancholy cannot be contained in a scientific theory and that a philosophical existential interpretation in required. Melancholy, deep melancholy, agitated melancholy, and depression are referred to side by side with schizophrenia and epilepsy in phenomenological analyses as particular constellations of symptoms rather than as whole morbid entities. This attitude results, as we have seen, from Jaspers's theoretical presupposition of the "idiocy" (in its original etymology) of the individual case that precludes any meaningful attempt at definition or generalization in the effort to grasp the whole.

Any theory that would attempt to comprehend the whole would do injustice to both its scientific ambition and the singular nature of the case. Jaspers proposes two alternatives: first, generating pathographies of great personalities that allow for a study of individual biographies of disease in parallel with biographies of artistic creation; and second, taking up the phenomenology of clinical cases into a philosophical reflection. These alternatives complement each other and allow for a glimpse into the depths of the ever-receding totality of Existenz. Jaspers poses the ancient and Renaissance question, made respectable again by Kant and the Romantics, concerning the relationship between diseased psyche and creativity: between genius and madman, on the one hand, between saint and fool, on the other. In part 5, section 4 of his study, he considers the relation between creativity and psychic pathos, especially in the case of melancholy and schizophrenia, explaining the value of self-understanding and interpretation of psychic distortions in the formation of Weltanschauung.[7] The paradox of discovering a positive significance of disease even as its negativity or evil is proposed for investigation emerges.

> The problem regarding the significance of illness for creativity. We need to investigate empirically which types of disease have not merely a destructive but a positive significance. Pathographies regarding outstanding personalities always pose the question whether the creativeness was in spite of the illness or came about among other things because of the illness (e.g., creativeness during hypomanic phases, aesthetic content arising from depressive states or metaphysical experiences in schizophrenic episodes). So too in events of historic moment, the problem arises, was the morbid event only destructive or was it an ally in positive creation? (729–30)

Whether creativity occurs in spite of illness or because of it, whether creativity emerges by overcoming morbidity or whether the latter creates the conditions for the possibility of creativity, is in fact a false distinction since the sickness, as the other of health or the negation of it, is—in Schellingian terms—both the negation and the ground of creativity. Jaspers distinguishes between mania, depression, and schizophrenia, and connects each with a distinctive manifestation: he relates mania with general creativeness, depression with art, and schizophrenia with metaphysical visions or religious dramas. This distinction is original and quite surprising since traditionally, from Aristotle to Kant, melancholia has been the cipher for both artistic genius and religious virtuoso. It is Jaspers, with his clinical psychiatric expertise, who qualifies and renames the different manifestations of psychic morbidity. He notes an uncanny closeness between specific illnesses and particular cosmologies, namely, between Gnosticism and compulsive disorder; journeys of the soul and schizophrenia; mythologies, superstition, witchcraft and dementia praecox; between sick individuals and religious figures such as shamans, saints, and founders of religion. Jaspers the existential philosopher, on the other hand, does not make distinctions among morbid manifestations: he considers the generic category of mental pathos in both religion and art as a cipher of tragic destiny and profound human mystery:

It has been a different situation with poetry and art. Here the sick person is often presented as sick and at the same time as a symbol of a profound human mystery. Philocretes, Ajax and Herakles all ended their tragic existence in madness; Lear and Ophelia go mad, Hamlet plays at madness. Don Quixote is almost a typical schizophrenic. In particular there is a repeated presentation of the Doppelganger experience (E. T. A. Hoffman, E. A. Poe, Dostoevsky). In contrast, with Goethe, madness plays scarcely any part and when it appears it is treated unrealistically (Gretchen in prison) if we compare it with the realistic presentations of Shakespeare and Cervantes. Velazquez painted idiots. Fools were maintained at the Royal Courts and enjoyed the freedom of fools in their talk. Dürer's engravings are melancholia itself; Hans Baldung Grien drew the Saturnine individual as typical of melancholic distress. . . . It is certain that some hidden correlation often stood in the background between the fact of illness and the profoundest of human possibilities, between human folly and wisdom. (730–31)[8]

Folly and wisdom, illness and health, the dialectical opposites coincide. Jaspers recalls illustrious figures of our cultural history who have opened for consciousness horizons of abysmal depths and soaring heights previously unknown. The list is a twentieth-century continuation of the Aristotelian list of remarkable melancholics, which indirectly proposes a sui generis hermeneutics of melancholy. What intrigues Jaspers in particular is the "coincidence of religion and madness." He wonders:

Could we interpret it that where the individual himself is in extremity, the extremity of his existing vital state provides a basis for meaningful experience. We may point to the empirical social fact that all effective movements of faith and all creeds have for the most part unconsciously and rarely consciously, been characterized precisely by the absurdity of the content of their faith (*credo quia absurdum*, as Tertullian and Kierkegaard emphasized).[9]

While Jaspers seems to embrace a Freudian antireligious interpretation of religion qua neurosis, he in fact develops an existentialist defense of religion through a defense of madness: yes, the religious virtuosi are mad, they are the mad par excellence, but that does not cancel the value of religion; on the contrary, religion gains its value thanks to the value contained in madness. A typology of religions is thus generated to correspond with a typology of psychoses in part 5, section 4, of his study. Such classifications may appear risqué, but their deeper meaning must be extracted from Jaspers's philosophy of the human being and his conception of illness and health.

The paradox of the identity of illness and health, as well as the paradox of the identity of madness and artistic creativity of outstanding morbid personalities, are thus elaborated. Being ill belongs to living as such, and man is the locus of this identity. "Man is exceptional among all living things. He has the largest potential scope and the biggest chances but with this goes the greatest risk. Thinkers have often conceived man's life as a whole in the form of a sickness, a disorder of living or a primeval disarray, a wounding of human nature through original sin" (785). If man's life is a form of sickness, this sickness has an exceptional ontology superior to health: Plato and Nietzsche are in agreement on this point and refer to illness not in the sense of being less than health and simply destructive, but rather more than health, as "an enlarged state, an enhanced state, a state of creativity" (786). Jaspers understands madness as an existential limit, a boundary or marginal situation that must be accepted as such; it is only in this acceptance and exposure that the message from the "margins of experience" can be received.

> In any case where there is an awakened sense of the human abyss . . . madness and psychopathy acquire a human significance. They are an actuality in which such possibilities are revealed, which the healthy person conceals from himself, avoids and guards himself against. But the healthy person who keeps his psyche marginally exposed and who investigates the psychopathological will find there what he potentially is or what is essentially there for him, distant and strange though it may be, a message from beyond the actual margins of his experience. (786–87)

Jaspers extracts the existential meaning of clinical and psychiatric material and articulates a Dasein analysis in part 6. Jaspers patiently collected the existential evidence that he would then put to use in his concluding philosophical reflections on the nature of being human and the sine qua non value of liminal situations for authentic Existenz. The shattering in madness is certainly a limit—a two-faced Janus, one face looking into the abyss, the other, as in Dante, at the stars. The reality of human incompleteness must be taken into consideration, for "we see the essence of Man as the incompleteness of his Being" (787). For a being defined by incompleteness, sickness must be an ontological condition, and to provoke the event or psychological state that indicates a descent into the abyss of anxiety is a task of pedagogical love. Jaspers acknowledges that his philosophical stance is grounded in but goes beyond clinical psychiatry and quotes Gebsattel:

> We cannot rid ourselves entirely of some basic philosophical viewpoint when formulating our psychotherapeutic goals . . . we cannot develop any psychotherapy that is purely medical, self-contained and appears to be its own justification. For instance, to dispel anxiety is generally thought to be a self-evident therapeutic aim. Gebsattel's dictum however is true, "We are doubtful whether we really want a life without anxiety as we are certain that we want a life without fear." Large numbers, particularly of modern people, seem to live

fearlessly because they lack imagination. There is as it were an impoverishment of the heart. This freedom from anxiety is but the other side of a deeper loss of freedom. Arousal of anxiety and with it of a more vital humanity might be just the task for someone possessed by *Eros paidagogos*. (803)

The existential philosopher in Jaspers sacrifices the clinical psychiatrist: existential and even ontological anxiety as revelatory ("apocalyptic" in its original etymology) and a condition for freedom, must be cultivated by the human individual whose horizon of being must be the actualization of Existenz. For Jaspers, as for all philosophers of life from Pascal and Böhme to Schelling, Kierkegaard, Nietzsche, and Heidegger, the beginning of authentic life originates in *Angst*. It is only through confrontation with the limit situation of the melancholic malady that the gifted personality reaches deep hidden sources of Existenz and, as a consequence, his creativity increases. Pegasus, symbol of divine creativity, is born from Medusa's blood.

JASPERS'S PATHOGRAPHIES

Jaspers continues his investigation of the correlation between creativity and pathology in his pathographies of Strindberg and van Gogh.[10] He tirelessly searches—though in vain—for irrefutable proof of a causal connection between the two: what he is capable of establishing with the available biographical, aesthetic, and pathological data is only a meaningful existential connection between the two histories of morbid psyche and artistic achievement. The meaningful connection reveals malady as a cipher of profound mystery, a limit situation whose essential nature is the shattering of the human personality, and thus a true *coincidentia oppositorum*: creative and destructive, revelatory and concealing, awakening, disturbing, and potentially self-illuminating. He suggests that every epoch is defined by its specific form of madness: hysteria for example was the medieval madness par excellence, which explains, he believes, the mysticism of medieval monasticism. Hysteria had an affinity with the spirit before the eighteenth century, while he notices an affinity between schizophrenia and the beginning of the twentieth century. Jaspers believes that schizophrenia, unlike the hysteria of medieval monasticism, is not a mode of milieu and contagion but the soil in which certain exceptional personalities developed. These exceptional personalities—such as Strindberg and van Gogh—open for us a deep source of existence for the space of an instant, as if the hidden depths were suddenly unearthed. Some of van Gogh's paintings vibrate with an intensity that is not endurable for long; it does not belong to our world, but brings with it a radical interrogation, a call addressed to our existence, thus provoking our own transformation.[11] Prophetically, continuing in the footsteps of Kierkegaard and Nietzsche, Jaspers calls the epigone time of his day to account and brings it under judgment: in this age, when the self is shattered and experience of God is the privilege of the sick, madness becomes the condition of authentic Existenz.

It is from this vantage point that Jaspers, in his essay "Origin of Our Contemporary Philosophical Situation," questions the meaning and value of the entire Western philosophical tradition.[12] The problem Jaspers identifies is the forsaking of the other-than-reason, the nonrational, in all of its forms: in knowledge, the opacity of the here and now; in matter, what is never consumed by rational form; in actual existence, that which is just as it is; in religious thought, the content of faith. In all these forms the nonrational remains unconquerable. It is Being itself which, while it cannot be completely dissolved into rationality, is by the arrogance of reason reduced to matter, primordial fact, impulse, or accident (19–20). The dialectics between reason and nonreason is at the foundation of all thinking and constitutes the history of Western philosophy.[13]

Against this background, where countermovements against rationality were "like a distant thunder announcing storms which could be released but which were not yet" (21–22), Kierkegaard and Nietzsche emerged as a shock that has provoked a radical and irremediable transformation in Western consciousness. They initiated a new philosophical attitude and atmosphere, a new type of thought, and therefore a new type of humanity, thus determining the philosophical situation of the twentieth century. The fundamental metamorphosis was produced by their relentless and honest questioning of reason from the depths of existence in search of genuine truth. The new intellectual attitude was "the medium of infinite reflection which is conscious of being unable to attain any real ground by itself" (24–25). Both make visible the limit of scientific knowledge and rationality that must humble itself and admit the existence of a radical otherness, something that one cannot understand. Their most ridiculed enemy is the System, whose closure and deadly perfection are contrary to existence. The ambiguity of existence and genuine truth can be adequately articulated only in indirect communication and through masks by engaging in the hermeneutical task of infinite interpretation. Faith and will replace thought: they are both grounded in the depth of personal existence: the faith of the martyrs and the will to power in a world in which God is dead.

Both saw before them a nothingness and had an apocalyptic vision of the end of history and a radical change in man. The distress of the epoch was experienced suicidally through "endless reflection, drive towards the basic, and, as they sank into the bottomless, hold upon the Transcendent" (30–31).

Jaspers explains the infinite melancholic reflection as a "reasoning without restraint," the "dissolving of all authority, and the "surrender of content that gives to thinking its measure, purpose, and meaning." But infinite reflection, Jaspers warns, is two-fold: it can lead to "complete ruin" or "authentic Existence" (31). Infinite melancholic reflection cannot exhaust or stop itself, is faithless, hinders decision, is never finished, can become dialectical twaddle, the poison of reflection; it is grounded in the endless ambiguity of existence and action, since anything can mean something else for reflection. Thus, Jaspers observes, while the endlessly active dialectic of infinite reflection is the condition of freedom, breaking out of the forms of the finite, awakening it risks generating the melancholic condition of Kierkegaard's aesthete, and ultimately even insanity (32).

To avoid the latter, an ethical decision or a decision of faith must restrain infinite reflection. Their self-reflection stopped only by the leap toward transcendence, Kierkegaard chose Christianity as an absurd paradox, world negation, and martyrdom, while Nietzsche embraced the death of God and the eternal return of the same (36). Jaspers emphasizes their exceptional and melancholic destinies, their loneliness, their lack of world fulfillment, their failure. Like Le Senne, he observes in both thinkers a physical developmental retardation and a lack of vitality. As a consequence, he remarks, they have been called simply insane and would be subjects of psychiatric analysis, if that would not detract from their height and nobility. Any diagnosis would fail due to their exceptional natures defying classification, for "with them a new form of human reality appears in history." Jaspers reflects:

> It is as though their very being, experiencing the abandonment of the age to the end, shattered, and, in the shattering itself, manifested a truth which otherwise would never have come to expression. If they won an unheard-of mastery over their own selves, they also were condemned to a world-less loneliness. . . . Both are irreplaceable as having dared to be shipwrecked. We orient ourselves by them. Through them we have intimations of something we could never have perceived without such sacrifices, of something that seems essential which even today we cannot adequately grasp. It is as if the Truth itself spoke, bringing an unrest into the depths of our consciousness of being. (37–38)

The shattering of their being manifests a hidden unexpressed and inexpressible truth; the sacrifice makes visible something essential, difficult or impossible to articulate that stirs the depths of our consciousness. Indeed, the consciousness of our age has been indelibly marked by the pathos of the morbid psyche of creator-revealers such as Kierkegaard and Nietzsche, Strindberg and Swedenborg, Hölderlin and van Gogh. In the foundering of these destinies, the depths of Existenz, its hidden possibilities, could be glimpsed. Philosophizing after Kierkegaard and Nietzsche must actualize the possibility of Existenz, Jaspers thinks, but without following them in their shipwreck.

Throughout his lifework, Jaspers was preoccupied with the questions first approached in *General Psychopathology*: what is the nature, significance, and role of otherness, of the nonrational and the incomprehensible? What is the relation between sickness or health and creativity? And ultimately, the question grounding all questions: what is a human being? The psychic malady, melancholia in particular, makes visible the metaphysical other: the otherness of reason and Being. Jaspers's clinical observations provide an existential argument for the Schellingian intuition of the primordial otherness of God: nonbeing, the negation and ground of Revelation. For both Schelling and Jaspers, being and reason are rooted in their respective others as their ultimate ground, and as such this otherness is the ground for freedom and creativity. Jaspers gives witness from the perspective and expertise of a clinical psychiatrist and philosopher to the Schellingian metaphysical intuition. Since his critique of Schelling was mainly directed toward the unverifiable theogonical vision, one could argue that he demythologizes Schelling's mythological construction. Schelling refers to human melancholy as a trace of primordial divine otherness, the ungrounded abysmal nought that provokes God's revelation by negating it—thus also ironically constituting its ground and condition. Jaspers agrees with Schelling that as the ground of freedom and creativity, melancholy must continually be conquered but never eliminated.

NOTES

1. In 1960, when *Mélancolie et Manie* was published, Binswanger was almost eighty years old. The study witnesses to the lifelong research of one of the prominent representatives of the Swiss School that includes Eugene Bleuler (1857–1939), elder and master, and Carl Gustav Jung, Binswanger remained an active element entertaining an ongoing dialogue with Freud, having Eugene Minkowski as disciple, and a fruitful collegial and doctrinal connection with Wilhelm Szilasi (1889–1966), Gebsattel, and Tellenbach. His thought was indelibly marked by early Husserl's phenomenology, so much so that Henry Maldiney (b. 1912), a French phenomenologist who was influenced by Binswanger's thought, could write, "The phenomenology of early Husserl appears as is refracted in the psychiatric thought of Binswanger. The refutation of psychologism done by the rigorous display of the notion of sense has had a disruptive effect on him" (Binswanger, *Melancholie* 424).

2. Ludwig Binswanger, *Mélancolie et manie: Études phénoménologiques*, trans. Jean Michel Azorin and Yves Tottoyan (Paris: Presses Universitaires de Frances, 1960; reprint, 1987). Binswanger (1881–1966), a Swiss psychiatrist and pioneer in the field of existential psychology, was influenced in particular by Husserl and Martin Buber. All quotations of Binswanger are my translations from the French edition.

3. Binswanger, *Mélancolie et manie*, "The woof of the threads of transcendental operations is nowhere as clearly visible as in the failure of these operations in the *Naturexperimente* which we call psychoses" (21).

4. Binswanger, *Mélancolie et manie*, 22, citing Husserl's *Formal and Transcendental Logic* (*Formale und Transzendentale Logik*, 1929).

5. Binswanger, *Mélancolie et manie*: In the contrast between melancholy-mania and schizophrenia, the specificity of the former is further clarified. Schizophrenia is an existential mode, and everybody has a private form of schizophrenia coming out of personal history whereas melancholy, despite the variety of themes of loss, undergoes a "generic form of menace against human Dasein grounded in its being forsaken" (134–35).

6. Karl Jaspers, *General Psychopathology*, 2d ed., trans. J. Hoenig and Marian W. Hamilton (Baltimore: Johns Hopkins University Press, 1997).

7. Jaspers, *General Psychopathology*: "Furthermore, Mind interprets the abnormal psychic phenomena and in so doing transforms them. I may know that my natural passions animae are subjecting me to distress, or I may blame myself and interpret my actions and feelings as wicked or I may believe I am exposed to the influences of gods and devils and am possessed by them or that others have a magic influence over me and that I am bewitched. These are all extremely different points of view" (728).

8. Jaspers, *General Psychopathology*: "It is not mere chance that all the world accepts the wisdom of fools" (786–87).

9. Jaspers, *General Psychopathology*, "We can go through the types of illness and notice what kinds of religious experiences have been observed in them. In this way contemporary phenomena can be demonstrated. Or we may see from history what outstanding religious individuals have shown abnormal traits and how mental illness and hysteria have played a part, particularly how individual religious phenomena can be grasped in psychological terms. Or we may ask how the priest or minister behaves towards people in practice when their religious behavior is rooted in and colored by illness and how religion may help the sick. Finally, we may go beyond the empirical field and ask how there could be any meaning in the *coincidence of religion and madness*" (731).

10. Karl Jaspers, *Strindberg et van Gogh, Swedenborg et Hölderlin*, trans. Helene Naef (Paris: Éditions de Minuit, 1953).

11. Jaspers, *Strindberg et van Gogh*, 234.

12. Karl Jaspers, "Origin of the Contemporary Philosophical Situation: The Historical Meaning of Kierkegaard and Nietzsche" in *Reason and Existence*, trans. William Earle (Marquette University Press, 1997), "The great history of Western philosophy from Parmenides and Heraclitus through Hegel can be seen as a thoroughgoing and completed unity. But the consciousness of a change into mere knowing about doctrines and history, of separation from life itself and actually believed truth has made us question the ultimate sense of this tradition: we question whether the truth of philosophizing has been grasped or ever if it can be grasped in this tradition" (22–23). All further quotations of Jaspers in this chapter are from this text.

13. In "Origin of the Contemporary Philosophical Situation," Jaspers engages in a brief historical review, calling out several paradoxical landmarks of the agonistic

combat between reason and its other (19–23). He notes that incomprehensible fate was the ultimate background of the Greek gods; Socrates listened to his daimon; Plato recognized madness as more than reason if divinely inspired, or less than reason if not so inspired; Aristotle considered the *alogoi*'s superior principle to deliberative reason; Christianity introduced the nonrational as faith, a complement to or contender with reason, whose idiom was antinomical and paradoxical. With Descartes began the grounding of reason upon itself alone, while, for the Enlightenment, rational thinking was considered a sufficient basis for human life. During the seventeenth and eighteenth centuries, countermovements emerged in support of the other-than-reason, which made reason possible while restraining it. Pascal, Giambattista Vico, and Pierre Bayle are mentioned as the primary contenders with rationalists and empiricists. German idealism followed, attempting to reconcile reason with its other. Jaspers remarks that, through rational understanding, the other of reason has either been converted into reason, recognized as a limit, or seen as the source of a new reason—thus ultimately Being has been grounded either in reason or in God.

Chapter 9

Postmodern Depression and Apocalypse

One aspect of the hermeneutical ground shared by the apocalyptic theologian Thomas J. J. Altizer and the secular theorist of culture Jean Baudrillard is concern for the ontological transformation suffered by postmodern self-consciousness. Since, according to Altizer, Western consciousness has been generated by our "evolving relationship to the biblical God" in such a way that our "deepest identity and actual becoming" have been indelibly marked by the destiny of our thinking of God, this transformation can only be understood through an investigation of its theological ground.[1] The present chapter inquires into postmodern melancholic subjectivity—a latter-day expression of Hegel's infinite grief and Heidegger's profound boredom—that intimately lives out the death or eclipse of God, as well as some of the philosophical and cultural implications of this theological death in the crepuscular light of our times. Once we have made visible its metaphysical ground, postmodern melancholy will stand forth as a disturbing sign or portent of full theological significance, rather than merely a symptom of existential failure, moral fault, or defective biology. If the soul experiences the death or absence of God through what Hegel knows as infinite grief and Ricoeur calls meontological moods—moods in which the void of nonbeing emerges—both Baudrillard and Altizer agree with Heidegger that melancholy in its hypostasis of acedia or depression is the contemporary mood par excellence.

Altizer's theology declares this death as God's progressive kenosis in Creation, Incarnation, Crucifixion, and Resurrection; the fulfillment of the Incarnation is a total reversal of transcendence into immanence initiated by a primordial Fall and resulting in a God *en abîme*—thus, issuing in an absolute *coincidentia oppositorum* between Godhead and its Other. This progressive descent presupposes a turn toward interiority, since the prime locus of this *coincidentia oppositorum* is our pathetic subjectivity, or according to Michel Henry, our "subjective body" in the pathos of being.[2] Indeed, it is helpful at this point to adduce Henry's concept of the pathetic subjective body as the body that can intimately live out the death of God. As we have seen (in chapter 7), Henry arrives at the notion of the primordial immanence of the subjective body. He finds in Meister Eckhart a confirmation of his own theology: since for Eckhart, God is discovered in the ground of the soul, God's death will be intimately experienced by the soul as its own melancholic pathos. Arguably, there is hardly a more significant mode of this, our postmodern subjectivity, than the meontological mood, acedic melancholy or depression, Tillich's anxiety of meaninglessness and emptiness. In "Postmodernity and Guilt," an essay andante coda to *The New Gospel of Christian Atheism*, Altizer reflects on postmodern consciousness, "So it is that an ancient melancholy is passing into a truly new depression, a depression wholly beyond all possible individual enactment, and hence beyond all individual responsibility, but precisely thereby it is all comprehensive as melancholy cannot possibly be."[3]

In a remarkably similar vein, Baudrillard muses in the last chapter of *Simulacra and Simulation*, "On Nihilism," on the eschatological novum of postmodernity in terms that echo Heidegger's concern for a bored and technological world:

> It is this melancholia that is becoming our fundamental passion. . . . . Melancholia is the fundamental tonality of functional systems, of current systems of simulation, of programming and information. Melancholia is the inherent quality of the mode of the disappearance of meaning, of the mode of the volatilization of meaning in operational systems. And we are all melancholic.[4]

If indeed depression—since Baudrillard seems in fact to mean by melancholia the acedic complex of boredom or depression—is all comprehensive today and is becoming our fundamental passion, the postmodern pathos par excellence, radical theology as thinking itself must begin here, with this condition, or in Heidegger's terms, with the contemporary ontological attunement to profound boredom, one in which the death of God is undergone by consciousness as the *infinite grief*.[5] As Lissa McCullough explains in her introduction to *Thinking Through the Death of God*, Altizer defines radical theology as a theology whose authority stems from visionary witness alone and not from validation by institutional authority or the established mandate of tradition; self-authorizing, it is a free witness to the sacred, a witness that unthinks established theological grounds while rethinking these grounds anew.[6] She maintains that Altizer's theology of darkness intends to speak to and redeem our world of tragedy and devastation, as a witness to the "final step in the process of desacralization"—that is, the death of God—which

Mircea Eliade judged to be the "sole religious creation of the modern Western world." The sacred has entered a "perfect state of camouflage, becoming wholly identified with the profane" (xix). Thus our task will be to understand Altizer's all-comprehensive depression and Baudrillard's melancholic passion theologically.

Altizer interrogates the meaning of the prevalent contemporary mood as "a melancholy from which guilt is totally absent," and which is reduced to "a comprehensive depression," taking on anguished tones. He observes a disturbing "innocence," the innocence of the amnesiac murderer of God and self. We postmoderns have already discarded our historical consciousness, the memory of God and of ourselves, by pursuing the instant and vicarious satisfaction of virtual instantaneity and simultaneity.[7] In revolting against the concept of sin and choosing instead the false ethical freedom of the victim, as Donald Capps's study reveals, postmodernity becomes "innocent" by living without the memory of its past history: it loses its delirium of guilt, thus incurring loss of the unity of the self, its self-identity, its courage, and self-responsibility; it loses transcendence and becomes fully immanent.[8] In the absence of the torment of self-contradiction and guilt—Ricoeur underlines the need to assume fault and sin in confession, in absence of which the ethical interrogation and vision are lost—the postmodern becomes acedic, that is, indifferent (careless) or depressed.[9] Now "innocent" through amnesia and indifference, the postmodern consciousness regresses, or simply dissolves, attaining—as Nietzsche's guilty consciousness dreamt—the easy bliss of the cow or the infant.[10] An apocalyptic theologian such as Altizer is profoundly disturbed by this guiltless consciousness, which according to him reveals a total inner emptiness and mutely witnesses to the end of self-consciousness and its history, a history that began with the agony of guilt as self-contradiction in Paul and Augustine. To forget God as our defining ground and the horizon of theological history means to "retreat into a disingenuous innocence," one that is denied to us, since "what has happened in our actual history is the comprehensive ground for everything that we are, the matrix of what we are becoming, giving rise to the most fundamental possible questions: who are we? What has happened?"[11] In this light, what does this theological innocence signify? Altizer distinguishes between melancholy as a condition marked principally by a sense of guilt, even a delirium of guilt, and the contemporary manifestation of depression or apathy, from which guilt is totally absent. As a dialectical theologian, Altizer can nonetheless discern in this apocalypse of self-consciousness—its dissolution into absolute Nothingness— the womb or *chora* of absolute fullness, which is the fullness of a new heaven and a new earth.

Although Baudrillard names the postmodern state of consciousness "melancholia," his description belies this and lets appear the undifferentiated mood of transparency or emptiness that Altizer calls "depression," characterized by a guiltless innocence. He too sees this consciousness as occurring outside the dialectical life and polarity proper to self-consciousness.

> Disappearance, aphanis, implosion, Fury of *Verschwindens*. Transpolitics is the elective sphere of the mode of disappearance (of the real, of meaning, of the stage, of history, of the social, of the individual). . . . In disappearance, in the desertlike, aleatory and indifferent form, there is no longer even pathos, the pathetic of nihilism—that mythical energy that is still the force of nihilism, of radicality, of mythic denial, dramatic anticipation. . . . It is simply disappearance. (162)

Baudrillard refers to a melancholy that is "incurable and beyond any dialectic" and unlike Altizer he refrains from interpreting the inner transparency and void as the womb of the novum. Our analysis of Schelling (chapter 6) helps us to see that Altizer's lamentation in the face of postmodern depression qua guiltless innocence and amnesia, and Baudrillard's critique of the melancholic transparency of virtual eternity, respectively, have to do not with melancholy, but on the contrary with its *absence*, thus with the emptiness of the acedic hypostasis, its impoverishing deficit of polarity and the dialectics of life. Altizer laments in postmodernity precisely the absence of self-dividedness, which is the ground of self-contradiction and guilt, but also of profound sorrow and joy that only a deepening self-consciousness makes possible. Meanwhile, Baudrillard notes the loss of the body and emphasizes the transparency of postmodern consciousness: the Schellingian God's nature and dark basis, its incarnating power, has been lost, according to Baudrillard, in the disembodying urge of virtual reality that de-realizes the ontology of the body. The body has been sacrificed for the sake of the promise of a disembodied freedom. In the desert of postmodern reality, bodies are transparent, they do not cast shadows; they are undead and haunting, carrying on a Levinasian nightmarish impersonal death-in-life existence. Can this contemporary condition be interpreted as a reactualization in consciousness of Schelling's absolute indifference or Hegel's primordial stage of the Concept? This self-emptiness is viewed by Altizer as the outcome of the divine kenosis, a Hegelian historical unfolding that originates with God's will to self-revelation and self-negation or sacrifice for the love of the other, a negation or sacrifice of the Godhead that begins with Creation and ends with Crucifixion-Resurrection. Although Creation is already the apocalypse of Godhead, the postmodern apocalypse of the self is the experience in consciousness of the last scene of the *Heilgeschichte*, the parousia, the fullness of time, the all in all, in which the intradivine Fall, Incarnation, Crucifixion, Resurrection, and Apocalypse coincide. The kenosis of God begun with Creation is now fulfilled historically in and for consciousness: there is nothing left of the transcendent Godhead since God has completely emptied himself into the world, a world that is now the divine dead body. Altizer's Creation is a cosmic Eucharistic sacrifice, God's total revealing and offering of himself to the world. This divine self-revelation and self-giving is also a fall into infinite abyss where God becomes his own Other: a perfect reversal and as such a *coincidentia oppositorum*. If this is now occurring in the fullness of time, what can follow but a new heaven and a new earth, an absolute novum made possible only by this apocalyptic death of God? For Altizer the death of God is truly a historical enactment of God's own sacrifice, a Hegelian movement of the spirit toward its fulfillment actualized in a total incarnation, which is a total kenosis. The fundamental difference between Altizer and Hegel on the one hand, and Schelling on the other, resides here. Schelling's intradivine dialectics is not kenotic since God is never only spirit, but eternally double, his dark nature is posited first and remains the ground of his existence, the irreducible remainder in both God and creation. Thus Schelling's God cannot die; one can mistakenly posit the death of God, that "God is not," while his envelopment and withdrawal persist, but that only means that God becomes manifest as nonbeing, not that "God is not at all."[12] The otherness of God is always present in the divine life and in creation as God's dark nature, the beginning, the oldest, the past in God. It is the "poison of life that needs to be overcome, yet without which life would pass away," the "first source of bitterness which is . . . the interior of all life and which immediately erupts whenever it is not soothed," the "unappeasable melancholy of all life."[13] As a Hegelian, by contrast, Altizer follows the total kenosis of the transcendent God into its Other without remainder as an apocalypse that is being enacted in postmodernity, but was initiated ab origine in God himself. The apocalyptic parousia is kairotically fulfilled in the world of creation and time, where God is all in all but as a God *en abîme*, completely and irreversibly incarnated and actualized as God's Other. In this context, what is the ground and meaning of the postmodern mood? Altizer interprets the guiltless depression as a sign of the end of Western self-consciousness that has been generated and shaped by its relation to the biblical God. It thus appears as if, in response to God's death or eclipse, consciousness either withdraws from its relation to the Christian God into a Schellingian primordial absolute indifference and potentiality, thus regaining its freedom for a totally new life, or it lives through the infinite grief of an eternal Golgotha and Good Friday. Both hypotheses embody a parousiac totality: the prelapsarian primordial and the eschatological, respectively. Postmodern depression would seem to suggest the former rather than the latter, a moment of absolute indifference antecedent to God himself that is nevertheless different from the primordial one and that contains the promise of a new horizon.

THE EVIL MELANCHOLY OF THE SYSTEMS

Baudrillard, in his turn, refers to the brave new world that has gradually replaced modernity with *the nothing* and can be named only apocalyptically—as a "post-"—in the aftermath of the disappearance of our concepts of life and history. Apocalyptic imagination, an intimation of our new reality, always gives birth to brave new worlds or utopias. But unlike Huxley, Baudrillard develops a sui generis apocalyptic metaphysics, taking up the role of Nietzsche's last man, a *vox clamantis in deserto* as we witness the dawning of a posthuman world. Due to the acceleration of technological advances, Baudrillard observes, we are now living the actualization of our sublime and obsessive Platonizing metaphors, from Descartes's disembodied mind of computerized virtual hyperreality to Hegel's spurious infinite of cloned eternity. Nietzsche was prophetic in his abhorrence of Platonism, and especially the Platonism for the masses, Christianity. Like Schelling and Kierkegaard before him, he recognized the dehumanizing potential inherent in idealism and rationalism, in any idea abstracted from the body, or as Schelling put it, "the unresisting ether of the concept," "lacking true life."[14] Baudrillard laments the literalism of the hermeneutics that grounds this actualization of our dreams and desires. Not being a theologian, but a theorist of culture with Marxist leanings, Baudrillard refuses to transcend in theological hope, philosophical paradox, or dialectics, the desert of postmodern hyperreality. He would agree with novelist Michel Houellebecq's speculation in his own apocalyptic utopia *The Elementary Particles* that we are living through the third (and last, for human beings) metaphysical crisis or change of metaphysical paradigm: the first was the advent of Christianity, the second was the medieval discovery of science that displaced the former, the third is the transition from the human to the posthuman.[15] The postmodern shift in metaphysical paradigm ushers us out of the human world of polarity, of good and evil, love and death, and into a Hegelian spurious infinite of the technological eternity of artifice and surface. The nightmarish Hegelianism envisioned by Kierkegaard, in which the world spirit has marched over the individual in an infamous leap of *Aufhebung*, is being actualized in the submission of the world to the *systems*, the universal web spun by the spider of Socrates's reason. In light of Nietzsche's prophetic warning against the irrationality of excessive rationality, it is as if the cunning of reason were fulfilling our innermost desire—that of self-transcendence—in a perverse way; or as if a malign demiurge were actualizing our dream literally, or the Greek divinity Nemesis were punishing by saturation our hubristic desire: self-transcendence has become a leaping over ourselves, a going beyond our humanity. The hellish punishment is, paradoxically, a mock fulfillment ensured by a literally minded demiurge, a lesser god, or by God's Other—thus ending desire, freedom, and Life. Baudrillard calls it the "saturation of systems," whose offspring is melancholia, "Melancholia is the brutal affection that characterizes our saturated systems. Once the hope of balancing good and evil, true and false, indeed of confronting some values of the same order, once the more general hope of a relation of forces and a stake has vanished. Everywhere, always, the system is too strong, hegemonic" (163).

The system appears as a life-annihilating otherness, a demonic reflection *en abîme* of divine atonement. In his commentary on Schelling's *Treatise on Freedom*, Heidegger endeavors to establish whether Schelling could find a place for freedom within his system. Heidegger discusses the will to a system of freedom and the "not-yet" of the *Ungrund* in Schelling.[16] At the end of his questioning Heidegger concludes that "freedom's incomprehensibility consists in the fact that it resists comprehension since . . . freedom transposes us into the occurrence of Being, not in the mere representation of it."[17] This is a clear affirmation of the fundamental impossibility of a system of freedom, or of comprehending the incomprehensible in a system, because it is the essential nature of freedom to evade conceptual encapsulation. The impossibility of "the jointure of Being" (as Heidegger defines the system) to contain freedom affirms freedom as essentially disruptive and conceptually unknowable. Indeed, Schelling relentlessly insists on a living God whose revelation is not a geometric necessity à la Spinoza, but the act of a free being. God's self-revelation was a conscious and free act undertaken in full knowledge of its consequences. He asserts that God himself is not a system but a life, and hence conditioned by a principle of darkness within, which he constantly overcomes through love. This conditioning factor is associated both with the possibility of freedom and of evil in God: "God himself, however, is not a system but a life, and this alone constitutes the answer to the question as to the possibility of evil in relation to God" (*Freedom* 78–79).

The actualization of our hyperrational visions in the web of systems appears to illustrate for us today the sin of limited and excessively literal interpretation as a *paradis artificiel*, a paradise from which the tree of good and evil is absent, and where the tree of life bears artificial or virtual fruit: a barren topos, a desert. Indeed, Baudrillard insists that the hyperreal world of postmodernity situates itself outside the dialectical play of polarity, which explains its dead and deadening nature; its beyondness is not the parousia of the kingdom of God but "a simulated transparency of all things . . . a simulacrum of the materialist or idealist realization of the world in hyperreality." The culmination of Baudrillard's vision of the apocalyptic negation of apocalypse, or the simulacrum of the novum, reaches the culmination of its mock parousia with the metamorphosis of God: in the world of the virtual, "*God is not dead, he has become hyperreal*" (159).

Hyperreal God, the God of the simulacra—outside polarity, nature, and life—is this not rather God's Other, indeed, as the tradition knows him, the master of lies, the Great Deceiver? Meanwhile, the desert of reality or the spurious infinity of a *paradis artificiel*—is this not rather an actualization of Hell? Or is it even beyond Heaven and Hell? If the latter, is it a complete reversal or withdrawal out of creation and into the absolute indifference of the before-the-beginning? Baudrillard explains it as the translation of the actual world into its simulation, which eliminates the mystery of Incarnation. By entering its mirrored image and assuming a virtual existence, postmodernity inhabits the land of the shadows and lives its own death eternally. One could conclude that Baudrillardian postmodernity is living through its own self-damnation. The bodies have been judged and will not be raised. Thus what is ultimately lamented in Baudrillard's hyperreality is a paradoxical twofold: on the one hand, the actualization of melancholic aspirations, dreams, and metaphors of self-transcendence, specifically transcending the pathetic experience of contingency and finitude, and on the other hand, the loss of the body. Both transcend embodied existence, the Incarnation. All Gnostic idealisms and rationalisms, as well as literal materialism, are refusals of the totality of being and denials of human metaxic existence. They all implicitly oppose the *Naturphilosophie* of a Böhme or a Schelling, the *Lebensphilosophie* of Nietzsche and Kierkegaard, which manifest concern for the preservation of embodied existence and the sacredness of the person.

Confronted with the postmodern mode of disappearance of body, dream, and freedom, Baudrillard identifies three historical modes of nihilism: the Romantic, the surrealist, and the postmodern. The distinctions are significant for the curve of the zeitgeist toward an eschatological moment: Romantic nihilism destroyed the order of appearances; surrealist nihilism undid the order of meaning; postmodern nihilism is a nihilism of transparency and has to do with the order of disappearance and its paradoxical accelerated inertia. He describes the latter's entropic excess, "A destiny of inertia for a saturated world. The phenomena of inertia are accelerating (if one can say that). The arrested forms proliferate, and growth is arrested in excrescence. Such is also the secret of hypertelie, of what goes further than its own end" (161). The hypertelic nature of hyperreality points to a cancerous proliferation beyond itself toward the saturation of the system; it is a system without precedent, at least in the ontological orders we have witnessed to date. Although Baudrillard identifies melancholia of the systems as our fundamental passion and makes reference to an eschatological crisis, he denies postmodern nihilism the darkness and apocalypticism previously associated with the final ending in our imagination:

Nihilism no longer wears the dark, Wagnerian, Spenglerian, fuliginous colors of the end of the century. It no longer comes from a weltanschauung of decadence nor from a metaphysical radicality born of the death of God and of all the consequences that must be taken from this death. Today's nihilism is one of transparency and it is in some sense more radical, more crucial than in its prior and historical forms, because this transparency, this irresolution is indissolubly that of the system, and that of all the theory that still pretends to analyze it. (159)

The nihilism of transparency appears as more radical than the melancholic and apocalyptic nihilism that dwelled in a world of meaning in the shadow of God, alive or dead. Baudrillard articulates the terror of a posthuman universe; in the world of transparency, polarities have vanished, hence there can be no apocalypse qua objective end of the world: neither apocalypse nor absolute novum, neither new heaven nor new earth; the reign is that of the same, indeed, it is Hegel's bad infinite actualized as infernal damnation. Clearly Baudrillard's melancholia emerges as indifference and inertia, a hypostasis of the acedic pole, or rather as the paradoxical acceleration of entropic systems, with their baroque convolutions and implosions—an inertia on the model of deadly proliferation. Thus Baudrillard is a postmodern Kierkegaard at war with the Hegelianism of the all-engulfing system, as he witnesses the end of the world of the person, the subjective body, and the actual; the beginning in its place of the simulacra of life and the simulated eternity of the virtual and the hyperreal. He is a prophet of the spurious infinite whose perfect illustration is the final scene in Stanley Kubrick's film *2001: A Space Odyssey*, suggesting the infinite regression and eternal damnation of the disembodied or virtually embodied space traveler.

For both Baudrillard and Altizer, postmodern consciousness lacks self-division and depth; the former describes it as a transparency, the latter as an empty and shallow innocence. While both Altizer and Baudrillard witness to a total reversal occurring in postmodernity, this reversal occurs in opposite directions: for Altizer, once God's kenosis is complete and God has poured himself without remainder into creation, transcendence converts to pure immanence and Godhead becomes its own Other by translating from the virtual to the actual. Altizer's theological dialectics therefore promise a new beginning, as postmodern apocalyptic fulfillment bears the seed of a new creation. The all-comprehensive acedic depression indicates the withdrawal of self-consciousness and its entering into concealment in the aftermath of the death of God. This concealment is not a Baudrillardian disappearing, but on the contrary an intimate living out of the consciousness of the death of God; or rather, since God has emptied himself into the world, it is God's Other as the nothing actually inhabiting consciousness. If, as Schelling explained,

God's self-negation always precedes God's revelation as its ground, then postmodernity can expect, with Altizer and Schelling, a new heaven and a new earth. An alternative interpretation would be Hegelian: the consciousness of infinite grief undergoes the death of God indefinitely. It has failed to live according to the Concept and enter the world of freedom and has instead developed a pathological condition. What can save humanity from itself? *Aletheia*, the labor of remembering, prepares a *metanoia* for which the entire history of consciousness has been a preparation, as D. G. Leahy convincingly argues in *Novitas Mundi*.[18]

In a move paradoxically similar but reversed, in Baudrillard's postmodernity God and creation are translated from the actual to the virtual—to the hyperreality of the simulacra. Actual embodied existence kenotically empties itself into its own reflection, its own disembodied shadow, the mirror of the virtual. Thus it participates in nothing and nonbeing; not in the nothing of primordial negation, nor in that of apocalypse, but rather in the nothing of the posthuman. For both thinkers, postmodern melancholia is not the delirium of the guilty conscience, since postmodern consciousness is "pure," transparent, "innocent" or rather unconscious of guilt and sin. It is essentially acedia, the phlegmatic condition that Kierkegaard liked to condemn as ethical evasion, lingering in the virtual as a way of refusing to choose oneself and self-actualization in existence. Acedia is "not guilty"; it is characterized by emptiness, indifference, and boredom, some of the characteristics of Kierkegaard's aesthetic as portrayed in *Either/Or*. For postmodernity, the melancholic mourning of God's death is no longer Hegelian infinite grief but the dissolution of self-consciousness itself.

NOTES

1. Lissa McCullough, "Theology as the Thinking of Passion Itself," in *Thinking Through the Death of God: A Critical Companion to Thomas J. J. Altizer*, ed. Lissa McCullough and Brian Schroeder (Albany: State University of New York Press, 2004), 29–32.

2. Michel Henry, "Le corps subjectif," in *Philosophie et phénoménologie du corps* (introduction, n. 1), 71–105.

3. Thomas J. J. Altizer, "Postmodernity and Guilt," in *A Call to Radical Theology* (introduction, n. 1); *The New Gospel of Christian Atheism* (Aurora: Davies Group, 2002).

4. Jean Baudrillard, *Simulacra and Simulation* (introduction, n. 1), 162. All further quotations of Baudrillard are taken from this text.

5. Martin Heidegger, "Awakening a Fundamental Attunement in our Philosophizing," in *The Fundamental Concepts of Metaphysics* (chapter 7, n. 9), 59–167.

6. Lissa McCullough, "Historical Introduction," in *Thinking Through the Death of God* (n. 1 above), xxi.

7. Recently the New York *Daily News* published an article by Rosemary Black, "Scientists Develop Pill that Erases Traumatic Memories" (June 4, 2010), which debates the advantages and disadvantages of such a remedy—another actualization of the dream of magically regaining one's purity. Instead of seeking grace, self-understanding, repentance, and *metanoia*, the guilty consciousness can annul itself and regain the tabula rasa of an innocent consciousness by taking a pill. Richard Condon's film *The Manchurian Candidate* (1959), remade twice (1962, 2004), and a romantic drama *Eternal Sunshine of the Spotless Mind* (directed by Michel Gondry, 2004) are reflections on the disturbing effects of the trauma-erasing pill.

8. Donald Capps, *The Depleted Self* (chapter 2, n. 27).

9. Paul Ricoeur, "Phenomenology of Confession," in *The Symbolism of Evil* (chapter 2, n. 23), 3–25.

10. Friedrich Nietzsche, "On the Uses and Disadvantages of History for Life," in *Untimely Meditations*, trans. R. J. Hollingdale (Cambridge: Cambridge University Press, 1983; reprint, 1996), 61.

11. McCullough, "Theology as the Thinking of Passion Itself," 31.

12. Schelling, *Ages* (chapter 6, n. 13): "Therefore, 'God is not' can mean two things. 'God is not existing [*existirend*].' This is being granted and maintained. 'God is not at all or God is absolutely not existing.' This is being denied. For God is precisely in that God does not have being. God is only as not having being, in the state of involution (*implicite, in statu involutionis*), which is a transport (intermediary) of real revelation" (86–87).

13. Schelling, *Ages,* "Here is the first source of bitterness which is, nay, must be, the interior of all life, and which immediately erupts whenever it is not soothed. For love is coerced into hatred and the silent and gentle spirit cannot act, but rather is oppressed by the enmity in which all of the forces are transposed by the necessity of life. From here comes the profound discontent that lies in all life and without which there is no actuality. This is the poison of life that needs to be overcome, yet without which, life would pass away" (89).

14. Schelling, *On the History of Modern Philosophy*, trans. Andrew Bowie (Cambridge: Cambridge University Press, 1994), 146, 143.

15. Michel Houellebecq, *The Elementary Particles*, trans. Frank Wynne (New York: Vintage, 2001).

16. Martin Heidegger, *Schelling's Treatise on the Essence of Human Freedom* (chapter 7, n. 23). If the *will to system* appears only with modernity and reaches its fulfillment in German idealism, German Protestantism as carried through in Nicolaus Cusanus, Luther, Sebastian Frank, Jakob Böhme, and Albrecht Dürer had already inscribed itself on that path. In this process, Heidegger believes, "through German Protestantism in the Reformation not only Roman dogma was changed, but also the Roman-Oriental form of the Christian experience of Being was transformed" to accommodate a wider horizon (31). System in its true sense as "the conscious joining of the jointure and coherence of Being itself" (28) is the true task of philosophy,

according to Heidegger, and "the possibility of the system of knowledge and the will to system as a manner of rediscovering the human being are the essential characteristics of the modern period" (29). System is made possible by and assures the predominance of mathematical thinking and self-certainty as the law of being and criterion of truth (30); but equally importantly, system effects "a setting free of man in the middle of beings as a whole, [for] that totality (God-world-man) must be understood and ordered in terms of the unity of a jointure and as such a unity" (32). The will to a *system* of freedom, however, appears as the will to comprehend the in-comprehensible, and Heidegger's reflections on Schelling polarize around this heroic attempt, this cause manquée.

17. Heidegger, *Schelling's Treatise*, 162.

18. D. G. Leahy, *Novitas Mundi: Perception of the History of Being* (Albany: State University of New York Press, 1994).

Chapter 10

Therapeutics of Melancholy

Thinking along with Ricoeur, it appears that the acedic meontological mood is the inverse of the desire for being, an instance of the Freudian death drive. Acedic will is infected by nothingness. The temptation to nothing or death drive can only be countered by the self's own will to exist. As Tillich maintained, only the courage to be, grounded in the power of Being itself, or God beyond God, can absorb the anxiety of emptiness. The formless meontological mood can be appeased or filled only by the equally formless ontological mood of infinite intellectual eros and potential beatitude corresponding to an absolute Object of desire beyond essence and form. Once again in Ricoeur and Tillich, the questionableness of the task of *apatheia*, the removal of desire and will, comes to the fore. If man is a being of desire, as philosophers from Plato to Spinoza have affirmed, the excision of desire means the death of man's being.

DESOILLE: A JUNGIAN REACTUALIZATION
OF FICINO'S THERAPEUTICS

At the end of his poetics of the earth, Gaston Bachelard mentions the method of healing through images recommended by Robert Desoille, a reactualization of Ficino's art.[1] Desoille's restoration of the function of the future by means of a radical shift in imagination implies the replacement of a morbid image by a salutary image. The morbid image stalls and weakens imagination, thus killing the future. The first effect of the therapeutic of imaginal redressing, according to Bachelard, is freeing imagination into and for the future, since irrespective of its etiology and ontology, melancholy is always manifest as a diseased imagination (392–93). As Binswanger and

Tellenbach among other psychiatrists have observed, the melancholic is victim to an imaginative delirium of loss, guilt, damnation, and emptiness. Le Senne, like Ficino, has emphasized the correlation between melancholic inhibition of action and excessive mental activity. While it is true that in some cases of melancholy, inhibition affects mental activity as well, in general the latter suffers from excess. Only this excessive thinking is "afflicted," a fact that makes Foucault insist on reestablishing the truth of the "synthesis of insanity and reason."[2] According to Foucault, the connection of afflicted reflection and inhibition of action translates itself into "weakness and thoughts," Ficino's "care and contemplation," or the insomniac brooding and thinking in circles; the object of this diseased reflection is the self itself, with its guilt or sin, its past, the unforgivable faux pas, its inadequacy, its failure, its emptiness, its self-condemnation, and impending punishment.[3] A victim of his own painful thoughts, the melancholic becomes increasingly incapable of escaping his fascination with evil; he is incapable of action and of the future, engulfed and consumed by his own imagination, like a fly caught in the net spun by his own spider-mind. He cannot escape unless rescued by a foreign agency.

As Bachelard notes, Desoille's method uses a therapeutic "cunning" that is discreet: nonaggressive, nonconceptual, indirect. It does not do violence to the deranged mind by rational demonstration of its morbid state, but remains in the medium of symbolic imaging and initiates a substitution of symbolic images. This method—the most discreet of all psychoanalyses—substitutes morbid image with salutary image, thus remaining in a symbolic milieu; it respects the anonymity of symbols by comparison with classical psychoanalysis, which hurries to reveal their clear signification. Moreover, inspired by the dialectics of Jungian alchemy, Desoille goes deeper: the reverie of descent is pursued before the reverie of ascent. Imaginal descent is a descent into the heart of earth or gross matter as the symbol of the abyss of the self—the main reason that Bachelard invokes Desoille's method in his analysis *La terre et les rêveries de la volonté*. It is in this descent into the intimacy of matter that the subject may stumble across "a moral concretion, a moral cyst" that must be dissolved. As Bachelard summarizes Desoille, this descent into the centre of self must reach the archaic and archetypal symbolism of the demonic and evil, the infernal dimension, which is marked in the case of the melancholic by a chthonic imaginal complex such as Dante's Medusa at the bottom of Hell (396). The descent, which means taking into possession and reassuming one's own abyss, is the prerequisite of authentic ascent. Thus, before the reverie of ascent that proposes the unity of the future, a reverie of descent is introduced in order to loosen the psyche bound to its painful past and help it discover through symbolic images the secret knot that blocks its free movement and ascent (394).

There is a profound metaphysical intuition that has informed all authentic systems of thought—religious, alchemical, literary, artistic—that the ascent into true being must be grounded in and assume the dark depths of the soul. Desoille's symbolic psychoanalytic trajectory is a discursive interpretation of this timeless intuition: the ascent always begins with a descent into Hell, of which the descent of Christ or of Dante are paradigmatic instances. The trajectory of the detour through Hell, and also that of the axis mundi uniting the two extreme poles of being and nonbeing, sacred and profane, is archetypal.[4] Such a detour is a therapeutic strategy inasmuch as it reintegrates the *other* as differently metaphorized—as the double, the shadow, the negative, the devil, chaos, evil—according to the respective symbol system to which it belongs. In fact, Jung goes so far as to interpret both the unleashed evil during World War II and the condition of the depleted soul at the end of the twentieth century as symptoms of prolonged erroneous therapeutics of the psyche that have rejected or ignored the shadow. He argues that Western culture has been indelibly marked by an entrenched Gnostic suspicion of passionate nature, and, in particular, by a reductive Christian theology that excluded and demonized the shadow.

DELIRIUM OF CULPABILITY AND THE THERAPEUTIC OF TRANSCENDENCE

Although it may be difficult to distinguish the melancholic's delirium of loss and culpability from healthy remorse, or Freudian melancholy from mourning, the difference between the two, according to Rudolf Otto, is what separates the religious from the moral dimension of meaning.[5] Otto proposes to illustrate the melancholic's specifically religious need for atonement by an analogy taken from the moral sphere. He distinguishes the healthy sense of culpability from a morbid sense of guilt and defilement (55–56). It is the latter that is in need of an atonement that, according to Otto, only religion, and Christianity in particular, can fulfill. Otto's concept of the culpable consciousness in need of religious atonement is identical, in its phenomenological emergence, with Binswanger's melancholic consciousness in its delirium of culpability or indebtedness. It becomes evident that melancholic consciousness gives rise to religious consciousness, a consciousness whose theme of loss—emerging as a delirium of ruin, disease, and guilt—can be healed only by translation into the religious sphere through self-transcendence and redemption. In other words, the melancholic consciousness can be healed through a complete *metanoia*, its transfiguration and rebirth as an absolute novum that can be brought about only by God as the absolute other.

The need of the melancholic consciousness for religious transcendence has been discussed by thinkers of melancholy including Henry of Ghent, Kant, Maine de Biran, Hegel, Schelling, Otto, Jaspers, Tillich, among others. In his study *Melancholy: History of the Problem* (1976), Hubertus Tellenbach (1914–1994), an existential psychiatrist, humanist, and theorist of melancholy, engages in an attempt to explain this dialectic.[6] He characterizes the *typus melancholicus* by two constellations of existential phenomena that translate Heidegger's notions of *entrancement (Bann)* and *suspension in limbo,* namely, *includence* and *remanence* (137–74). *Includence* refers to the melancholic relation to space, designating the encapsulation or self-enclosure of *typus melancholicus* within limits that he is no longer able to transcend (137). The symbol of *includence* suggests a self-imposed, oppressive, narrowly circumscribed space that significantly limits or even abolishes the freedom of being. Tellenbach emphasizes that *includence* is secreted by the melancholic consciousness itself. The critical moment comes either with feeling overwhelmed by and trapped in one's own self and situation or with the forced collapse of a familiar structure and, consequently, feeling compelled to change (146). Tellenbach exemplifies *includence* by citing Kierkegaardian self-contradiction, the situation in which one is called to mutually exclusive moral tasks whose fulfillment implies conditions impossible for the individual to meet. *Typus melancholicus,* unable to endure this contradiction for very long, moves from the pre-melancholic phase to pathological melancholy (147).

While *includence* refers to spatial constriction, the constellation of *remanence* refers to time, that is, to temporal entrapment: it describes the familiar phenomenon of the course of existence seeming to slow down and verge on stagnation (148). Tellenbach's explanation of *remanence* draws a correlation between entrapment in time and the delirium of guilt, of feeling in debt or in default. In cases of *remanence* and *includence* alike, *typus melancholicus* enters into self-contradiction, a state in which one experiences a sense of culpability, of failing, and of being in debt to oneself or one's ideal. The melancholic's burden of debt perceived as guilt becomes the *delusion of guilt or indebtedness,* and makes advancement toward the future difficult or impossible (149). The constriction of spatial *includence* and the retardation of temporal *remanence* point to one and the same ontological disorder, manifested differentially in relation to space and time, respectively (165). This spatio-temporal imprisonment in painful self-contradiction and self-accusation, lived as eternal, is clearly an experience of Hell: encapsulated being in a situation that becomes non-*transcendendum*—that which cannot be transcended (142). It is this un-transcendability of entrapment that constitutes the essence of the melancholic experience of damnation and Hell.

In the Hegelian dialectic, Tellenbach notes, melancholy inhabits the locus of intersection between necessity and freedom (146, 208, 213). The melancholic needs to transcend himself, thus effecting a restructuration of personality that would help the self ascend out of Hell and regain the freedom of being. In order to clarify the understanding of melancholic entrapment and the radical necessity of self-transcendence, Tellenbach adduces the Platonist theory of scholastic philosopher Henry of Ghent (1217–1293) concerning the mathematical-imaginative melancholics as "the best mathematicians and the worst metaphysicians," and affirms that the one thing the melancholic lacks—and therefore needs—is self-transcendence (13, 119). He explains that according to Henry of Ghent, the inner structure that characterizes the mathematical-imaginative human type imposes limits that cannot be transcended: on the one hand, one's nature urges one beyond oneself, on the other, one's own imaginal limits forbid the desired self-transcendence. This inner contradiction is the source of the melancholic theme of resignation and despair, since cognition of the mathematical-imaginative order alone is insufficient for attaining the Platonic Ideas:

> Henry of Ghent has described two basic modes of being human, which define differing possible accesses to knowledge. What is important is the ability to ascend, to surpass: in short, to be able to transcend, and this he denies to the mathematical-imaginative type. This represents a decisive step toward defining more precisely the gift of genius to which Aristotle links melancholy. Henry of Ghent, however, sees only that endowment predestined to melancholy which shows itself above all in mathematical thought, that is to say, in thought and experience of the firm intramundane orders, which are . . . also limits. Within these limits such a spirit can move confidently, but it cannot overstep them. The inner structural character of this type sets limits he cannot transcend. That he cannot do so can drive him into melancholy, for his nature continually urges him upward and beyond, while simultaneously his limits prevent him. Thus, a sense of agonizing dissatisfaction must grow in him, one which paralyzes and finally brings him down in depression; cognition of the (mathematical) order alone does not allow him to attain the absolute, to the vision of the platonic ideas. This resignation and despair of incapacity is in fact an exquisite theme of melancholy. (13–14)

As already mentioned in relation to Kant's analysis of the sublime, Henry of Ghent relates melancholy, geometry, and imagination (338–45). The metaphysical incapacity of the melancholic is explained by a "darkening of the intellect" due to the "preponderantly imaginative disposition" that correlates with a capacity for mathematics, geometry in particular. Henry of Ghent argues that it is this intellectual limitation and the resultant feeling of imprisonment that causes melancholy. Thus, melancholy is caused by the mind's incapacity to rise above spatial notions and its consequent imprisonment in figural representation. This origin could equally be the ground for artistic genius, religious fervor, and melancholic despair.

Henry of Ghent's theory has its artistic illustration in Dürer's engraving *Melencolia I*.[7] The enigmatic potency of *Melencolia I* begins with the "I" in its title. One of the tentative explanations is that Dürer was influenced by Cornelius Agrippa of Nettensheim's complex theory of a three-leveled melancholy—imaginative, intellectual, and spiritual—and that the "I" stands for the Roman numeral one and thus for imaginative melancholy, the type that corresponds to Henry of Ghent's theory.[8] In Agrippa's classification of the condition, according to "a threefold apprehension of the soul, imaginative, rational and mental," melancholy's comportment corresponds to the level of the soul affected by it. Agrippa further invokes Pseudo-Aristotle's theory of melancholy in *Problem 30.1*, as well as Plato's theory of madness, poetry, and divination in *Ion* as endorsement for his own vision. The first type of melancholy affects imagination and is the ground for manual arts; the second type affects reason and the result is special knowledge and understanding of human and natural things; the third kind elevates the mind into understanding, thus making it receptive to sublime and divine things. Prophets and visionaries are the products of this higher melancholy.[9]

The melancholy affecting the imaginative soul is a condition favoring special gifts in the arts of geometry, architecture, and construction. Both Agrippa and Henry of Ghent portray the melancholic genius as bearing the artistic or religious propensity and destiny par excellence. The imaginative-mathematical melancholic is torn between an elevated ideal and a limited aptitude; the discrepancy crucifies such a one, who feels overwhelmed by anxiety and guilt, crushed under the burden of nothingness, bound in self-contradiction between desire of the absolute Object and perceived inadequacy. As the ideal seems increasingly more elusive, the individual becomes depressed, apathetic, slothful, bored, or on the contrary, desperate and enraged. Otto argues that the imaginative-mathematical melancholic can be saved only by divine intervention. Here the healing and salvific value of religious symbolism and sacramental life become evident: the melancholic can be saved from melancholy only by divine grace through a transfiguration or a Lazarus-like event. Indeed, self-transcendence through the experience of the sublime and the *mysterium tremenduum et fascinans* is the archetypal form of therapeutic for the melancholic soul: *typus melancholicus* is fundamentally *homo religiosus*. The melancholic delirium of culpability and loss can be appeased only by God; the pathetic self, imprisoned in time and space—*entrapment* and *suspension in limbo* according to Heidegger, *remanence* and *includence* according to Tellenbach—can regain freedom in a new heaven and a new earth, the absolute novum of new creation made possible by divine agapeic love and forgiveness.

TILLICH: THE COURAGE TO BE IN SPITE OF NONBEING

Articulations of the correlation between melancholy and God are addressed and deepened by Paul Tillich in *The Courage to Be* (1952), a study of anxiety in its three cultural-historical and existential forms: that is, anxiety of fate and death, anxiety of guilt and condemnation, and anxiety of emptiness and meaninglessness.[10] Tillich traces anxiety in its three main emphases through the cultural sensibility and philosophical thinking of Western history. As explained by Hegelian dialectic, anxiety as unhappy consciousness always expresses a crisis and emerges at the end of a major cultural epoch or stage of consciousness, being related to a collapse in the prior familiar system of meaning. Since anxiety is the sign of a necessary crisis, existential or metaphysical, it can never be removed: the melancholic can either succumb to it, or assume and overcome it. Tillich's *courage to be*, as a modern theological-existentialist injunction, develops Aquinas's fortitude, Kant's affects of the vigorous kind, and Maine de Biran's will and effort to be. He defines anxiety as the "existential awareness of nonbeing as part of one's being."[11] The courage to be, grounded in the power of being itself, assumes the anxiety of nonbeing into itself.

Anxiety has various emphases and forms corresponding to the different orders of nonbeing: ontic, moral, and spiritual. The *ontic* threat of nonbeing calls forth the anxiety of fate and death, the *moral* threat of nonbeing calls forth the anxiety of guilt and condemnation, and the *spiritual* threat of nonbeing provokes the anxiety of meaninglessness and emptiness. Tillich has no intention of providing a psychotherapeutic of neurotic anxiety. He acknowledges the difficulty of discriminating between existential and pathological anxiety due to boundary confusion. According to him, anxiety needs to be assumed with the courage to be in spite of nonbeing or else it becomes pathological anxiety or neurosis, that is, a mode of "avoiding nonbeing by avoiding being"—since avoiding being is the only way to avoid despair if the individual fails to assume the burden of anxiety (66). According to Tillich, the predominant type of anxiety after the Second World War was the anxiety of emptiness and meaninglessness.

Tillich sanctions Heidegger's observation about the bored condition of contemporary Dasein and profound boredom as a fundamental attunement of contemporary Dasein. The anxiety of meaninglessness is a response to the absolute threat of "the loss of an ultimate concern, of a meaning which gives meaning to all meanings," caused by the "loss of a spiritual center, of an answer, however symbolic and indirect to the question of the meaning of existence."[12] The anxiety of emptiness is a milder form of the anxiety of meaninglessness, being provoked by the loss of relative concerns, the concerns of everyday existence. The anxiety of emptiness and meaninglessness is a mood reflecting a total breakdown of familiar values due to having been misunderstood in their original power, or having proved incapable of addressing a critical new existential situation.

Ultimately it is the threat of spiritual nonbeing stemming from loss of meaning that is eluded by the suicidal individual through ontic annihilation. The therapeutic for this malady of the soul, Tillich affirms, is the assumption of risk involved in the courage to be in spite of nonbeing. This courage must be grounded in a self-transcending power of Being, or God beyond God as the power of Being Itself. The movement of transcendence grounded in the God beyond God is a lonely and perilous journey through a dark night and entails undergoing this abysmal condition with lucidity. It may begin, as Heidegger suggests, while strolling through empty city streets on a Sunday afternoon when profound boredom is allowed to appear. One does not turn to the Other for help, as did Evagrius and Pascal: the pathetic condition does not have a transcendent cause but is the ground of one's own self. In order to conquer it, one must own it and assume it without remainder. Dante knew that Paradise is reached by traversing Hell, for descent into Hell is the condition for ascent: the magnum opus of the maturity and freedom of the self begins in depression, in the hellish abyss within.

NOTES

1. Gaston Bachelard, *La terre et les rêveries de la volonte* (The earth and the reveries of the will) (Paris: Jose Conti, 1948). All quotations of Bachelard in this chapter are taken from this text; the translations are mine. Robert Desoille (1890–1966), a French psychotherapist and a graduate of the Sorbonne, became known for his studies of waking dreams and for creating the concept of directed daydreaming. Through the directed waking dreams, negative reflexes are dissolved and new dynamic stereotypes are formed initially in imagination. See Robert Desoille, *Le rêve éveillé dirigé en psychothérapie* (The waking dream in psychotherapy), (Ramonville Saint-Agnes: Édition Erès, 1973; reprint, 2000).

2. Wolf Lepenies, "Reflection and the Inhibition of Action," in *Melancholy and Society* (introduction, n. 2), 163.

3. Michel Foucault, *Madness and Civilization: A History of Insanity in the Age of Reason*, trans. Richard Howard (New York: Vintage, 1988), 159–62.

4. The scholarly work of Mircea Eliade (1907–1986) is tireless in detecting and documenting such archetypes in all orders of experience and discourse.

5. Rudolf Otto, "The Holy as a Category of Value-Sin and Atonement," in *The Idea of the Holy*, trans. John W. Harvey (London: Oxford University Press, 1923; reprint, 1958).

6. Hubertus Tellenbach, *Melancholy, History of the Problem: Endogeneity, Typology, Pathogenesis, and Clinical Considerations* (chapter 5, n. 18).

7. The second part of Panovsky, Klibansky and Saxl's *Saturn and Melancholy* is dedicated to a thorough study of Dürer's engraving. Erwin Panofsky, one of the coauthors of the work, also authored *The Life and Art of Albrecht Dürer*.

8. According to Panofsky, although Agrippa's *Three Books of Occult Philosophy* was published in 1531, its original version was already known in 1509 in Dürer's circles (Erwin Panofsky, *The Life and Art of Albrecht Dürer*, 157–71).

9. Cornelius Agrippa of Nettesheim, "Chapter 60: Of madness and divinations . . . and of the power of a melancholy humor," in *Three Books* (chapter 5, n. 9), 188–92.

10. Paul Tillich, *The Courage to Be*, 2d ed. (introduction, n. 3).

11. Tillich, *The Courage to Be*: "Anxiety is the state in which a being is aware of its possible nonbeing . . . anxiety is the existential awareness of nonbeing . . . awareness that nonbeing is a part of one's own being. Anxiety is finitude, experienced as one's own finitude. This is the natural anxiety of man as man. . . . It is the anxiety of nonbeing, the awareness of one's finitude as finitude" (35–36).

12. Tillich, *The Courage to Be*: "A belief breaks down through external events or inner processes: one is cut off from creative participation in a sphere of culture, one feels frustrated about something which one had passionately affirmed, one is driven from devotion to an object to devotion to another and again on to another, because the meaning of each of them vanishes and the creative eros is transformed into indifference or aversion. Everything is tried and nothing satisfies. The contents of the tradition, however excellent, however praised, however loved once, lose their power to give content today. And present culture is even less able to provide the content" (47–48).

Afterthoughts

Now at the conclusion of the present study, we must question whether the task proposed in the Introduction has been fulfilled and what the yield of this investigation ultimately is. In our search for the origins of the condition, we have discovered and attended to the essential and structural identity and specific difference between melancholy and acedia. The distinction between the two humors, between phlegm and melancholy, as well as the distinction between the two sins of acedia and of tristitia, have brought terminological and conceptual clarity into the discussion of a condition that is still burdened by conceptual frames that are either excessive or rigidly reductive. The genealogical investigation has made visible the value inherent in the symbolism of melancholy-acedia, and furthermore a hermeneutics of its symbolism based on this value. The condition emerged in symbols of heterogeneous traditions and systems, namely, theological, metaphysical, medical, astrological, mythological, psychological, phenomenological, and existential. In these symbolic representations or paradigms, the condition offered itself to be anatomized. Thus the limbs of the Dame—as both melancholy and acedia used to be referred to in medieval allegories—could be identified and the Dame remembered imaginatively. Its symbolic life has been one of countless metamorphoses: a constitutive metaphysical element of the world, humor, sin, the passion of nothing, innate capacity for the sublime and the tragic, metaphysical potency of nonbeing, diminished psychic function of activity, non-*transcendentum* mathematical imagination, ontological attunement of Dasein, nigredo stage in the alchemy of consciousness, immanent pathetic subjectivity. Through the different modes of this symbolic and hermeneutic life, the relation of acedia-melancholy to time, self, and God has emerged as constitutive.

In connection with its principal theological interpretation as mortal sin, as well as with its ancient symbolic personification as Saturn, there surfaced the question of the relevance of the symbol of sin as an appropriate hermeneutics of acedia-melancholy and the question of the value of the mythical dialectics respectively. In this respect, Donald Capps's suggestion to substitute for the concept of sin in the present Narcissistic Age the concept of shame, for the figure of Job that of Jonas, emphasizes the aporias of a contemporary hermeneutics of melancholy, while continuing to situate the condition within a theological frame.

What does this arguably negative condition reveal directly or indirectly that is intrinsically valuable to an understanding of the human; what does it make visible about the latter that is fundamental to the meaning of human ontology and destiny? With this question we have entered the domain of the second concern of the present investigation, namely, the hermeneutical task. The present investigation has furthered the Ricoeurian program of a philosophical reflection on fallibility. Since Ricoeur's intention implied a progressively more embodied analysis of the pathos of misery in his works, from *Voluntary and Involuntary* to *Fallible Man* to *The Symbolism of Evil*, the subsequent stage of his philosophical project thereafter was meant as a more intensive observation and analysis of the symbols of evil indicative of pathos in their rapport with fallibility. Our investigation has made visible the hermeneutical significance of divine and human otherness for the life of consciousness, as well as the absolute necessity to assume melancholic pathos as one's own and engage in the labor of self-transformation. The negative affection has only gradually surfaced in consciousness as the abysmal locus of the encounter with the meontological ground of God and Being. Thus, there are two principal ideational nuclei for the entire study. The first is Schelling's theogonic speculation in the *Ages of the World*, since it is here that previous intimations of the primordial nonbeing appearing in the dark mood are validated, and once validated metaphysically, a new destiny of the hermeneutic of melancholy is made possible. The post-Schellingean theories of melancholy suffer a dramatic shift due to the radical transformation in the understanding of the negative mood ushered in by Schelling's theogony. God and creature, their freedom and creativity, are both grounded in the otherness of primordial nonbeing that the melancholic comes gradually to know as his or her own essence.

It is only by after-thinking Schelling that the moment of Nietzsche and Kierkegaard can occur and, in its aftermath, Heidegger's invitation to boredom as well as Jaspers's study of psychopathology, liminal situation, and insight. Thus Heidegger echoes the Christian moral theologians, Pascal in particular, in his sui generis remedial regimen to be observed in *profound boredom*, resisting the temptation to flee by immersion in boredom as one's own abysmal ground of being. This paradoxical anti-therapeutic is a reinterpretation and a deepening of the theology of sin and, in its lucid and tragic heroism, marks the coming of age of self-consciousness. All subsequent serious thinking of acedia-melancholy, culminating in the death of God theology, will witness to this newly achieved superior degree of self-understanding while following and qualifying the consequences of the Schellingian revolution in ontotheological thinking; thus we situate Michel Henry, the phenomenologist of immanent self-affection, and more recently the theologies of Jean Luc Marion's "God without being," Richard Kearney's "possible God," John Caputo's "weakness of God," heralded by Thomas Altizer's death of God kerygma.

The second ideational nucleus in the economy of the present investigation is Hegelian, namely, the stage of negation in Hegel's dialectics of the evolution of consciousness, and in particular the notion of *infinite grief* as the experience of the death of God undergone by the soul. This nucleus indicates the sine qua non value of melancholy in the constitution of self-consciousness, on the one hand, and the relation between melancholy and the death of God, on the other. With Schelling's meontological metaphysics of melancholic madness, Hegel's dialectics of the Idea, and their further reverberations in later thinkers, melancholic pathos appears in its all-encompassing totality as a perduring condition of the soul, a theological coincidentia oppositorum of cross and redemption. The claim of the present work, that melancholy is not reducible to contingent social-cultural or psychological factors but rather is a human ontological condition par excellence, fraught with theological meaning in its origin, its implications, and its therapeutics, has been argued and vindicated.

Viewed in this light, the utopian ambitions of eliminating the condition appear as naively pseudo-scientific. Schelling's conclusion and Jaspers's endorsement of it, that madness must be controlled by reason but never eliminated, deserve to be reiterated. The present author also endorses Tillich's conviction that the regimen of psychiatric treatment is certainly efficient when applied with expert caution but ultimately it is only a temporary solution toward conscious self-restoration: medicine and theology must join in the therapeutics of the human, the being whose body is subjective, whose soul is embodied; in contrast to the Cartesian rationalism that reifies the body, thus allowing for correspondingly separated therapeutics, Henry's reminder that the "bodies will be judged" reintroduces theological thinking into phenomenology and indicates further deepening of self-consciousness.

While taking Ricoeur's philosophical reflection one step further into the *pathétique* of misery, the present study of melancholy intends to place itself within the movement of a phenomenological retrieval of theological existential meaning as inspired by Heidegger and continued by Michel Henry. At the same time, the author hopes that an extended horizon of symbolic and conceptual signification will aid in alleviating melancholic suffering by deepening reflection, thus ontologically grounding the suffering self; the symbol, insisted Ricoeur, gives rise to thought. Ultimately, I maintain that familiarity with the hermeneutic of melancholy is of profound significance for a true understanding of what it means to be a human being; only such an understanding can give a foundation for deliberate existence and ethical action. A melancholy-less world is no longer a human world.

Throughout its hermeneutic history melancholy has functioned as a complex symbol signifying the anomic exception with its two diametric valuations symbolically unified in the *coincidentia oppositorum* of the servant-king, the God-man, or God-Satan; thus marked, like a scapegoat, it has been repeatedly expelled literally or metaphorically from the inner or outer citadel to the desert, itself a figura of primordial chaos and of the liminal. Its vilification as universal folly, moral sin, or disease has called for reductive and often utopian remedies as forms of secular or religious exorcism ranging from surgical excision of the "stone of madness" to imprisonment and execution.[1] Phenomenologically complex and symbolically ambiguous, melancholy has given rise to abundant reflection on the contradictory possibilities, ontological and existential, of the human condition. Human melancholy is the indelible trace of God's abysmal otherness, God's dark nature and ground of nonbeing, the paradoxical negation-and-ground-of-revelation. For Jakob Böhme (1575–1624), the visionary mystic and artisan, source of the theogony of German idealism, melancholy is present in the dialectics of concealment-revelation as the solid and dark core of sound and light. Böhme's bell and candle symbolize this negation-and-ground-of-revelation; the sound of the bell and the light of the candle are imprisoned in the body of metal and the body of wax, while the ringing and the light cannot exist in the absence of their dark bodies.[2] They illustrate the way in which the God of love can be manifest only by confronting the God of wrath, and the self knows its light only by knowing its darkness.

In the struggle to master and control the inner obstacle of melancholy, the self comes to know itself and becomes a self for itself. The nothing concealed in the depths of the self and emerging in profound boredom, depression, or melancholy is also, paradoxically, the ground of self-genesis. The negation of God, in the absence or death of God, is also the ground of God's revelation. As a result of tracing melancholy's symbolic expressions from its genesis and taking note of its defining moments, the progressive awareness and acceptance of melancholy by consciousness as its own nonbeing emerges. The Evagrian demon of acedia has finally been completely assimilated in Michel

Henry's philosophy as the very ground of subjectivity. According to Jung the assumption of melancholy as the dark shadow is the task of consciousness and indicates its maturity. Heidegger's Dasein is called back to the clearing opened up in *profound boredom* that lets its essence appear. There is a profound theological wisdom in this sui generis form of self-acceptance: it is the acceptance of absolute nonbeing symbolized by the death of God. As an archetypal experience defining and circumscribing human destiny in the image and likeness of the divine, melancholy is an ontological-pathetic condition of the soul that leads it from the abyss to the stars.

NOTES

1. A reference to Hieronymus Bosch's painting *The Extraction of the Stone of Madness* (see chapter 3, n. 25)

2. Jakob Böhme, *Six Theosophic Points*, trans. John Rolleston Earle (Kila: Kessinger, 1992), "What rings in the light knocks and thumps in the dark as is to be seen in the thing men use to strike upon, that it gives a ringing sound. For the sound is not the thing; as a bell that is rung is itself not a sound but only a hardness and a cause of the sound. . . . The reason is this that in the matter of the bell there is an element which at creation in the motion of the omnipresent god was shut up in the darkness" (48); see also Böhme, *On the Election of Grace*, trans. John Rolleston Earle (New York: Richard R. Smith, 1930), 23–24.

Bibliography

Adorno, Theodor W. *Kierkegaard: Construction of the Aesthetic*. Translated by Robert Hullot-Kentor. Minneapolis: University of Minnesota Press, 1989.

Agamben, Giorgio. *The Man without Content*. Translated by Georgia Albert. Stanford: Stanford University Press, 1999.

Altizer, Thomas J. J. *The Contemporary Jesus*. Albany: State University of New York Press, 1997.

———. *Genesis and Apocalypse: A Theological Voyage Toward Authentic Christianity*. Louisville: Westminster John Knox Press, 1990.

———. *Godhead and the Nothing*. Albany: State University of New York Press, 2003.

———. *History as Apocalypse*. Albany: State University of New York Press, 1985.

———. *The New Gospel of Christian Atheism*. Aurora, Col.: Davies Group, 2002.

———. "Postmodernity and Guilt." In *A Call to Radical Theology*. Edited by Lissa McCullough. Albany: State University of New York Press, forthcoming.

———. *The Self-Embodiment of God*. New York: Harper & Row, 1977.

Aquinas, Thomas. *Hope*. Translated by W. J. Hill. Vol. 33 of *Summa Theologiae*. 60 vols. New York: Blackfriars in conjunction with McGraw-Hill, 1966.

———. *Charity*. Translated by Thomas R. Heath. Vol. 35 of *Summa Theologiae*. 60 vols. New York: Blackfriars in conjunction with McGraw-Hill, 1972.

Aristotle. *The Basic Works of Aristotle*. Edited by Richard McKeon. New York: Random House, 1941.

———. Question 1 in "Book 30: Problems Connected with Thought, Intelligence, and Wisdom." *Problems II, Books 22–38, and Rhetorica ad Alexandrum*, 155–69. Translated by W. S. Hett and H. Rackham. Loeb Classical Library, no. 317. Cambridge: Harvard University Press, 1983.

Augustine. *The Confessions of Saint Augustine*. Translated by Rex Warner. New York: Penguin, 1963.

Bachelard, Gaston. *La poétique de la rêverie*. Paris: Presses Universitaires de France, 1960.

———. *La terre et les rêveries de la volonté*. Paris: J. Conti, 1948.

———. *La terre et les rêveries du repos*. Paris: J. Conti, 1948.

Badiou, Alain. *Saint Paul: The Foundation of Universalism*. Translated by Ray Brassier. Stanford: Stanford University Press, 2003.

Balthasar, Hans Urs von. *The Realm of Metaphysics in the Modern Age*. Vol. 5 of *The Glory of the Lord: A Theological Aesthetics*. Translated by Oliver Davies, Andrew Louth, Brian McNeil, John Saward, and Rowan Williams. San Francisco: Ignatius, 1991.

Baudrillard, Jean. *The Illusion of the End*. Translated by Chris Turner. Stanford: Stanford University Press, 1994.

———. *Simulacra and Simulation*. Translated by Sheila Faria Glaser. Ann Arbor: University of Michigan Press, 1994.

Benjamin, Walter. *The Origin of German Tragic Drama*. Translated by John Osborne. New York: Verso, 1998.

Binswanger, Ludwig. *Mélancolie et manie: Études phénoménologiques*. Translated by Jean Michel Azorin, Yves Totoyan, and Arthur Tatossian. Paris: Presses Universitaires de France, 1987.

Bodei, Remo. *Geometrie des passions. Peur, espoir, bonheur: De la philosophie a l'usage politique*. Paris: Presses universitaires de France, 1997.

Böhme, Jakob. *De electione gratiae* and *Quaestiones theosophicae*. Translated by John Rolleston Earle. New York: Richard R. Smith, 1930.

———. *Six Theosophic Points*. Translated by John Rolleston Earle. Kila: Kessinger Publishing, 1992.

Brodsky, Joseph. *On Grief and Reason*. New York: Farrar, Straus & Giroux, 1995.

Burke, Edmund. *A Philosophical Enquiry into the Origin of our Ideas of the Sublime and the Beautiful*. Oxford: Oxford University Press, 1990.

Burton, Robert. *The Anatomy of Melancholy*. Introduction by William Gass. Edited by Holbrook Jackson. New York: New York Review Books, 2001.

———. *The Anatomy of Melancholy*. 3 vols. Introduction by J. B. Bamborough. Edited by Thomas C. Faulkner, Nicholas K. Kiessling, and Rhonda L. Blair. Commentary edited by J. B. Bamborough and Martin Dodsworth. London: Oxford University Press, 1989.

Capps, Donald. *Deadly Sins and Saving Virtues*. Philadelphia: Fortress, 1987.

———. *The Depleted Self: Sin in a Narcissistic Age*. Minneapolis: Fortress, 1993.

———. *Men and Their Religion: Honor, Hope and Humor*. Harrisburg: Trinity Press International, 2002.

———. *Men, Religion, and Melancholy: James, Otto, Jung, and Erickson*. New Haven: Yale University Press, 1997.

Caputo, John D. *The Mystical Element in Heidegger's Thought*. New York: Fordham University Press, 1986.

———. *The Weakness of God: A Theology of the Event*. Bloomington: Indiana University Press, 2006.

———.ed. *Transcendence and Beyond: A Postmodern Inquiry.* Bloomington and Indianapolis: Indiana University Press, 2007.

———. Caputo, John D., and Gianni Vattimo. *After the Death of God.* Edited by Jeffrey W. Robbins. New York: Columbia University Press, 2007.

Cassian, John. *The Conferences.* Translated by Boniface Ramsey. New York: Paulist, 1997.

———. *The Monastic Institutes: Consisting of the Training of a Monk and the Eight Deadly Sins.* Translated by Jerome Bertram. London: St. Austin, 1999.

Chevalier, Jean, and Alain Gheerbrant. *The Penguin Dictionary of Symbols.* Translated by John Buchanan-Brown. London: Penguin, 1996.

Cioran, Emil M. *On the Heights of Despair.* Translated by Ilinca Zarifopol-Johnston. Chicago: Chicago University Press, 1992.

———. *The Temptation to Exist.* Translated by Richard Howard. Chicago: Chicago University Press, 1998.

Courtine, Jean-Francois, ed. *Figures de la subjectivité: Approches phénoménologiques et psychiatriques.* Paris: Éditions du Centre National de la Recherche Scientifique, 1992.

Clair, Jean. *Mélancolie: Génie et folie en Occident.* Paris: Gallimard, 2005.

Dante, Alighieri. *The Divine Comedy.* Translated by H. R. Huse. Chicago: Holt, Rinehart and Winston, 1954.

Davy, Carozza A., and James Shey. *Petrarch's Secretum.* New York: American University Studies, 1989.

Deleuze, Gilles. *Essays Critical and Clinical.* Translated by Daniel W. Smith and Michael A. Greco. Minneapolis: University of Minnesota Press, 1997.

Derrida, Jacques. *Of Spirit: Heidegger and the Question.* Translated by Geoffrey Bennington and Rachel Bowlby. Chicago: Chicago University Press, 1989.

———. *On the Name.* Translated by David Wood, John P. Leavey, and Ian McLeod. Stanford: Stanford University Press, 1995.

Descartes, Rene. *The Passions of the Soul.* Translated by Stephen Voss. Indianapolis: Hackett, 1989.

Desmond, William. *Being and the Between.* Albany: State University of New Press, 1995.

———. *Perplexity and Ultimacy.* Albany: State University of New York Press, 1995.

Desoille, Robert. *Le rêve éveillé dirigé en psychothérapie: Ces étranges chemins de l'imaginaire.* Ramonville Saint-Agnes: Édition Erès, 1973; reprint, 2000.

Dodds, E. R. *The Greeks and the Irrational.* Berkeley: University of California Press, 1951.

Evagrius Ponticus. *The Praktikos* and *Chapters on Prayer.* Translated by John Eudes Bamberger. Kalamazoo: Cistercian, 1981.

———. *Le gnostique ou a celui qui est devenu digne de la science.* Translated by Antoine Guillaumont and Claire Guillaumont. Paris: Éditions du Cerf, 1989.

———.*Sur les pensées.* Translated by Paul Gehin, Claire Guillaumont, and Antoine Guillaumont. Paris: Éditions du Cerf, 1998.

Ficino, Marsilio. *Three Books on Life.* Translated by Carol V. Kaske and John R. Clark. New York: Medieval and Renaissance Texts and Studies, 1989.

Forthomme, Bernard. *De l'acedie monastique a l'anxio-depression: Histoire philoso-phique de la transformation d'un vice en pathologie*. Paris: Sanofi-Synthélabo, 2000.

Foucault, Michel. *The Care of the Self*. Translated by Robert Hurley. New York: Vintage, 1988.

———. *Madness and Civilization*. Translated by Richard Howard. New York: Vintage, 1973.

Freud, Sigmund. *Civilization and Its Discontents*. Translated by James Strachey. New York: Norton, 1989.

———. *On Murder, Mourning, and Melancholy*. Translated by Shaun Whiteside. New York: Penguin, 2005.

Hadot, Pierre. *Philosophy as a Way of Life*. Translated by Michael Chase. Oxford: Blackwell, 1995.

Hart, Ray L. "Afterthinking Meister Eckhart." In *The Otherness of God*. Edited by Orrin F. Summerell. Charlottesville: University Press of Virginia, 1998.

———. "La negativité dans l'ordre du divin." In *Voici Maitre Eckhart*. Edited by Emilie Zum Brunn. Grenoble: Jerome Millon, 1994.

———. *Unfinished Man and the Imagination*. Atlanta: Herder and Herder, 1968; reprint, Louisville, KY: Westminster John Knox, 2001.

———. *God-Being-Nothing*. Unpublished manuscript.

Healy, Desmond. *Boredom and Culture*. London: Associated University Presses, 1984.

Hegel, G. W. F. *Faith and Knowledge*. Translated by Walter Cerf and H. S. Harris. Albany: State University of New York, 1977.

———. *Lectures on the Philosophy of Religion: One-Volume Edition; The Lectures of 1827*. Translated by R. F. Brown, P. C. Hodgson, J. M. Stewart, and H. S. Harris. Berkeley: University of California Press, 1988.

———. *The Phenomenology of Spirit*. Translated by A. V. Miller. Oxford: Oxford University Press, 1977.

———. *The Philosophy of Mind*. Translated by A. V. Miller. Oxford: Clarendon, 1991.

Heidegger, Martin. *Basic Writings*. Edited by David F. Krell. San Francisco: Harper & Row, 1977.

———. *Being and Time*. Translated by John Macquarrie and Edward Robinson. San Francisco: Harper & Row, 1962.

———. *Contributions to Philosophy (From Enowning)*. Translated by Parvis Emad and Kenneth Maly. Bloomington: Indiana University Press, 1999.

———. *Fundamental Concepts of Metaphysics*. Translated by William McNeill and Nicholas Walker. Bloomington: Indiana University Press, 1995.

———. *Schelling's Treatise on the Essence of Human Freedom*. Translated by Joan Stambaugh. Athens: Ohio University Press, 1985.

Henry, Michel. *L'essence de la manifestation*. Vol. 2. Épiméthée-essais phi-losophiques, series edited by Jean Hyppolite. Paris: Presses Universitaires de France, 1963.

———. *Philosophie et phénoménologie du corps*. Épiméthée-essais philosophiques, series edited by Jean Hyppolite. Paris: Presses Universitaires de France, 1965. English translation by Girard Etzkorn under the title, *Philosophy and Phenomenology of the Body*. The Hague: Nihhoff, 1975.

Hippocrates. *Regimen 1* and *Regimen 2*. Vol. 4 of *Hippocrates*, 225–365. Translated by W. H. S. Jones. Loeb Classical Library, no. 150. Cambridge: Harvard University Press, 1931.

Hume, David. *A Treatise on Human Nature*. New York: Penguin, 1985.

Husserl, Edmund. *The Crisis of European Sciences and Transcendental Phenomenology*. Translated by David Carr. Evanston: Northwestern University Press, 1970.

———. *On the Phenomenology of the Consciousness of Internal Time*. Translated by John Barnett Brough. Boston: Kluwer, 1991.

Huxley, Aldous. "Accidie." In *On the Margin*. London: Morrison & Gibb, 1923.

Guardini, Romano. *Melancolie*. Translated by Jeanne Ancelet-Hustache. Paris: Éditions du Seuil, 1992.

Irigaray, Luce. *Passions élémentaires*. Paris: Éditions de Minuit, 1982.

James, William. *The Varieties of Religious Experience*. 1902. New York: Penguin, 1982.

Jankelevitch, Vladimir. *L'aventure, l'ennui, le serieux*. Paris: Éditions Montaigne, 1963.

Jaspers, Karl. *General Psychopathology*. 2nd ed. Translated by J. Hoenig and Marian W. Hamilton. Baltimore: Johns Hopkins University Press, 1997.

———. *Reason and Existence: Five Lectures*. Translated by William Earle. Milwaukee: Marquette University Press, 1997.

———. *Strindberg et van Gogh, Swedenborg et Hölderlin*. Translated by Helene Naef. Preface Maurice Blanchot. Paris: Éditions de Minuit, 1953.

Jequier, Claire. *La folie, un pêche médiéval: La tentation de la solitude*. Paris: L'Harmattan, 2001.

Jung, Carl G. *Aion: Researches into the Phenomenology of the Self*. Translated by R. F. C. Hull. Princeton: Princeton University Press, 1979.

———. *Mysterium Coniunctionis: An Inquiry into the Separation and Synthesis of Psychic Opposites in Alchemy*. Translated by R. F. C. Hull. Princeton: Princeton University Press, 1989.

———. *Psychological Types or the Psychology of Individuation*. Translated by H. Godwin Baynes. New York: Pantheon, 1962.

Kant, Immanuel. *Anthropology from a Pragmatic Point of View*. Translated by Victor Lyle Dowdell. Carbondale: Southern Illinois University Press, 1978; reprint, 1996.

———. *Critique of Judgment*. Translated by Werner S. Pluhar. Indianapolis: Hackett, 1987.

———. *Critique of Pure Reason*. Translated by J. M. D. Meiklejohn. New York: Prometheus, 1990.

———. *Groundwork of the Metaphysics of Morals.* Translated by Mary J. Gregor. Cambridge: Cambridge University Press, 1998.

———. *Observations on the Feeling of the Beautiful and Sublime.* Translated by John T. Goldthwaite. Berkeley: University of California Press, 1960; reprint, 1991.

Kearney, Richard. *The God Who May Be.* Bloomingdale: Indiana University Press, 2001.

———. *Strangers, Gods, and Monsters.* London: Routledge, 2003.

Kierkegaard, Soren. *The Concept of Anxiety.* Translated by Reidar Thomte and Albert B. Anderson. Princeton: Princeton University Press, 1980.

———. *Either/Or.* Translated by David F. Swenson and Lillian Marvin Awenson. Princeton: Princeton University Press, 1971.

The Sickness unto Death. Translated by Howard V. Hong and Edna H. Hong. Princeton: Princeton University Press, 1980.

Kinsman, Robert S. *The Darker Vision of the Renaissance: Beyond the Fields of Reason.* Berkeley: University of California Press, 1974.

Klein, Marjorie H., ed. *Personality and Depression: A Current View.* New York: Guilford, 1993.

Klibansky, Raymond, Erwin Panofsky, and Fritz Saxl. *Saturn and Melancholy.* London: Thomas Nelson & Sons, 1964.

Kristeller, Paul Oskar. *The Philosophy of Marsilio Ficino.* Translated by Virginia Conant. Gloucester: Peter Smith, 1964.

Kristeva, Julia. *Black Sun: Depression and Melancholia.* Translated by Leon S. Roudiez. New York: Columbia University Press, 1989.

Kuhn, Reinhard. *The Demon of Noontide: Ennui in Western Literature.* Princeton: Princeton University Press, 1976.

Larue, Anne. *L'autre mélancolie: Acedia ou les chambres de l'esprit.* Paris: Hermann, 2001.

Leahy, D. G. *Novitas Mundi: Perception of the History of Being.* New York: New York University Press, 1980.

Lepenies, Wolf. *Melancholy and Society.* Translated by Jeremy Gaines and Doris Janes. Cambridge: Harvard University Press, 1992.

Le Senne, René. *Obstacle and Value.* Translated by Bernard P. Dauenhauer. Evanston: Northwestern University Press, 1972.

———. *Traité de caractérologie: suivi de Précis d'idiologie,* a commentary by Édouard Morot-Sir. Paris: Presses Universitaires de France, 1973.

Levinas, Emmanuel. *Existence and Existents.* Translated by Alphonso Lingis. Pittsburgh: Duquesne University Press, 2001.

———. *Time and the Other.* Translated by Richard A. Cohen. Pittsburgh: Duquesne University Press, 1987.

Libis, Jean. *Bachelard et la mélancolie: L'ombre de Schopenhauer dans la philosophie de Gaston Bachelard.* Villeneuve d'Ascq: Presses Universitaires du Septentrion, 2000.

Livingston, Donald W. *Philosophical Melancholy and Delirium: Hume's Pathology of Philosophy.* Chicago: University of Chicago Press, 1998.

Lyonnet, Stanislas. "Pêche." In *Dictionnaire de spiritualité ascetique et mystique: Doctrine et histoire*, vol. 12, pt. 1 (Pacaud–Photius), 790–815. Paris: Beauchesne, 1984.

Maine de Biran, Pierre. *Le premier journal*. Vol. 1 of *Oeuvres complètes*. Geneva: Sladkine, 1982.

Marion, Jean-Luc. *God without Being*. Translated by Thomas A. Carlson. Chicago: Chicago University Press, 1991.

Maritain, Jacques. *The Dream of Descartes*. Translated by Mabelle L. Andison. New York: Philosophical Library, 1944.

McCullough, Lissa, and Brian Schroeder, eds. *Thinking through the Death of God: A Critical Companion to Thomas J. J. Altizer*. Albany: State University of New York Press, 2004.

Meister Eckhart. *Meister Eckhart*. Translated by Bernard McGinn. New York: Paulist, 1986.

———. *Meister Eckhart*. Vols. 1 and 3. Edited and translated by M. O'C. Walshe. Rockport: Element, 1990 and 1991.

Mettra, Claude. *Saturne ou l'herbe des âmes*. Paris: Éditions Seghers, 1981.

Miller, David L. "Until God's Absence Helps!" In thematic issue entitled God Must Not Die! (Or Must He?): Jung and Christianity. *Spring: A Journal of Archetype and Culture* 84 (Fall 2010): 73–91.

Montassut, Marcel. *La dépression constitutionnelle: L'ancienne neurasthénie dans ses rapports avec la médicine générale. Clinique, biologie, thérapeutique*. Paris: Masson, 1931.

Moore, Thomas. *The Planets Within: Marsilio Ficino's Astrological Psychology*. London: Associated University Press, 1982.

Nemo, Philippe. *Job and the Excess of Evil*. Postface by Emmanuel Levinas. Translated by Michael Kigel. Pittsburgh: Duquesne University Press, 1998.

Nettesheim, Henry Cornelius Agrippa of. *Three Books of Occult Philosophy*. Translated by James Freake. Saint Paul: Llewellyn, 2000.

Neville, Robert C. *The Truth of Broken Symbols*. Albany: State University of New York Press, 1996.

Nietzsche, Friedrich. *On the Genealogy of Morals*. Translated by Walter Kaufmann and R. J. Hollingdale. New York: Vintage, 1989.

———. *Untimely Meditations*. Translated by R. J. Hollingdale. Cambridge: Cambridge University Press, 1996.

Norris, Kathleen. *Acedia and Me*. New York: Penguin, 2008.

Olson, Alan M. *Hegel and the Spirit: Philosophy as Pneumatology*. Princeton: Princeton University Press, 1992.

———. ed. *Disguises of the Demonic: Contemporary Perspectives on the Power of Evil*. New York: Association Press, 1975.

———. ed. *Heidegger and Jaspers*. Philadelphia: Temple University Press, 1994.

O'Regan, Cyril. *The Heterodox Hegel*. Albany: State University of New York Press, 1994.

Otto, Rudolf. *The Idea of the Holy*. Translated by John W. Harvey. London: Oxford University Press, 1923; reprint, 1958.

Pascal, Blaise. *Pensées*. Translated by A. J. Krailsheimer. London: Penguin, 1995.

Plato. *Plato: The Collected Dialogues*. Edited by Edith Hamilton and Huntington Cairns. Bollingen Series, no. 71. Princeton: Princeton University Press, 1961.

Poe, Edgar Allan. *The Complete Tales of Edgar Allan Poe*. New York: Barnes & Noble, 1999.

Prigent, Hélène. *Mélancolie: Les métamorphoses de la dépression*. Paris: Gallimard, 2005.

Radden, Jennifer. *Moody Minds Distempered: Essays on Melancholy and Depression*. Oxford: Oxford University Press, 2009.

———. *The Nature of Melancholy from Aristotle to Kristeva*. Edited by Jennifer Radden. Oxford: Oxford University Press, 2000.

Raposa, Michael L. *Boredom and the Religious Imagination*. Charlottesville: University Press of Virginia, 1999.

Ricoeur, Paul. *Fallible Man*. Translated by Charles A. Kelbley. New York: Fordham University Press, 1986.

———. *The Symbolism of Evil*. Translated by Emerson Buchanan. Boston: Beacon, 1967.

Rorty, Richard, and Gianni Vattimo. *The Future of Religion*. Edited by Santiago Zabala. New York: Columbia University Press, 2005.

Sallis, John. *Chorology: On Beginning in Plato's "Timaeus."* Bloomington: Indiana University Press, 1999.

Schelling, F. W. J. *The Ages of the World*. Translated by Jason M. Wirth. New York: State University of New York Press, 2000.

———. *Philosophical Inquiries into the Nature of Human Freedom*. Translated by James Gutmann. Chicago: Open Court, 1936.

———. *On the History of Modern Philosophy*. Translated by Andrew Bowie. Cambridge: Cambridge University Press, 1994.

Schopenhauer, Arthur. *The World as Will and Idea*. Translated by Jill Berman. London: Dent, 1995.

Seznec, Jean. *La survivance des dieux antiques: Essai sur le rôle de la tradition mythologique dans l'humanisme et dans l'art de la Renaissance*. London: Warburg Institute, 1940.

Solomon, Andrew. *The Noonday Demon: An Atlas of Depression*. New York: Simon & Schuster, 2001.

Sontag, Susan. *Illness as Metaphor*. New York: Farrar, Straus and Giroux, 1988.

———. *Under the Sign of Saturn*. New York: Farrar, Straus and Giroux, 1980.

Sousa, Ronald de. *The Rationality of Emotion*. Cambridge: MIT, 1997.

Spacks, Patricia Meyer. *Boredom: The Literary History of a State of Mind*. Chicago: University of Chicago Press, 1995.

Taylor, Charles. *Sources of the Self: The Making of Modern Identity*. Cambridge: Harvard University Press, 1989.

Taylor, Mark C. *After God*. Chicago: University of Chicago Press, 2007.

———. *Erring: A Postmodern A/theology*. Chicago: University of Chicago Press, 1984.

Tellenbach, Hubertus. *Melancholy: History of the Problem, Endogeneity, Typology, Pathogenesis, and Clinical Considerations.* Translated by Erling Enq. Pittsburg: Duquesne University Press, 1980.

Tillich, Paul. *The Courage to Be.* New Haven: Yale University Press, 1959.

———. *Dynamics of Faith.* New York: Harper & Row, 2001.

———. *The Meaning of Health: Essays in Existentialism, Psychoanalysis and Religion.* Chicago: Exploration Press, 1984.

Vattimo, Gianni. *After Christianity.* Translated by Luca D'Isanto. New York: Columbia University Press, 2002.

———. *Christianity, Truth, and Weakening Faith: A Dialogue.* Translated by McCuaig. New York: Columbia University Press, 2010.

———. *The End of Modernity: Nihilism and Hermeneutics in Postmodern Culture.* Baltimore: Johns Hopkins University Press, 1991.

Wenzel, Siegfried. *The Sin of Sloth: Acedia in Medieval Thought and Literature.* Chapel Hill: University of North Carolina Press, 1967.

Žižek, Slavoj. *The Abyss of Freedom: Ages of the World.* Ann Arbor: University of Michigan Press, 1997.

———. *The Indivisible Remainder: On Schelling and Related Matters.* New York: Verso, 1996.

———. *The Puppet and the Dwarf.* Cambridge: MIT, 2003.

Žižek, Slavoj, and John Milbank. *The Monstrosity of Christ: Paradox or Dialectic?* Edited by Creston Davis. Cambridge: MIT, 2009.

Index

About the Author

Alina N. Feld (Ph.D., Boston University) teaches religious studies, ethics, and Western and Eastern philosophy at Hofstra University and Dowling College in New York. Her core interest has been philosophical investigation of the meaning of being human and related questions of moral responsibility, with special attention to issues of transcendence and fallibility. Her scholarly work has been cross-cultural and interdisciplinary, attempting to mediate between different philosophical and spiritual traditions, and between theological and cultural dimensions of modernity.